The Sphere Project

Humanitarian Charter and Minimum Standards in Disaster Response

Published by:

The Sphere Project
Copyright © The Sphere Project 2004
PO Box 372, 17 chemin des Crêts CH-1211 Geneva 19, Switzerland
Tel: +41 22 730 4501 Fax: +41 22 730 4905
Email: info@sphereproject.org Web: http://www.sphereproject.org

The Sphere Project

The Sphere Project is a programme of the Steering Committee for Humanitarian Response (SCHR) and InterAction with VOICE and ICVA. The project was launched in 1997 to develop a set of universal minimum standards in core areas of humanitarian assistance. The aim of the project is to improve the quality of assistance provided to people affected by disasters, and to enhance the accountability of the humanitarian system in disaster response. The Humanitarian Charter and Minimum Standards in Disaster Response are the product of the collective experience of many people and agencies. They should not therefore be seen as representing the views of any one agency.

First trial edition 1998
First final edition 2000
This edition 2004

ISBN 92-9139-097-6

A catalogue record for this publication is available from The British Library and the US Library of Congress.

Distributed for the Sphere Project worldwide by Oxfam GB.
Available from: Oxfam Publishing, 274 Banbury Road, Oxford OX2 7DZ, UK
Tel: +44 1865 311 311 Fax: +44 1865 312 600
Email: publish@oxfam.org.uk Web: www.oxfam.org.uk/publications
and from its agents and representatives throughout the world. Oxfam GB is a registered charity, no 202918, and is a member of Oxfam International.

Designed by: DS Print and Redesign, London.
Printed by: Musumeci, Aosta, Italy.

Contents

Annexes

Overall Handbook Structure

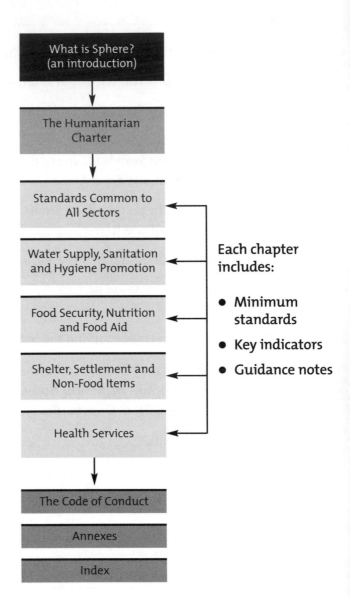

What is Sphere?

Sphere is based on two core beliefs: first, that all possible steps should be taken to alleviate human suffering arising out of calamity and conflict, and second, that those affected by disaster have a right to life with dignity and therefore a right to assistance. Sphere is three things: a handbook, a broad process of collaboration and an expression of commitment to quality and accountability.

The initiative was launched in 1997 by a group of humanitarian NGOs and the Red Cross and Red Crescent movement, who framed a Humanitarian Charter and identified Minimum Standards to be attained in disaster assistance, in each of five key sectors (water supply and sanitation, nutrition, food aid, shelter and health services). This process led to the publication of the first Sphere handbook in 2000. Taken together, the Humanitarian Charter and the Minimum Standards contribute to an operational framework for accountability in disaster assistance efforts.

The cornerstone of the handbook is the Humanitarian Charter, which is based on the principles and provisions of international humanitarian law, international human rights law, refugee law and the *Code of Conduct for the International Red Cross and Red Crescent Movement and Non-Governmental Organisations (NGOs) in Disaster Relief*. The Charter describes the core principles that govern humanitarian action and reasserts the right of populations affected by disaster, whether natural or man-made (including armed conflict), to protection and assistance. It also reasserts the right of disaster-affected populations to life with dignity.

The Charter points out the legal responsibilities of states and warring parties to guarantee the right to protection and assistance. When the relevant authorities are unable and/or unwilling to fulfil their responsibilities, they are obliged to allow humanitarian organisations to provide humanitarian assistance and protection.

The Minimum Standards and the key indicators have been developed using broad networks of practitioners in each of the sectors. Most of the standards, and the indicators that accompany them, are not new, but consolidate and adapt existing knowledge and practice. Taken as a whole, they represent a remarkable consensus across a broad spectrum, and reflect a continuing determination to ensure that human rights and humanitarian principles are realised in practice.

To date, over 400 organisations in 80 countries, all around the world, have contributed to the development of the Minimum Standards and key indicators. This new (2004) edition of the handbook has been significantly revised, taking into account recent technical developments and feedback from agencies using Sphere in the field. In particular, a sixth sector, food security, has been added and integrated with those of nutrition and food aid. Another new chapter details a number of process standards common to all sectors. These include participation, assessment, response, targeting, monitoring, evaluation, and staff competencies and management. In addition, seven cross-cutting issues (children, older people, disabled people, gender, protection, HIV/AIDS and the environment) with relevance to all sectors have been taken into account.

When to use this book

The Sphere handbook is designed for use in disaster response, and may also be useful in disaster preparedness and humanitarian advocacy. It is applicable in a range of situations where relief is required, including natural disasters as well as armed conflict. It is designed to be used in both slow- and rapid-onset situations, in both rural and urban environments, in developing and developed countries, anywhere in the world. The emphasis throughout is on meeting the urgent survival needs of people affected by disaster, while asserting their basic human right to life with dignity.

Despite this focus, the information contained in the handbook is not prescriptive. It can be applied flexibly to other situations, such as disaster preparedness and the transition out of disaster relief. It is not designed for use in response to technological disasters, such as those involving transport, industrial, chemical, biological or nuclear calamity. However, while not addressing these types of disaster specifically, it is relevant to situations where population movements or other consequences triggered by such an event create a need for humanitarian assistance.

Timeframe

The timeframe in which the handbook is used depends largely on the context. It may take days, weeks or even months before agencies are able to achieve the Minimum Standards and indicators specified in a particular sector. In some situations, the Minimum Standards may be achieved without the need for external intervention. A timeframe for implementation needs to be agreed in any given situation. Where relevant, guidance notes suggest realistic timescales for the implementation of the standards and indicators.

There are different approaches among humanitarian agencies as to how to carry out relief activities, based on differences in identities, mandates and capabilities. These differences point to the concept of complementarity, which means that humanitarian agencies use different modes of action or techniques in fulfilling their responsibility to provide assistance. In all contexts, disaster response should support and/or complement existing government services in terms of structure, design and long-term sustainability.

How to use this book

There are already many field manuals that offer practical guidance to humanitarian workers. This book is not a 'how to' manual. Instead, it offers a set of Minimum Standards and key indicators that inform different aspects of humanitarian action, from initial assessment through to coordination and advocacy. The standards are general statements that define the minimum level to be attained in a given context; the indicators act as 'signals' that determine whether or not a standard has been attained; while the guidance notes provide additional information.

Each of the four technical chapters – water supply, sanitation and hygiene promotion; food security, nutrition and food aid; shelter, settlement and non-food items; and health services – has its own set of standards and indicators. The initial chapter on common standards sets out guidelines for programme design and implementation, which are applicable to all sectors. This chapter should be read first, before turning to the relevant technical chapter.

The guidance notes in each chapter relate to specific points that should be considered when applying the standards in different situations. They offer advice on priority issues and on tackling practical difficulties, and may also describe dilemmas, controversies or gaps in current knowledge. Guidance notes always relate to a specific key indicator, and the link is signalled in the text. Key indicators should always be read in conjunction with the relevant guidance note.

Each chapter also contains a brief introduction setting out the major issues relevant to that sector and appendices containing select lists of references detailing further sources of technical information, assessment checklists and, where relevant, formulas, tables and examples of report forms. It is important to remember that all the chapters are interconnected, and that frequently standards described in one sector need to be addressed in conjunction with standards described in others.

The difference between standards and indicators

The standards are based on the principle that populations affected by disaster have the right to life with dignity. They are qualitative in nature, and are meant to be universal and applicable in any operating environment. The key indicators, as measures to the standards, can be qualitative or quantitative in nature. They function as tools to measure the impact of processes used and programmes implemented. Without them, the standards would be little more than statements of good intent, difficult to put into practice.

The standards for the different sectors do not stand alone: they are interdependent. However, there is inevitably a tension between the formulation of universal standards and the ability to apply them in practice. Every context is different. In some instances, local factors may make the realisation of all standards and indicators unattainable. When this is the case, the gap between the standards and indicators listed in the handbook and the ones reached in actual practice must be described, and the reasons for it and what needs to be changed must be explained.

Recognising vulnerabilities and capacities of disaster-affected populations

In order to maximise the coping strategies of those affected by disasters, it is important to acknowledge the differing vulnerabilities, needs and capacities of affected groups. Specific factors, such as gender, age, disability and HIV/AIDS status, affect vulnerability and shape people's ability to cope and survive in a disaster context. In particular, women, children, older people and people living with HIV/AIDS (PLWH/A) may suffer specific disadvantages in coping with a disaster and may face physical, cultural and social barriers in accessing the services and support to which they are entitled. Frequently ethnic origin, religious or political affiliation, or displacement may put certain people at risk who otherwise would not be considered vulnerable.

Failure to recognise the differing needs of vulnerable groups and the barriers they face in gaining equal access to appropriate services and support can result in them being further marginalised, or even denied vital assistance. Providing information to disaster-affected populations about their right to assistance and the means of accessing this assistance is essential. The provision of such information to vulnerable groups is particularly important as they may be less able to cope and recover than others when faced with the erosion or loss of their assets, and may need more support. For these reasons, it is essential to recognise specific vulnerable groups, to understand how they are affected in different disaster contexts, and to formulate a response accordingly. Special care must be taken to protect and provide for all affected groups in a non-discriminatory manner and according to their specific needs.

However, disaster-affected populations must not be seen as helpless victims, and this includes members of vulnerable groups. They possess, and acquire, skills and capacities and have structures to cope with and respond to a disaster situation that need to be recognised and supported. Individuals, families and communities can be remarkably resourceful and resilient in the face of disaster, and initial assessments should take account of the capacities and skills as much as of the needs and deficiencies of the affected population. Irrespective of whether a disaster is of sudden onset or develops gradually, individuals and communities will be actively coping and recovering from its effects, according to their own priorities.

The key vulnerable groups are women, children, older people, disabled people, PLWH/A and ethnic minorities. This is not an exhaustive list of vulnerable groups, but it includes those most frequently identified. Throughout the handbook, when the term 'vulnerable groups' is used, it refers to all these groups. There may be circumstances in which one particular group of vulnerable people is more at risk than another, but at any time of threat to one group, it is likely that others will also be at risk. In general, the handbook avoids specifying between different vulnerable groups. When any one group is at risk, users are strongly urged to think clearly of all the groups mentioned in this list.

Cross-cutting issues

In revising the handbook, care has been taken to address a number of important issues that have relevance to all sectors. These relate to 1) children, 2) older people, 3) disabled people, 4) gender, 5) protection, 6) HIV/AIDS and 7) the environment. They have been incorporated into the relevant sections of each chapter, rather then being dealt with in parallel. These particular issues were chosen on account of their relation to vulnerability, and because they were the ones most frequently raised in feedback from users of Sphere in the field. The handbook cannot address all cross-cutting issues comprehensively, but it recognises their importance.

Children Special measures must be taken to ensure the protection from harm of all children and their equitable access to basic services. As children often form the larger part of an affected population, it is crucial that their views and experiences are not only elicited during emergency assessments and planning but that they also influence humanitarian service delivery and its monitoring and evaluation. Although vulnerability in certain specificities (e.g. malnutrition, exploitation, abduction and recruitment into fighting forces, sexual violence and lack of opportunity to participate in decision-making) can also apply to the wider population, the most harmful impact is felt by children and young people.

According to the Convention on the Rights of the Child, a child is considered to be an individual below the age of 18. Depending on cultural and social contexts, however, a child may be defined differently amongst some population groups. It is essential that a thorough analysis of how a client community defines children be undertaken, to ensure that no child or young person is excluded from humanitarian services.

Older people Older women and men are those aged over 60, according to the United Nations. However, cultural and social factors mean that this definition varies from one context to another. Older people make up a large proportion of the most vulnerable in disaster-affected populations, but they also have key contributions to make in survival and rehabilitation. Isolation is the most significant factor creating vulnerability for older people in disaster situations. Along with the disruption to livelihood strategies and family and community support structures, isolation exacerbates existing vulnerabilities derived from chronic health and mobility problems and potential mental deficiencies. However, experience shows that older people are more likely to be aid givers than receivers. If supported, they can play important roles as carers, resource managers and income generators, while using their knowledge and experience of community coping strategies to help preserve the community's cultural and social identities and encourage conflict resolution.

Disabled people In any disaster, disabled people – who can be defined as those who have physical, sensory or emotional impairments or learning difficulties that make it more difficult for them to use standard disaster support services – are particularly vulnerable. To survive a period of dislocation and displacement, they need standard facilities to be as accessible for their needs as possible. They also need an enabling social support network, which is usually provided by the family.

Gender The equal rights of women and men are explicit in the human rights documents that form the basis of the Humanitarian Charter. Women and men, and girls and boys, have the same entitlement to humanitarian assistance; to respect for their human dignity; to acknowledgement of their equal human capacities, including the capacity to make choices; to the same opportunities to act on those choices; and to the same level of power to shape the outcome of their actions.

Humanitarian responses are more effective when they are based on an understanding of the different needs, vulnerabilities, interests, capacities and coping strategies of men and women and the differing impacts of disaster upon them. The understanding of these differences, as well as of inequalities in women's and men's roles and workloads, access to and control of resources, decision-making power and opportunities for skills development, is achieved through gender analysis. Gender cuts across all the other cross-cutting issues. Humanitarian aims of proportionality and impartiality mean that attention must be paid to achieving fairness between women and men and ensuring equality of outcome.

Protection Assistance and protection are the two indivisible pillars of humanitarian action. Humanitarian agencies are frequently faced with situations where human acts or obstruction threaten the fundamental well-being or security of whole communities or sections of a population, such as to constitute violations of the population's rights as recognised by international law. This may take the form of direct threats to people's well-being, or to their means of survival, or to their safety. In the context of armed conflict, the paramount humanitarian concern is to protect people against such threats.

The form of relief assistance and the way in which it is provided can have a significant impact (positive or negative) on the affected population's security. This handbook does not provide detailed descriptions of protection strategies or mechanisms, or of how agencies should implement their responsibility. However, where possible, it refers to protection aspects or rights issues – such as the prevention of sexual abuse and exploitation, or the need to ensure adequate registration of the population – as agencies must take these into account when they are involved in providing assistance.

HIV/AIDS The coping mechanisms and resilience of communities are reduced when there is a high prevalence of HIV/AIDS and consequently the threshold for external stressors to cause a disaster may be lowered, while the amount of time a community needs to recover may be prolonged. People living with HIV/AIDS (PLWH/A) often suffer from discrimination, and therefore confidentiality must be strictly adhered to and protection made available when needed. This debilitating disease not only affects individuals but also their families and communities, as young people in their most productive years, especially women, are disproportionately affected – physically, psychologically and financially. As the pandemic matures and more people die, the demographic characteristics of communities change to leave a disproportionate number of children, including orphans, and older people. These vulnerable groups require special attention and relief programmes may need to be modified accordingly.

Environment The environment is understood as the physical, chemical and biological surroundings in which disaster-affected and local communities live and develop their livelihoods. It provides the natural resources that sustain individuals, and determines the quality of the surroundings in which they live. It needs protection if these essential functions are to be maintained. The Minimum Standards address the need to prevent over-exploitation, pollution and degradation of environmental conditions. Their proposed minimal preventive actions aim to secure the life-supporting functions of the environment, and seek to introduce mechanisms that foster the adaptability of natural systems for self-recovery.

Scope and limitations of the Sphere handbook

Agencies' ability to achieve the Minimum Standards will depend on a range of factors, some of which are within their control while others, such as political and security factors, may lie outside their control. Of particular importance are the extent to which agencies have access to the affected population, whether they have the consent and cooperation of the authorities in charge, and whether they can operate in conditions of reasonable security. Equally critical is the availability of sufficient financial, human and material resources.

While the Humanitarian Charter is a general statement of humanitarian principles, this handbook alone cannot constitute a complete evaluation guide or set of criteria for humanitarian action. First, the Minimum Standards do not cover all the possible forms of appropriate humanitarian assistance. Second, there will inevitably be situations where it may be difficult, if not impossible, to meet all of the standards. There are many factors – including lack of access or insecurity, insufficient resources, the involvement of other actors and non-compliance with international law – that contribute to creating extremely difficult conditions in which to carry out humanitarian work.

For example, agencies may find that the resources at their disposal are insufficient to meet the needs of the affected population; prioritisation of needs and response and advocacy for the removal of the obstacles that hinder adequate assistance and protection may then be necessary. In situations where the vulnerability of local populations to disaster is high or where there is widespread poverty or prolonged conflict, it can be the case that the Minimum Standards exceed normal everyday living conditions. Since this can give rise to resentment, local conditions must be taken into account, and programmes should always be designed with equality of the affected and surrounding populations in mind.

It is recognised that in many cases not all of the indicators and standards will be met – however, users of this book should strive to meet them as well as they can. In the initial phase of a response, for example, providing basic facilities for all the affected population may be more important than reaching the Minimum Standards and indicators for only a proportion of the population. This handbook cannot cover every question or resolve every dilemma. What it can do is serve as a starting point, using standards and indicators based on consensus derived from years of experience and good practice; guidance notes designed to offer practical direction; and the Humanitarian Charter, which suggests a legal framework and a basis for advocacy.

The Humanitarian Charter and Minimum Standards will not solve all of the problems of humanitarian response, nor can they prevent all human suffering. What they offer is a tool for humanitarian agencies to enhance the effectiveness and quality of their assistance, and thus to make a significant difference to the lives of people affected by disaster.

The Humanitarian Charter

The Humanitarian Charter

Humanitarian agencies committed to this Charter and to the Minimum Standards will aim to achieve defined levels of service for people affected by calamity or armed conflict, and to promote the observance of fundamental humanitarian principles.

The Humanitarian Charter expresses agencies' commitment to these principles and to achieving the Minimum Standards. This commitment is based on agencies' appreciation of their own ethical obligations, and reflects the rights and duties enshrined in international law in respect of which states and other parties have established obligations.

The Charter is concerned with the most basic requirements for sustaining the lives and dignity of those affected by calamity or conflict. The Minimum Standards which follow aim to quantify these requirements with regard to people's need for water, sanitation, nutrition, food, shelter and health care. Taken together, the Humanitarian Charter and the Minimum Standards contribute to an operational framework for accountability in humanitarian assistance efforts.

1 Principles

We reaffirm our belief in the humanitarian imperative and its primacy. By this we mean the belief that all possible steps should be taken to prevent or alleviate human suffering arising out of conflict or calamity, and that civilians so affected have a right to protection and assistance.

It is on the basis of this belief, reflected in international humanitarian law and based on the principle of humanity, that we offer our services as humanitarian agencies. We will act in accordance with the principles of humanity and impartiality, and with the other principles set out in the *Code of Conduct for the International Red Cross and Red Crescent Movement and Non-Governmental Organisations (NGOs) in Disaster Relief* (1994). **This Code of Conduct appears in full on page 315.**

The Humanitarian Charter affirms the fundamental importance of the following principles:

1.1 The right to life with dignity

This right is reflected in the legal measures concerning the right to life, to an adequate standard of living and to freedom from cruel, inhuman or degrading treatment or punishment. We understand an individual's right to life to entail the right to have steps taken to preserve life where it is threatened, and a corresponding duty on others to take such steps. Implicit in this is the duty not to withhold or frustrate the provision of life-saving assistance. In addition, international humanitarian law makes specific provision for assistance to civilian populations during conflict, obliging states and other parties to agree to the provision of humanitarian and impartial assistance when the civilian population lacks essential supplies.[1]

1.2 The distinction between combatants and non-combatants

This is the distinction which underpins the 1949 Geneva Conventions and their Additional Protocols of 1977. This fundamental principle has been increasingly eroded, as reflected in the enormously increased proportion of civilian casualties during the second half of the twentieth century. That internal conflict is often referred to as 'civil war' must not blind us to the need to distinguish between those actively engaged in hostilities, and civilians and others (including the sick, wounded and prisoners) who play no direct part. Non-combatants are protected under international humanitarian law and are entitled to immunity from attack.[2]

1.3 The principle of non-refoulement

This is the principle that no refugee shall be sent (back) to a country in which his or her life or freedom would be threatened on account of race, religion, nationality, membership of a particular social group or political opinion; or where there are substantial grounds for believing that s/he would be in danger of being subjected to torture.[3]

2 Roles and Responsibilities

2.1 We recognise that it is firstly through their own efforts that the basic needs of people affected by calamity or armed conflict are met, and we acknowledge the primary role and responsibility of the state to provide assistance when people's capacity to cope has been exceeded.

2.2 International law recognises that those affected are entitled to protection and assistance. It defines legal obligations on states or warring parties to provide such assistance or to allow it to be provided, as well as to prevent and refrain from behaviour that violates fundamental human rights. These rights and obligations are contained in the body of international human rights law, international humanitarian law and refugee law (see sources listed below).

2.3 As humanitarian agencies, we define our role in relation to these primary roles and responsibilities. Our role in providing humanitarian assistance reflects the reality that those with primary responsibility are not always able or willing to perform this role themselves. This is sometimes a matter of capacity. Sometimes it constitutes a wilful disregard of fundamental legal and ethical obligations, the result of which is much avoidable human suffering.

2.4 The frequent failure of warring parties to respect the humanitarian purpose of interventions has shown that the attempt to provide assistance in situations of conflict may potentially render civilians more vulnerable to attack, or may on occasion bring unintended advantage to one or more of the warring parties. We are committed to minimising any such adverse effects of our interventions in so far as this is consistent with the obligations outlined above. It is the obligation of warring parties to respect the humanitarian nature of such interventions.

2.5 In relation to the principles set out above and more generally, we recognise and support the protection and assistance mandates of the International Committee of the Red Cross and of the United Nations High Commissioner for Refugees under international law.

3 Minimum Standards

The Minimum Standards which follow are based on agencies' experience of providing humanitarian assistance. Though the achievement of the standards depends on a range of factors, many of which may be beyond our control, we commit ourselves to attempt consistently to achieve them and we expect to be held to account accordingly. We invite other humanitarian actors, including states themselves, to adopt these standards as accepted norms.

By adhering to the standards set out in chapters 1-5 we commit ourselves to make every effort to ensure that people affected by disasters have access to at least the minimum requirements (water, sanitation, food, nutrition, shelter and health care) to satisfy their basic right to life with dignity. To this end we will continue to advocate that governments and other parties meet their obligations under international human rights law, international humanitarian law and refugee law.

We expect to be held accountable to this commitment and undertake to develop systems for accountability within our respective agencies, consortia and federations. We acknowledge that our fundamental accountability must be to those we seek to assist.

Notes

1. Articles 3 and 5 of the *Universal Declaration of Human Rights* 1948; Articles 6 and 7 of the *International Covenant on Civil and Political Rights* 1966; common Article 3 of the four *Geneva Conventions* of 1949; Articles 23, 55 and 59 of the *Fourth Geneva Convention*; Articles 69 to 71 of *Additional Protocol I* of 1977; Article 18 of *Additional Protocol II* of 1977 as well as other relevant rules of international humanitarian law; *Convention against Torture and Other Cruel, Inhuman or Degrading Treatment or Punishment* 1984; Articles 10, 11 and 12 of the *International Covenant on Economic, Social, and Cultural Rights* 1966; Articles 6, 37 and 24 of the *Convention on the Rights of the Child* 1989; and elsewhere in international law.

2. The distinction between combatants and non-combatants is the basic principle underlying international humanitarian law. See in particular common Article 3 of the four *Geneva Conventions of 1949 and Article 48 of Additional Protocol I of 1977*. See also Article 38 of the *Convention on the Rights of the Child* 1989.

3. Article 33 of the *Convention on the Status of Refugees* 1951; Article 3 of the *Convention against Torture and Other Cruel, Inhuman or Degrading Treatment or Punishment* 1984; Article 22 of the *Convention on the Rights of the Child* 1989.

Charter

Sources

The following instruments inform this Charter:

Universal Declaration of Human Rights 1948.

International Covenant on Civil and Political Rights 1966.

International Covenant on Economic, Social and Cultural Rights 1966.

International Convention on the Elimination of All Forms of Racial Discrimination 1969.

The four Geneva Conventions of 1949 and their two Additional Protocols of 1977.

Convention relating to the Status of Refugees 1951 and the Protocol relating to the Status of Refugees 1967.

Convention against Torture and Other Cruel, Inhuman or Degrading Treatment or Punishment 1984.

Convention on the Prevention and Punishment of the Crime of Genocide 1948.

Convention on the Rights of the Child 1989.

Convention on the Elimination of All Forms of Discrimination Against Women 1979.

Convention relating to the Status of Stateless Persons 1960.

Guiding Principles on Internal Displacement 1998.

Chapter 1: Minimum Standards Common to All Sectors

How to use this chapter

This chapter details eight core 'process and people' standards that are relevant to each of the technical sectors. The standards are: 1) participation, 2) initial assessment, 3) response, 4) targeting, 5) monitoring, 6) evaluation, 7) aid worker competencies and responsibilities and 8) supervision, management and support of personnel. Each contains the following:

● *the minimum standards:* these are qualitative in nature and specify the minimum levels to be attained;

● *key indicators:* these are 'signals' that show whether the standard has been attained. They provide a way of measuring and communicating the impact, or result, of programmes as well as the process or methods used. The indicators may be qualitative or quantitative;

● *guidance notes:* these include specific points to consider when applying the standards and indicators in different situations, guidance on tackling practical difficulties, and advice on priority issues. They may also include critical issues relating to the standards or indicators, and describe dilemmas, controversies or gaps in current knowledge.

The chapter is followed by a select list of references, which point to sources of information on both general and specific technical issues relating to the standards.

Contents

Common
Standards

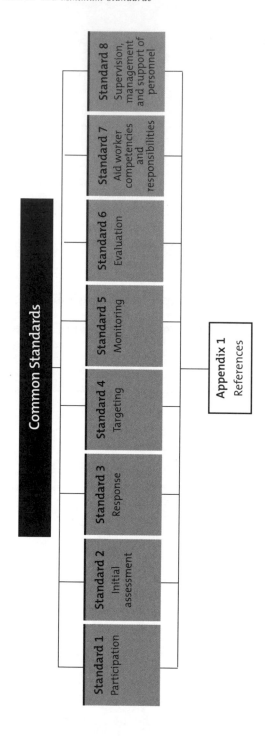

Introduction

These common standards relate to each of the chapters in this handbook and are integral to all of them. By implementing the standards described here, agencies will support the realisation of the standards outlined in the technical chapters.

Links to international legal instruments

Everyone has the right to life with dignity and respect for their human rights. Humanitarian agencies have the responsibility to provide assistance in a manner that is consistent with human rights, including the right to participation, non-discrimination and information, as reflected in the body of international human rights, humanitarian and refugee law. In the Humanitarian Charter and the *Code of Conduct for the International Red Cross and Red Crescent Movement and Non-Governmental Organisations (NGOs) in Disaster Relief,* humanitarian agencies undertake to make themselves accountable to those they seek to assist. The common standards outline the responsibilities of organisations and individuals when providing protection and assistance.

The importance of the standards common to all sectors

Programmes that meet the needs of disaster-affected populations must be based on a clear understanding of the context. Initial assessments will analyse the nature of the disaster and its effect on a population. The affected people's capacities and available resources should be identified at the same time as assessing their needs and vulnerabilities and any gaps in essential services. No single sector can be considered in isolation from the others, or in isolation from economics, religious and traditional beliefs, social practices, political and security factors, coping mechanisms or anticipated future developments. Analysis of the causes and effects of the disaster is critical. If the problem is not correctly identified and understood then it will be difficult, if not impossible, to respond appropriately.

Response depends on a number of factors, including an organisation's capacity, area(s) of expertise, budget constraints, familiarity with the region or situation and security risks for staff. The response standards detailed here are designed to clarify 'who does what when'. Once an appropriate response has been determined, targeting mechanisms should be established that enable agencies to provide assistance impartially and without discrimination, according to need.

Monitoring systems should be established early in the process to continuously measure progress against objectives and to check on the continuing relevance of the programme within an evolving context. An evaluation, which may be carried out during or at the end of the response, determines the overall effectiveness of the programme and identifies lessons that may improve similar programmes in future.

The quality of humanitarian assistance will depend on the skills, abilities, knowledge and commitment of staff and volunteers working in difficult and sometimes insecure conditions. Sound management and supervision are key elements of an assistance programme and, along with capacity building, can help to ensure that minimum standards of humanitarian assistance are respected. Given the importance of gender and other cross-cutting issues, diversity in human resources should be taken into account when building a team.

The participation of disaster-affected people – including the vulnerable groups outlined below – in the assessment, development, implementation and monitoring of responses should be maximised to ensure the appropriateness and quality of any disaster response. Systematic sharing of knowledge and information among all those involved in the response is fundamental to achieving a common understanding of problems and effective coordination among agencies.

Links to other chapters

It is critical that this chapter be read first, before turning to the relevant technical sector.

Vulnerabilities and capacities of disaster-affected populations

The groups most frequently at risk in disasters are women, children, older people, disabled people and people living with HIV/AIDS (PLWH/A). In certain contexts, people may also become vulnerable by reason of ethnic origin, religious or political affiliation, or displacement. This is not an exhaustive list, but it includes those most frequently identified. Specific vulnerabilities influence people's ability to cope and survive in a disaster, and those most at risk should be identified in each context.

Throughout the handbook, the term 'vulnerable groups' refers to all these groups. When any one group is at risk, it is likely that others will also be threatened. Therefore, whenever vulnerable groups are mentioned, users are strongly urged to consider all those listed here. Special care must be taken to protect and provide for all affected groups in a non-discriminatory manner and according to their specific needs. However, it should also be remembered that disaster-affected populations possess, and acquire, skills and capacities of their own to cope, and that these should be recognised and supported.

Common
Standards

The Minimum Standards

Common standard 1: participation

The disaster-affected population actively participates in the assessment, design, implementation, monitoring and evaluation of the assistance programme.

Key indicators (to be read in conjunction with the guidance notes)

- Women and men of all ages from the disaster-affected and wider local populations, including vulnerable groups, receive information about the assistance programme, and are given the opportunity to comment to the assistance agency during all stages of the project cycle (see guidance note 1).

- Written assistance programme objectives and plans should reflect the needs, concerns and values of disaster-affected people, particularly those belonging to vulnerable groups, and contribute to their protection (see guidance notes 1-2).

- Programming is designed to maximise the use of local skills and capacities (see guidance notes 3-4).

Guidance notes

1. *Representation of all groups:* the participation of disaster-affected people in decision-making throughout the project cycle (assessment, design, implementation, monitoring and evaluation) helps to ensure that programmes are equitable and effective. Special effort should be made to ensure the participation of a balanced representation of people within the assistance programme, including vulnerable and marginalised groups. Participation should ensure that programmes are based on the willing cooperation of disaster-affected people and that they respect local culture, where this does not undermine the rights of individuals. Assistance programmes should reflect the interdependency of individuals, households and communities and ensure that protection elements are not overlooked.

2. **Communication and transparency:** the sharing of information and knowledge among all those involved is fundamental to achieving a better understanding of the problem and to providing coordinated assistance. The results of assessments should be actively communicated to all concerned organisations and individuals. Mechanisms should be established to allow people to comment on the programme e.g. by means of public meetings or via community-based organisations. For individuals who are homebound or disabled, specific outreach programmes may be required.

3. **Local capacity:** participation in the programme should reinforce people's sense of dignity and hope in times of crisis, and people should be encouraged to participate in programmes in different ways. Programmes should be designed to build upon local capacity and to avoid undermining people's own coping strategies.

4. **Long-term sustainability:** long-term benefits are usually realised during the course of strengthening local capacities to deal with disasters. A disaster response programme should support and/or complement existing services and local institutions in terms of structure and design and be sustainable after the external assistance stops. Local and national governmental organisations have fundamental responsibilities for populations and must be consulted in the longer-term design of programmes when feasible.

Common standard 2: initial assessment

Assessments provide an understanding of the disaster situation and a clear analysis of threats to life, dignity, health and livelihoods to determine, in consultation with the relevant authorities, whether an external response is required and, if so, the nature of the response.

Key indicators (to be read in conjunction with the guidance notes)

● Information is gathered using standardised procedures and made available to allow for transparent decision-making (see guidance notes 1-6).

- The assessment considers all technical sectors (water and sanitation, nutrition, food, shelter, health), and the physical, social, economic, political and security environment (see guidance note 7).

- Through consultation, the assessment takes into account the responses of the local and national authorities and other actors and agencies (see guidance note 7).

- Local capacities and strategies to cope with the disaster, both those of the affected population and the surrounding population, are identified (see guidance note 8).

- Whenever feasible, data are disaggregated by sex and by age (see guidance note 9).

- The assessment is underpinned by the rights of those affected by disasters, as defined by international law.

- The assessment takes into account the responsibility of relevant authorities to protect and assist the population on the territory over which they have control, and also takes into account national law, standards and guidelines applicable where the affected population is found, as they conform with international law.

- The assessment includes an analysis of the operating environment, including factors affecting the personal safety and security of the affected population and of humanitarian staff (see guidance note 10).

- Estimates of population numbers are cross-checked and validated with as many sources as possible, and the basis for the estimate made known.

- Assessment findings are made available to other sectors, national and local authorities and representatives of the affected population. Recommendations are made on the need for external assistance, and on appropriate responses that should be linked with exit or transition strategies (see guidance note 11).

Assessment checklists for individual sectors can be found in the appendices at the end of each technical chapter.

Guidance notes

1. *Initial assessments* provide the basis for delivering any immediate assistance that may be needed and also identify the areas on which a more detailed assessment should focus. An initial assessment is not an end in itself, but should be seen as a first step in a continuous process of reviewing and updating as part of the monitoring process, particularly when the situation is evolving rapidly, or when there are critical developments such as large population movements or an outbreak of disease. Frequently it may not be possible to adequately address or consult all sectors or groups within the population. When this is the case, it should be clearly stated which groups have been omitted, and efforts should be made to return to them at the first opportunity.

2. *Checklists:* these are a useful way of ensuring that key areas have been examined, and examples of checklists are provided in appendices to each of the technical chapters of this handbook. Additional information can be found in Appendix 1: References on page 43.

3. *Timeliness:* an initial assessment should be carried out as soon as possible after the disaster occurs, while addressing any life-threatening or other critical needs. The report should normally be generated within days and its format and content should allow planners and analysts to easily identify priorities and provide sufficient information to rapidly design an appropriate programme. A more in-depth assessment will be needed later to identify gaps in assistance and to provide baseline information.

4. *Assessment team:* a gender-balanced team, composed of generalists and relevant technical specialists and with clear terms of reference, which seeks to actively involve the population in a culturally acceptable manner, will improve the quality of an assessment. Local knowledge and previous experience of disasters in the country or region are critical.

5. *Collecting information:* team members should be clear on the objectives and methodology of the assessment and on their own roles before field work begins, and a mix of quantitative and qualitative methods appropriate to the context should normally be used. Some individuals or groups may not be able to speak openly, and special arrangements may be considered to collect sensitive information. Information must be treated with the utmost

Common Standards

care and confidentiality must be ensured. Following the individual's consent, consideration may be given to passing on this information to appropriate actors or institutions. Staff operating in conflict situations need to be aware that information collected may be sensitive, could be misused and could compromise the agency's own ability to operate.

6. **Sources of information:** information for the assessment report can be compiled from primary sources, including direct observation and discussions with key individuals, such as agency staff, local authorities, community leaders (of both sexes), elders, children, health staff, teachers, traders and other relevant actors, and from secondary sources, such as existing literature and reports (both published and unpublished), relevant historical material and pre-emergency data. National or regional disaster-preparedness plans also provide an important source of information. Comparing secondary information with direct observation and judgement is crucial in order to minimise potential biases. The methods used for collecting information and the limitations of the resulting data must be clearly communicated to portray a realistic picture of the situation. The assessment report should clearly indicate specific concerns and recommendations expressed by all groups, notably those who are particularly vulnerable.

7. **Sectoral assessments:** a multi-sectoral assessment may not always be possible in the initial phase of a disaster and may delay action to meet critical needs in specific sectors. When individual sectoral assessments are carried out, extra attention should be paid to linkages with other sectors and to broader contextual and protection issues, in consultation with other actors and agencies.

8. **Relationship with host population:** the provision of facilities and support for displaced populations can cause resentment amongst the host community, especially where existing resources are limited and have to be shared with new arrivals. In order to minimise tensions, host populations should be consulted and, where appropriate, the development of infrastructure and services for displaced populations should lead also to a sustainable improvement in the livelihoods of the host population.

9. **Disaggregation of data** is important for various reasons. It enables users of an assessment to check the accuracy of results and allows comparison with earlier studies on the same area. In addition to age, gender, vulnerability, etc., it is useful to include average family size and number of households as

key disaggregated information, as this will help in planning a more appropriate response. In the early stages of a disaster, it may be difficult to disaggregate data by age and gender. However, mortality and morbidity for children under five years old should be documented from the outset, as this section of the population is usually at special risk. As time and conditions allow, more detailed disaggregation should be sought, to detect further differences according to age, sex and vulnerability.

10. **Underlying context:** the assessment and subsequent analysis should take account of underlying structural, political, security, economic, demographic and environmental issues. Likewise, any changes in living conditions and community structures of both host and displaced populations in relation to the pre-disaster phase should be considered.

11. **Recovery:** analysis and planning for the post-disaster recovery period should be part of the initial assessment, as external aid can slow recovery if not provided in a way that supports the local population's own survival mechanisms.

Common standard 3: response

A humanitarian response is required in situations where the relevant authorities are unable and/or unwilling to respond to the protection and assistance needs of the population on the territory over which they have control, and when assessment and analysis indicate that these needs are unmet.

Key indicators (to be read in conjunction with the guidance notes)

- Where people's lives are at risk as a result of disaster, programmes prioritise life-saving needs (see guidance note 1).

- Programmes and projects are designed to support and protect the affected population and to promote their livelihoods, so that they meet or exceed the Sphere Minimum Standards, as illustrated by the key indicators (see guidance note 2).

- There is effective coordination and exchange of information among those affected by or involved in the disaster response. Humanitarian

Common Standards

agencies undertake activities on the basis of need, where their expertise and capacity can have the greatest impact within the overall assistance programme (see guidance note 3).

● Organisations, programmes and projects that either cannot address identified needs or are unable to attain the Minimum Standards make any gaps known so that others may assist (see guidance notes 4-5).

● In conflict situations, the assistance programme takes into account the possible impact of the response on the dynamics of the situation (see guidance note 6).

Guidance notes

1. ***Responding to actual need:*** humanitarian response must be organised to meet assessed needs. Care should be taken that superfluous items that could interfere with the delivery of essential items are not included in the delivery channels.

2. ***Meeting the Minimum Standards:*** response programmes and projects should be designed to close the gap between existing living conditions and the Sphere Minimum Standards. It is nevertheless important to make a distinction between the emergency needs and the chronic needs of an affected population. In many cases, humanitarian needs and the resources that would be required to bring a community, area, region or even country up to the Minimum Standards are far greater than the resources available. An agency cannot expect to bring this about single-handedly and communities, their neighbours, host governments, donors and other local and international organisations all have an important role to play. Coordination among those responding to a disaster situation is essential to address critical gaps.

3. ***Capacity and expertise:*** in situations where an organisation is highly specialised, or mandated to respond to particular needs (or groups), it should aim to provide the greatest humanitarian impact possible using its own resources and skills base. Even within the specific limits of an agency's expertise or mandate, however, it is likely that the overall humanitarian need will outstrip its organisational resources. Where the agency finds itself with excess capacity, it should make that capacity known to the wider humanitarian response community and contribute when and where necessary.

4. **Making gaps known:** while humanitarian agencies prefer to demonstrate programme successes and positive evaluations of ongoing initiatives to help fund future programmes, they must nevertheless be prepared to promptly acknowledge gaps in their capacity to meet basic needs.

5. **Sharing information:** organisations identifying critical needs should make them known to the wider community as quickly as possible, to enable those agencies with the most appropriate resources and capacity to respond. Wherever possible, recognised terminology, standards and procedures should be used to help others mobilise their responses more quickly and more effectively. The use of standard survey formats and associated guidelines, agreed among the host government and agencies at country level, can help significantly in this regard.

6. **Maximising positive impact and limiting harm:** conflict and competition for scarce resources often lead to increased insecurity, misuse or misappropriation of aid, inequitable distribution or diversion of aid. Understanding the nature and source of conflict helps to ensure that aid is distributed in an impartial way and reduces or avoids negative impact. In conflict-affected settings, an analysis of the actors, mechanisms, issues and context of the conflict should be carried out prior to programme planning.

Common standard 4: targeting

Humanitarian assistance or services are provided equitably and impartially, based on the vulnerability and needs of individuals or groups affected by disaster.

Key indicators (to be read in conjunction with the guidance notes)

- Targeting criteria must be based on a thorough analysis of vulnerability (see guidance note 1).

- Targeting mechanisms are agreed among the affected population (including representatives of vulnerable groups) and other appropriate actors. Targeting criteria are clearly defined and widely disseminated (see guidance notes 2-3).

Common Standards

● Targeting mechanisms and criteria should not undermine the dignity and security of individuals, or increase their vulnerability to exploitation (see guidance notes 2-3).

● Distribution systems are monitored to ensure that targeting criteria are respected and that timely corrective action is taken when necessary (see guidance notes 4-5).

Guidance notes

1. *The purpose of targeting* is to meet the needs of the most vulnerable, while providing aid efficiently and in a way that minimises dependency.

2. *Targeting mechanisms* are the ways in which assistance is made available impartially and without discrimination, according to need. Options include community-based targeting, administrative targeting, self-targeting, and combinations of these methods. Agency workers should be aware that self-targeting can sometimes exclude certain vulnerable groups. To ensure that the disaster-affected population is consulted and is in agreement with the targeting decisions, a representative group of women and men, boys and girls and people from vulnerable groups should be included in the consultation process. In conflict situations, it is essential to understand the nature and source of the conflict and how this might influence administrative and community decisions about targeting assistance.

3. *Targeting criteria* are usually linked to the level or degree of vulnerability of a community, household or individual, which in turn are determined by the risks presented by the disaster and the coping capacity of the recipients. Individual dignity may be unintentionally undermined by improper targeting criteria and mechanisms and appropriate measures must be taken to avoid this. Some examples include:

   – administrative and community-based targeting mechanisms may ask for information about an individual's assets. Such questions may be perceived as intrusive and can potentially undermine social structures.

   – households with malnourished children are often targeted for selective food assistance. This may undermine people's dignity since it may encourage parents to keep their children thin so that they continue to receive selective rations. This can also apply when general rations are provided.

- where assistance is targeted through local clan systems, people who fall outside such systems (e.g. displaced individuals) are likely to be excluded.

- displaced women, girls and boys may be exposed to sexual coercion.

- people suffering from HIV/AIDS may be exposed to stigma. Confidentiality should be observed at all times.

4. *Access to and use of facilities and services:* people's use of facilities and goods provided are affected by many factors, such as access, security, convenience, quality and whether they are appropriate to needs and customs. Access may be particularly constrained in situations of armed conflict, and by factors such as corruption, intimidation and exploitation (including for sex). Wherever possible, factors that limit the use of facilities should be dealt with through community mobilisation or revisions to the programme. It is essential to ensure that consultation before and during programme implementation includes adequate discussion with women, children and other vulnerable groups, for whom the constraints on use are likely to be greatest.

5. *Monitoring errors of exclusion and inclusion:* when a targeting system fails to reach all of the vulnerable people in need following a disaster, individuals or groups can quickly develop critical needs. Provision should be made for updating and refining targeting and distribution systems to achieve more effective coverage.

Common standard 5: monitoring

The effectiveness of the programme in responding to problems is identified and changes in the broader context are continually monitored, with a view to improving the programme, or to phasing it out as required.

Key indicators (to be read in conjunction with the guidance notes)

● The information collected for monitoring is timely and useful, it is recorded and analysed in an accurate, logical, consistent, regular and transparent manner and it informs the ongoing programme (see guidance notes 1-2).

● Systems are in place to ensure regular collection of information in each of the technical sectors and to identify whether the indicators for each standard are being met.

● Women, men and children from all affected groups are regularly consulted and are involved in monitoring activities (see guidance note 3).

● Systems are in place that enable a flow of information between the programme, other sectors, the affected groups of the population, the relevant local authorities, donors and other actors as needed (see guidance note 4).

Guidance notes

1. *Use of monitoring information:* disaster situations are volatile and dynamic. Regularly updated information is therefore vital in ensuring that programmes remain relevant and effective. Regular monitoring allows managers to determine priorities, identify emerging problems, follow trends, determine the effect of their responses, and guide revisions to their programmes. Information derived from continual monitoring of programmes can be used for reviews, evaluations and other purposes. In some circumstances a shift in strategy may be required to respond to major changes in needs or in the context.

2. *Using and disseminating information:* information collected should be directly relevant to the programme – in other words, it should be useful and acted upon. It should also be documented and made available proactively as needed to other sectors and agencies, and to the affected population. The means of communication used (dissemination methods, language, etc.) must be appropriate and accessible for the intended audience.

3. *People involved in monitoring:* people who are able to collect information from all groups in the affected population in a culturally acceptable manner should be included, especially with regard to gender and language skills. Local cultural practices may require that women or minority groups be consulted separately by individuals who are culturally acceptable.

4. Information sharing: monitoring and evaluation activities require close consultation and cooperation across sectors. For example, during a cholera epidemic, information should be continually shared between water and sanitation agencies and health agencies. Coordination mechanisms such as regular meetings and the use of notice boards can facilitate this exchange of information.

Common standard 6: evaluation

There is a systematic and impartial examination of humanitarian action, intended to draw lessons to improve practice and policy and to enhance accountability.

Key indicators (to be read in conjunction with the guidance notes)

● The programme is evaluated with reference to stated objectives and agreed minimum standards to measure its overall appropriateness, efficiency, coverage, coherence and impact on the affected population (see guidance note 1).

● Evaluations take account of the views and opinions of the affected population, as well as the host community if different.

● The collection of information for evaluation purposes is independent and impartial.

● The results of each evaluation exercise are used to improve future practice (see guidance note 2).

Guidance notes

1. Establishing criteria: evaluating humanitarian assistance programmes is not an easy task since disasters are characterised by rapid changes and a high degree of uncertainty. While qualitative methods are more likely to capture the intricate nature of disaster responses, those evaluating such programmes should be prepared to use different methods and compare and weigh the results to arrive at valid conclusions.

Common Standards

2. *Subsequent use of information:* evaluations should result in written reports, which are shared to contribute to transparency and accountability, and which allow for lessons to be learned across programmes and agencies that lead to improvements in humanitarian policies and practices.

Common standard 7: aid worker competencies and responsibilities

Aid workers possess appropriate qualifications, attitudes and experience to plan and effectively implement appropriate programmes.

Key indicators (to be read in conjunction with the guidance notes)

● Aid workers have relevant technical qualifications and knowledge of local cultures and customs, and/or previous emergency experience. Workers are also familiar with human rights and humanitarian principles.

● Staff are knowledgeable about the potential tensions and sources of conflict within the disaster-affected population itself and with host communities. They are aware of the implications of delivering humanitarian assistance, and pay particular attention to vulnerable groups (see guidance note 1).

● Staff are able to recognise abusive, discriminatory or illegal activities, and refrain from such activities (see guidance note 2).

Guidance notes

1. *Staff need to be aware* of the extent to which crimes of violence, including rape and other forms of brutality against women, girls and boys, can increase during times of crisis. Fear of harassment and rape forces women into forming alliances with soldiers and other men in positions of authority or power. Young males are vulnerable to forced conscription into fighting forces. Staff and field partners should know how to refer women, men and children seeking redress for human rights violations, and be familiar with procedures for referring survivors of rape and sexual violence for counselling, medical or contraceptive care.

2. **Staff must understand** that responsibility for control over the management and allocation of the valuable resources involved in disaster response programmes puts them and others involved in their delivery in a position of relative power over other people. Staff must be alert to the danger that this power may be corruptly or abusively exercised. Staff should be aware that women and children are frequently coerced into humiliating, degrading or exploitative behaviour. Sexual activity cannot be required in exchange for humanitarian assistance nor should aid workers be party to any such forms of exchange. Activities such as forced labour and illicit drug use and trading are also prohibited.

Common standard 8: supervision, management and support of personnel

Aid workers receive supervision and support to ensure effective implementation of the humanitarian assistance programme.

Common Standards

Key indicators (to be read in conjunction with the guidance notes)

● Managers are accountable for their decisions and for ensuring adequate security and compliance with codes/rules of conduct as well as support for their staff (see guidance note 1).

● Technical and managerial staff are provided with the necessary training, resources and logistical support to fulfil their responsibilities (see guidance note 2).

● Staff working on programmes understand the purpose and method of the activities they are asked to carry out, and receive subsequent feedback on their performance.

● All staff have written job descriptions, with clear reporting lines, and undergo periodic written performance assessment.

● All staff are oriented regarding relevant health and safety issues for the region and environment in which they are to work (see guidance note 3).

● Staff receive appropriate security training.

● Capacity-building systems for staff are set up and these are subject to routine monitoring (see guidance notes 4-5).

● The capacity of national and local organisations is built up to promote long-term sustainability.

Guidance notes

1. *Managers at all levels* have particular responsibilities to establish and/or maintain systems that promote the implementation of programmes, of relevant policies, and to ensure compliance with rules/codes of conduct. Some humanitarian agencies already have codes or rules that relate to staff and institutional conduct with respect to issues such as child protection or sexual exploitation and abuse. As the importance of such rules is widely recognised, many humanitarian agencies are in the process of developing codes of conduct. Managerial accountability for ensuring compliance is a crucial aspect in the success of such codes.

2. *Humanitarian agencies* should ensure that their staff are qualified and competent, and properly trained and prepared, before assignment to an emergency situation. When deploying emergency teams, agencies should seek to ensure that there is a balance of women and men among staff and volunteers. Ongoing support and training may be necessary to ensure that staff can fulfil their responsibilities.

3. *All staff* should receive appropriate briefings on security and health issues, both prior to their deployment and when they arrive on-site. They should receive vaccinations and malaria prophylaxis medications (where needed) prior to deployment. Upon arrival, they should receive information aimed at minimising security risks, and should also be briefed on food and water safety, prevention of HIV/AIDS and other endemic infectious diseases, medical care availability, medical evacuation policies and procedures, and workers' compensation.

4. *Special efforts* should be made to promote diversity within the various levels of an organisation.

5. *Capacity building* is an explicit objective during the rehabilitation phase following a disaster. It should also be undertaken, to the extent possible, during the disaster/relief phase itself, especially when this is protracted.

Appendix 1

References

Thanks to the Forced Migration Online programme of the Refugee Studies Centre at the University of Oxford, many of these documents have received copyright permission and are posted on a special Sphere link at: http://www.forcedmigration.org

Participation

ALNAP Global Study: *Participation by Affected Populations in Humanitarian Action: Practitioner Handbook* (forthcoming). http://www.alnap.org

http://www.hapgeneva.org

Assessment and response

UNHCR, *Handbook for Emergencies* (2000). http://www.unhcr.ch

Field Operations Guidelines for Assessment and Response (FOG, 1998). USAID. http://www.info.usaid.gov/ofda

Demographic Assessment Techniques in Complex Humanitarian Emergencies: Summary of a Workshop (2002). http://books.nap.edu/books/0309084970/html

Humanity Development Library: http://humaninfo.org

OCHA Humanitarian Information Centres: http://www.humanitarianinfo.org

OCHA (1999), *Orientation Handbook on Complex Emergencies*. Office for the Coordination of Humanitarian Affairs. United Nations. New York.

Relief Web Humanitarian Library: http://www.reliefweb.int/library

Telford, J (1997), *Good Practice Review 5: Counting and Identification of Beneficiary Populations in Emergency Operations: Registration and its Alternatives*. Relief and Rehabilitation Network/Overseas Development Institute. London.

Targeting

Humanitarian Ethics in Disaster and War. IFRC, 2003.
http://www.ifrc.org/publicat/wdr2003/chapter1.asp

International Food Policy Research Institute Training Material, *Targeting: Principles and Practice.*
http://www.reliefweb.int/training/ti1227.html

Vincent, M, Refslund Sorensen, B. (eds.) (2001), *Caught Between Borders, Response Strategies of the Internally Displaced.* Norwegian Refugee Council.

International Strategy for Disaster Reduction, *Countering Disasters, Targeting Vulnerability.* UN/ISDR, 2001. http://www.unisdr.org

Monitoring and evaluation

ALNAP Annual Review (2001), *Humanitarian Action: Learning from Evaluation.* http://www.alnap.org

ALNAP Annual Review (2003), *Humanitarian Action: Improving Monitoring to Enhance Accountability and Learning.*
http://www.alnap.org

Guidance for Evaluation of Humanitarian Assistance in Complex Emergencies, (1999). Organisation for Economic Cooperation for Development (OECD). Paris. http://www.oecd.org/dac

Manual for the Evaluation of Humanitarian Aid. European Community Humanitarian Office Evaluation Unit, Brussels, 2002. http://europa.eu.int

Personnel

The People in Aid Code of Good Practice in the Management and Support of Aid Personnel 2003. People in Aid. http://peopleinaid.org

Children

Action for the Rights of the Child (ARC). Save the Children Alliance and UNHCR, 1998.

Children Not Soldiers, Guidelines for Working with Child Soldiers and Children Associated with Fighting Forces. Save the Children.

Gosling, L and Edwards, M, *Toolkits – A Practical Guide to Planning, Monitoring, Evaluation and Impact Assessment*. Save the Children.

Inter-Agency Working Group on Unaccompanied and Separated Children, *Inter-Agency Guiding Principles on Unaccompanied and Separated Children* (forthcoming).

Disability

http://www.annenberg.nwu.edu/pubs/disada/

http://www.fema.gov/rrr/assistf.shtm

http://www.redcross.org/services/disaster/beprepared/disability.pdf

Environment

http://www.benfieldhrc.org/disastersstudies/projects/REA

Environmental assessment resources for small-scale activities: http://www.encapafrica.org

www.reliefweb.int/ochaunep

Gender

Beck, T and Stelcner, M (1996), *Guide to Gender-Sensitive Indicators*. Canadian International Development Agency (CIDA). Quebec.

Dugan, J, *Assessing the Opportunity for Sexual Violence against Women and Children in Refugee Camps*. Journal of Humanitarian Assistance, August 2000. http://www.jha.ac/articles

Common Standards

Enarson, E (2000), *Gender and Natural Disasters,* Working Paper, In Focus Programme on Crisis Response and Reconstruction. ILO.

FAO, *Gender in Emergencies Annex:* manuals, guidelines, major documents: http://www.fao.org

FAO/WFP (2003), *Passport to Mainstreaming a Gender Perspective in Emergency Programmes.*

Gender and Disaster Network: http://www.anglia.ac.uk

Gender and Humanitarian Assistance Resource Kit: http://www.reliefweb.int/library/GHARkit

UNHCR, *Guidelines on the Protection of Refugee Women.*

UNICEF (1999), *Mainstreaming Gender in Unstable Environments.* http://www.reliefweb.int/library

HIV/AIDS

Holmes W (2003), *Protecting the Future: HIV Prevention, Care, and Support Among Displaced and War-Affected Populations. International Rescue Committee.* Kumarian Press, New York.

Inter-Agency Field Manual. Reproductive Health in Refugee Situations. UNHCR/WHO/UNFPA. Geneva, 1999.

Inter-Agency Standing Committee (IASC) on HIV/AIDS in Emergency Settings. *Guidelines for HIV/AIDS Interventions in Emergency Settings* (draft). IASC, 2003: 85. Geneva.

Family Health International (FHI) (2001), *HIV/AIDS Prevention and Care in Resource-Constrained Settings: A Handbook for the Design and Management of Programs.* Virginia.

Older people

HelpAge International, *Older People in Disaster and Humanitarian Crises: Guidelines for Best Practice.* Available in English, French, Spanish and Portuguese. http://www.helpage.org

Madrid International Plan of Action on Ageing, Report of the Second World Assembly on Ageing, Madrid, 8-12 April 2002, A/CONF.197/9 Paragraphs 54-56. http://www.un.org

UNHCR, *Policy on Older Refugees* (as endorsed at the 17th Meeting of the Standing Committee February/March 2000). EC/50/SC/CRP.13

United Nations Principles for Older Persons. http://www.un.org

Protection

Agenda for Protection. UNHCR. Geneva, 2002.

Frohardt, M, Paul, D and Minear, L (1999), *Protecting Human Rights: The Challenge to Humanitarian Organisations.* Occasional Paper 35, Thomas J. Watson Jr. Institute for International Studies, Brown University.

Growing the Sheltering Tree: Protecting Rights Through Humanitarian Action, Programmes and Practice Gathered from the Field. Inter-Agency Standing Committee, Geneva.

Protecting Refugees: A Field Guide for NGOs. UNHCR. Geneva, 1999.

Strengthening Protection in War: A Search for Professional Standards. ICRC. Geneva, 2001.

OCHA, *Protection of Civilians in Armed Conflict.*
http://www.reliefweb.int/ocha_ol/civilians/

Common
Standards

Notes

Notes

Notes

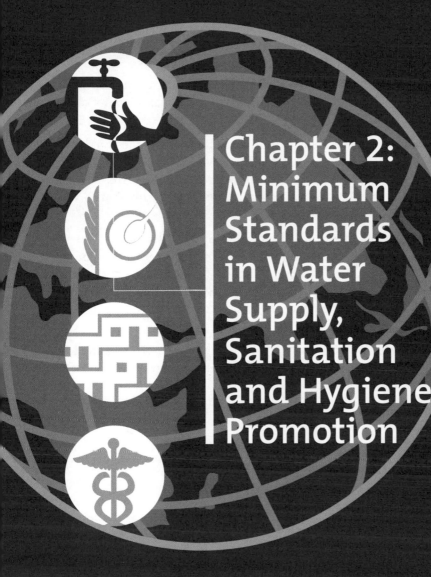

Chapter 2:
Minimum
Standards
in Water
Supply,
Sanitation
and Hygiene
Promotion

How to use this chapter

This chapter is divided into six main sections: Hygiene Promotion, Water Supply, Excreta Disposal, Vector Control, Solid Waste Management and Drainage. Each contains the following:

● *the minimum standards:* these are qualitative in nature and specify the minimum levels to be attained in the provision of water and sanitation responses;

● *key indicators:* these are 'signals' that show whether the standard has been attained. They provide a way of measuring and communicating the impact, or result, of programmes as well as the process, or methods, used. The indicators may be qualitative or quantitative;

● *guidance notes:* these include specific points to consider when applying the standard and indicators in different situations, guidance on tackling practical difficulties, and advice on priority issues. They may also include critical issues relating to the standard or indicators, and describe dilemmas, controversies or gaps in current knowledge.

The appendices include a select list of references, which point to sources of information on both general issues and specific technical issues relating to this chapter.

Contents

HP/
Wat San

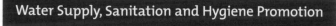

Water Supply, Sanitation and Hygiene Promotion

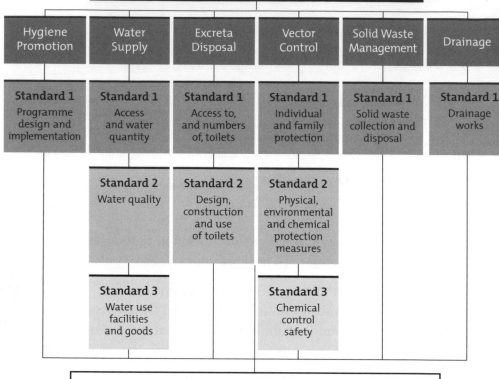

Hygiene Promotion	Water Supply	Excreta Disposal	Vector Control	Solid Waste Management	Drainage
Standard 1 Programme design and implementation	**Standard 1** Access and water quantity	**Standard 1** Access to, and numbers of, toilets	**Standard 1** Individual and family protection	**Standard 1** Solid waste collection and disposal	**Standard 1** Drainage works
	Standard 2 Water quality	**Standard 2** Design, construction and use of toilets	**Standard 2** Physical, environmental and chemical protection measures		
	Standard 3 Water use facilities and goods		**Standard 3** Chemical control safety		

Appendix 1

Water and Sanitation Initial Needs Assessment Checklist

Appendix 2

Planning Guidelines for Minimum Water Quantities for Institutions and Other Uses

Appendix 3

Planning Guidelines for Minimum Numbers of Toilets at Public Places and Institutions

Appendix 4

Water-and Excreta-Related Diseases and Transmission Mechanisms

Appendix 5

References

Introduction

Links to international legal instruments

The Minimum Standards in Water, Sanitation and Hygiene Promotion are a practical expression of the principles and rights embodied in the Humanitarian Charter. The Humanitarian Charter is concerned with the most basic requirements for sustaining the lives and dignity of those affected by calamity or conflict, as reflected in the body of international human rights, humanitarian and refugee law.

Everyone has the right to water. This right is recognised in international legal instruments and provides for sufficient, safe, acceptable, physically accessible and affordable water for personal and domestic uses. An adequate amount of safe water is necessary to prevent death from dehydration, to reduce the risk of water-related disease and to provide for consumption, cooking, and personal and domestic hygienic requirements.

The right to water is inextricably related to other human rights, including the right to health, the right to housing and the right to adequate food. As such, it is part of the guarantees essential for human survival. States and non-state actors have responsibilities in fulfilling the right to water. In times of armed conflict, for example, it is prohibited to attack, destroy, remove or render useless drinking water installations or irrigation works.

The Minimum Standards in this chapter are not a full expression of the Right to Water. However, the Sphere standards reflect the core content of the Right to Water and contribute to the progressive realisation of this right globally.

The importance of water supply, sanitation and hygiene promotion in emergencies

Water and sanitation are critical determinants for survival in the initial stages of a disaster. People affected by disasters are generally much more susceptible to illness and death from disease, which are related to a large extent to inadequate sanitation, inadequate water supplies and poor hygiene. The most significant of these diseases are diarrhoeal diseases and infectious diseases transmitted by the faeco-oral route (see Appendix 4). Other water- and sanitation-related diseases include those carried by vectors associated with solid waste and water.

The main objective of water supply and sanitation programmes in disasters is to reduce the transmission of faeco-oral diseases and exposure to disease-bearing vectors through the promotion of good hygiene practices, the provision of safe drinking water and the reduction of environmental health risks and by establishing the conditions that allow people to live with good health, dignity, comfort and security. The term 'sanitation', throughout Sphere, refers to excreta disposal, vector control, solid waste disposal and drainage.

Simply providing sufficient water and sanitation facilities will not, on its own, ensure their optimal use or impact on public health. In order to achieve the maximum benefit from a response, it is imperative to ensure that disaster-affected people have the necessary information, knowledge and understanding to prevent water- and sanitation-related disease, and to mobilise their involvement in the design and maintenance of those facilities.

In most disaster situations the responsibility for collecting water falls to women and children. When using communal water and sanitation facilities, for example in refugee or displaced situations, women and adolescent girls can be vulnerable to sexual violence or exploitation. In order to minimise these risks, and to ensure a better quality of response, it is important to encourage women's participation in water supply and sanitation programmes wherever possible. An equitable participation of women and men in planning, decision-making and local management will help to ensure that the entire affected population has safe and easy access to water supply and sanitation services, and that services are equitable and appropriate.

Links to other chapters

Many of the standards in the other sector chapters are relevant to this chapter. Progress in achieving standards in one area often influences and even determines progress in other areas. For a response to be effective, close coordination and collaboration are required with other sectors. Coordination with local authorities and other responding agencies is also necessary to ensure that needs are met, that efforts are not duplicated, and that the quality of water and sanitation responses is optimised.

For instance, where nutritional standards have not been met, the urgency to improve the standard of water and sanitation increases, as people's vulnerability to disease will have significantly increased. The same applies to populations where HIV/AIDS prevalence is high or where there is a large proportion of older or disabled people. Priorities should be decided on the basis of sound information shared between sectors as the situation evolves. Reference to specific standards or guidance notes in other technical chapters is made where relevant.

HP/
Wat San

Links to the standards common to all sectors

The process by which an intervention is developed and implemented is critical to its effectiveness. This chapter should be utilised in conjunction with the standards common to all sectors, which cover participation, initial assessment, response, targeting, monitoring, evaluation, aid worker competencies and responsibilities, and the supervision, management and support of personnel (see chapter 1, page 21). In particular, in any response the participation of disaster-affected people – including the vulnerable groups outlined below – should be maximised to ensure its appropriateness and quality.

Vulnerabilities and capacities of disaster-affected populations

The groups most frequently at risk in emergencies are women, children, older people, disabled people and people living with HIV/AIDS (PLWH/A). In certain contexts, people may also become vulnerable by reason of ethnic origin, religious or political affiliation, or displacement. This is not an exhaustive list, but it includes those most frequently identified. Specific vulnerabilities influence people's ability to cope and survive in a disaster, and those most at risk should be identified in each context.

Throughout the handbook, the term 'vulnerable groups' refers to all these groups. When any one group is at risk, it is likely that others will also be threatened. Therefore, whenever vulnerable groups are mentioned, users are strongly urged to consider all those listed here. Special care must be taken to protect and provide for all affected groups in a non-discriminatory manner and according to their specific needs. However, it should also be remembered that disaster-affected populations possess, and acquire, skills and capacities of their own to cope, and that these should be recognised and supported.

The Minimum Standards

1 Hygiene Promotion

The aim of any water and sanitation programme is to promote good personal and environmental hygiene in order to protect health. Hygiene promotion is defined here as the mix between the population's knowledge, practice and resources and agency knowledge and resources, which together enable risky hygiene behaviours to be avoided. The three key factors are 1) a mutual sharing of information and knowledge, 2) the mobilisation of communities and 3) the provision of essential materials and facilities. Effective hygiene promotion relies on an exchange of information between the agency and the affected community in order to identify key hygiene problems and to design, implement and monitor a programme to promote hygiene practices that will ensure the optimal use of facilities and the greatest impact on public health. Community mobilisation is especially pertinent during disasters as the emphasis must be on encouraging people to take action to protect their health and make good use of facilities and services provided, rather than on the dissemination of messages. It must be stressed that hygiene promotion should never be a substitute for good sanitation and water supplies, which are fundamental to good hygiene.

Hygiene promotion is integral to all the standards within this chapter. It is presented here as one overarching standard with related indicators. Further specific indicators are given within each standard for water supply, excreta disposal, vector control, solid waste management and drainage.

HP/
Wat San

Hygiene promotion standard 1: programme design and implementation

All facilities and resources provided reflect the vulnerabilities, needs and preferences of the affected population. Users are involved in the management and maintenance of hygiene facilities where appropriate.

Key indicators (to be read in conjunction with the guidance notes)

● Key hygiene risks of public health importance are identified (see guidance note 1).

● Programmes include an effective mechanism for representative and participatory input from all users, including in the initial design of facilities (see guidance notes 2, 3 and 5).

● All groups within the population have equitable access to the resources or facilities needed to continue or achieve the hygiene practices that are promoted (see guidance note 3).

● Hygiene promotion messages and activities address key behaviours and misconceptions and are targeted for all user groups. Representatives from these groups participate in planning, training, implementation, monitoring and evaluation (see guidance notes 1, 3 and 4 and Participation standard on page 28).

● Users take responsibility for the management and maintenance of facilities as appropriate, and different groups contribute equitably (see guidance notes 5-6).

Guidance notes

1. ***Assessing needs:*** an assessment is needed to identify the key hygiene behaviours to be addressed and the likely success of promotional activity. The key risks are likely to centre on excreta disposal, the use and maintenance of toilets, the lack of hand washing with soap or an alternative, the unhygienic collection and storage of water, and unhygienic food storage and preparation. The assessment should look at resources available to the population as well as local behaviours, knowledge and

practices so that messages are relevant and practical. It should pay special attention to the needs of vulnerable groups. If consultation with any group is not possible, this should be clearly stated in the assessment report and addressed as quickly as possible (see Participation standard, page 28 and the assessment checklist in Appendix 1).

2. **Sharing responsibility:** the ultimate responsibility for hygiene practice lies with all members of the affected population. All actors responding to the disaster should work to enable hygienic practice by ensuring that both knowledge and facilities are accessible, and should be able to demonstrate that this has been achieved. As a part of this process, vulnerable groups from the affected population should participate in identifying risky practices and conditions and take responsibility to measurably reduce these risks. This can be achieved through promotional activities, training and facilitation of behavioural change, based on activities that are culturally acceptable and do not overburden the beneficiaries.

3. **Reaching all sections of the population:** hygiene promotion programmes need to be carried out with all groups of the population by facilitators who can access, and have the skills to work with, different groups (for example, in some cultures it is not acceptable for women to speak to unknown men). Materials should be designed so that messages reach members of the population who are illiterate. Participatory materials and methods that are culturally appropriate offer useful opportunities for groups to plan and monitor their own hygiene improvements. As a rough guide, in a camp scenario there should be two hygiene promoters/community mobilisers per 1,000 members of the target population. For information on hygiene items, see Non-food items standard 2 on page 232.

4. **Targeting priority hygiene risks and behaviours:** the objectives of hygiene promotion and communication strategies should be clearly defined and prioritised. The understanding gained through assessing hygiene risks, tasks and responsibilities of different groups should be used to plan and prioritise assistance, so that misconceptions (for example, how HIV/AIDS is transmitted) are addressed and information flow between humanitarian actors and the affected population is appropriate and targeted.

HP/
Wat San

5. ***Managing facilities:*** where possible, it is good practice to form water and/or sanitation committees, made up of representatives from the various user groups and half of whose members are women. The functions of these committees are to manage the communal facilities such as water points, public toilets and washing areas, be involved in hygiene promotion activities and also act as a mechanism for ensuring representation and promoting sustainability.

6. ***Overburdening:*** it is important to ensure that no one group is overburdened with the responsibility for hygiene promotional activities or management of facilities and that each group has equitable influence and benefits (such as training). Not all groups, women or men have the same needs and interests and it should be recognised that the participation of women should not lead to men, or other groups within the population, not taking responsibility.

2 Water Supply

Water is essential for life, health and human dignity. In extreme situations, there may not be sufficient water available to meet basic needs, and in these cases supplying a survival level of safe drinking water is of critical importance. In most cases, the main health problems are caused by poor hygiene due to insufficient water and by the consumption of contaminated water.

Water supply standard 1: access and water quantity

All people have safe and equitable access to a sufficient quantity of water for drinking, cooking and personal and domestic hygiene. Public water points are sufficiently close to households to enable use of the minimum water requirement.

Key indicators (to be read in conjunction with the guidance notes)

- Average water use for drinking, cooking and personal hygiene in any household is at least 15 litres per person per day (see guidance notes 1-8).

- The maximum distance from any household to the nearest water point is 500 metres (see guidance notes 1, 2, 5 and 8).

- Queuing time at a water source is no more than 15 minutes (see guidance note 7).

- It takes no more than three minutes to fill a 20-litre container (see guidance notes 7-8).

- Water sources and systems are maintained such that appropriate quantities of water are available consistently or on a regular basis (see guidance notes 2 and 8).

Guidance notes

1. **Needs:** the quantities of water needed for domestic use may vary according to the climate, the sanitation facilities available, people's normal habits, their religious and cultural practices, the food they cook, the clothes they wear, and so on. Water consumption generally increases the nearer the water source is to the dwelling.

Simplified table of basic survival water needs		
Survival needs: water intake (drinking and food)	2.5-3 litres per day	Depends on: the climate and individual physiology
Basic hygiene practices	2-6 litres per day	Depends on: social and cultural norms
Basic cooking needs	3-6 litres per day	Depends on: food type, social as well as cultural norms
Total basic water needs	7.5-15 litres per day	

See Appendix 2 for guidance on minimum water quantities needed for institutions and other uses.

2. **Water source selection:** the factors that need to be taken into account are the availability and sustainability of a sufficient quantity of water; whether water treatment is required and, if so, the feasibility of this; the availability of the time, technology or funding required to develop a source; the proximity of the source to the affected population; and the existence of any social, political or legal factors concerning the source. Generally, groundwater sources are preferable as they require less treatment, especially gravity-flow supplies from springs, which require no pumping. Disasters often require a combination of approaches and sources in the initial phase. All sources need to be regularly monitored to avoid over-exploitation.

3. **Measurement:** measuring solely the volume of water pumped into the reticulation system or the time a handpump is in operation will not give an accurate indication of individual consumption. Household surveys,

observation and community discussion groups are a more effective method of collecting data on water use and consumption.

4. *Quality and quantity:* in many emergency situations, water-related disease transmission is due as much to insufficient water for personal and domestic hygiene as to contaminated water supplies. Until minimum standards for both quantity and quality are met, the priority should be to provide equitable access to an adequate quantity of water even if it is of intermediate quality, rather than to provide an inadequate quantity of water that meets the minimum quality standard. It should be taken into account that people living with HIV/AIDS need extra water for drinking and personal hygiene. Particular attention should be paid to ensuring that the water requirements of livestock and crops are met, especially in drought situations where lives and livelihoods are dependent on these (see Appendix 2).

5. *Coverage:* in the initial phase of a response the first priority is to meet the urgent survival needs of all the affected population. People affected by an emergency have a significantly increased vulnerability to disease and therefore the indicators should be reached even if they are higher than the norms of the affected or host population. In such situations it is recommended that agencies plan programmes to raise the levels of water and sanitation facilities of the host population also, to avoid provoking animosity.

6. *Maximum numbers of people per water source:* the number of people per source depends on the yield and availability of water at each source. For example, taps often function only at certain times of day and handpumps and wells may not give constant water if there is a low recharge rate. The rough guidelines (for when water is constantly available) are:

250 people per tap	based on a flow of 7.5 litres/minute
500 people per handpump	based on a flow of 16.6 l/m
400 people per single-user open well	based on a flow of 12.5 l/m.

These guidelines assume that the water point is accessible for approximately eight hours a day only; if access is greater than this, people can collect more than the 15 litres per day minimum requirement. These

HP/
Wat San

targets must be used with caution, as reaching them does not necessarily guarantee a minimum quantity of water or equitable access.

7. **Queuing time:** excessive queuing times are indicators of insufficient water availability (either due to an inadequate number of water points or inadequate yields of water points). The potential negative results of excessive queuing times are: 1) reduced per capita water consumption; 2) increased consumption from unprotected surface sources; and 3) reduced time for water collectors to tend to other essential survival tasks.

8. **Access and equity:** even if a sufficient quantity of water is available to meet minimum needs, additional measures may be needed to ensure that access is equitable for all groups. Water points should be located in areas that are accessible to all regardless of e.g. sex or ethnicity. Some handpumps and water carrying containers may need to be designed or adapted for use by people living with HIV/AIDS, older and disabled people and children. In urban situations, it may be necessary to supply water into individual buildings to ensure that toilets continue to function. In situations where water is rationed or pumped at given times, this should be planned in consultation with the users. Times should be set which are convenient and safe for women and others who have responsibility for collecting water, and all users should be fully informed of when and where water is available.

Water supply standard 2: water quality

Water is palatable, and of sufficient quality to be drunk and used for personal and domestic hygiene without causing significant risk to health.

Key indicators (to be read in conjunction with the guidance notes)

- A sanitary survey indicates a low risk of faecal contamination (see guidance note 1).

- There are no faecal coliforms per 100ml at the point of delivery (see guidance note 2).

- People drink water from a protected or treated source in preference to other readily available water sources (see guidance note 3).

● Steps are taken to minimise post-delivery contamination (see guidance note 4).

● For piped water supplies, or for all water supplies at times of risk or presence of diarrhoea epidemic, water is treated with a disinfectant so that there is a free chlorine residual at the tap of 0.5mg per litre and turbidity is below 5 NTU (see guidance notes 5, 7 and 8).

● No negative health effect is detected due to short-term use of water contaminated by chemical (including carry-over of treatment chemicals) or radiological sources, and assessment shows no significant probability of such an effect (see guidance note 6).

Guidance notes

1. ***A sanitary survey*** is an assessment of conditions and practices that may constitute a public health risk. The assessment should cover possible sources of contamination to water at the source, in transport and in the home, as well as defecation practices, drainage and solid waste management. Community mapping is a particularly effective way of identifying where the public health risks are and thereby involving the community in finding ways to reduce these risks. Note that while animal excreta is not as harmful as human excreta, it can contain cryptosporidium, giardia, salmonella, campylobacter, caliciviruses and some other common causes of human diarrhoea and therefore does present a significant health risk.

2. ***Microbiological water quality:*** faecal coliform bacteria (>99% of which are *E. coli*) are an indicator of the level of human/animal waste contamination in water and the possibility of the presence of harmful pathogens. If any faecal coliforms are present the water should be treated. However, in the initial phase of a disaster, quantity is more important than quality (see Water supply standard 1, guidance note 4).

3. ***Promotion of protected sources:*** merely providing protected sources or treated water will have little impact unless people understand the health benefits of this water and therefore use it. People may prefer to use unprotected sources, e.g. rivers, lakes and unprotected wells, for reasons such as taste, proximity and social convenience. In such cases

HP/
Wat San

technicians, hygiene promoters and community mobilisers need to understand the rationale for these preferences so that consideration of them can be included in promotional messages and discussions.

4. ***Post-delivery contamination:*** water that is safe at the point of delivery can nevertheless present a significant health risk due to re-contamination during collection, storage and drawing. Steps that can be taken to minimise such risk include improved collection and storage practices, distributions of clean and appropriate collection and storage containers (see Water supply standard 3), treatment with a residual disinfectant, or treatment at the point of use. Water should be routinely sampled at the point of use to monitor the extent of any post-delivery contamination.

5. ***Water disinfection:*** water should be treated with a residual disinfectant such as chlorine if there is a significant risk of water source or post-delivery contamination. This risk will be determined by conditions in the community, such as population density, excreta disposal arrangements, hygiene practices and the prevalence of diarrhoeal disease. The risk assessment should also include qualitative community data regarding factors such as community perceptions of taste and palatability (see guidance note 6). Piped water supply for any large or concentrated population should be treated with a residual disinfectant and, in the case of a threat or the existence of a diarrhoea epidemic, all drinking water supplies should be treated, either before distribution or in the home. In order for water to be disinfected properly, turbidity must be below 5 NTU.

6. ***Chemical and radiological contamination:*** where hydrogeological records or knowledge of industrial or military activity suggest that water supplies may carry chemical or radiological health risks, those risks should be assessed rapidly by carrying out chemical analysis. A decision that balances short-term public health risks and benefits should then be made. A decision about using possibly contaminated water for longer-term supplies should be made on the basis of a more thorough professional assessment and analysis of the health implications.

7. ***Palatability:*** although taste is not in itself a direct health problem (e.g. slightly saline water), if the safe water supply does not taste good, users may drink from unsafe sources and put their health at risk. This may also be a risk when chlorinated water is supplied, in which case promotional activities are needed to ensure that only safe supplies are used.

8. ***Water quality for health centres:*** all water for hospitals, health centres and feeding centres should be treated with chlorine or another residual disinfectant. In situations where water is likely to be rationed by an interruption of supply, sufficient water storage should be available at the centre to ensure an uninterrupted supply at normal levels of utilisation (see Appendix 2).

Water supply standard 3: water use facilities and goods

People have adequate facilities and supplies to collect, store and use sufficient quantities of water for drinking, cooking and personal hygiene, and to ensure that drinking water remains safe until it is consumed.

Key indicators (to be read in conjunction with the guidance notes)

● Each household has at least two clean water collecting containers of 10-20 litres, plus enough clean water storage containers to ensure there is always water in the household (see guidance note 1).

● Water collection and storage containers have narrow necks and/or covers, or other safe means of storage, drawing and handling, and are demonstrably used (see guidance note 1).

● There is at least 250g of soap available for personal hygiene per person per month.

● Where communal bathing facilities are necessary, there are sufficient bathing cubicles available, with separate cubicles for males and females, and they are used appropriately and equitably (see guidance note 2).

● Where communal laundry facilities are necessary, there is at least one washing basin per 100 people, and private laundering areas are available for women to wash and dry undergarments and sanitary cloths.

● The participation of all vulnerable groups is actively encouraged in the siting and construction of bathing facilities and/or the production and distribution of soap, and/or the use and promotion of suitable alternatives (see guidance note 2).

Guidance notes

1. ***Water collection and storage:*** people need vessels to collect water, to store it and to use it for washing, cooking and bathing. These vessels should be clean, hygienic and easy to carry and be appropriate to local needs and habits, in terms of size, shape and design. Children, disabled people, older people and PLWH/A may need smaller or specially designed water carrying containers. The amount of storage capacity required depends on the size of the household and the consistency of water availability e.g. approximately 4 litres per person would be appropriate for situations where there is a constant daily supply. Promotion and monitoring of safe collection, storage and drawing provide an opportunity to discuss water contamination issues with vulnerable groups, especially women and children.

2. ***Communal washing and bathing facilities:*** people may need a space where they can bathe in privacy and dignity. If this is not possible at the household level, central facilities may be needed. Where soap is not available or commonly used, alternatives can be provided such as ash, clean sand, soda or various plants suitable for washing and/or scrubbing. Washing clothes is an essential hygiene activity, particularly for children, and cooking and eating utensils also need washing. The numbers, location, design, safety, appropriateness and convenience of facilities should be decided in consultation with the users, particularly women, adolescent girls and any disabled people. The location of facilities in central, accessible and well-lit areas can contribute to ensuring the safety of users.

3 Excreta Disposal

Safe disposal of human excreta creates the first barrier to excreta-related disease, helping to reduce transmission through direct and indirect routes. Safe excreta disposal is therefore a major priority, and in most disaster situations should be addressed with as much speed and effort as the provision of safe water supply. The provision of appropriate facilities for defecation is one of a number of emergency responses essential for people's dignity, safety, health and well-being.

Excreta disposal standard 1: access to, and numbers of, toilets

People have adequate numbers of toilets, sufficiently close to their dwellings, to allow them rapid, safe and acceptable access at all times of the day and night.

Key indicators (to be read in conjunction with the guidance notes)

- A maximum of 20 people use each toilet (see guidance notes 1-4).

- Use of toilets is arranged by household(s) and/or segregated by sex (see guidance notes 3-5).

- Separate toilets for women and men are available in public places (markets, distribution centres, health centres, etc.) (see guidance note 3).

- Shared or public toilets are cleaned and maintained in such a way that they are used by all intended users (see guidance notes 3-5).

- Toilets are no more than 50 metres from dwellings (see guidance note 5).

- Toilets are used in the most hygienic way and children's faeces are disposed of immediately and hygienically (see guidance note 6).

HP/
Wat San

Guidance notes

1. ***Safe excreta disposal:*** the aim of a safe excreta disposal programme is to ensure that the environment is free from contamination by human faeces. The more all groups from the disaster-affected population are involved, the more likely the programme is to succeed. In situations where the population has not traditionally used toilets, it may be necessary to conduct a concerted education/promotion campaign to encourage their use and to create a demand for more toilets to be constructed. Disasters in urban areas where the sewerage system is damaged may require solutions such as isolating parts of the system that still work (and re-routing pipes), installing portable toilets and using septic tanks and containment tanks that can be regularly desludged.

2. ***Defecation areas:*** in the initial phase of a disaster, before any toilets can be constructed, it may be necessary to mark off an area to be used as a defecation field or for trench latrines. This will only work if the site is correctly managed and maintained.

3. ***Public toilets:*** in some initial disaster situations and in public places where it is necessary to construct toilets for general use, it is very important to establish systems for the proper regular cleaning and maintenance of these facilities. Disaggregated population data should be used to plan the ratio of women's cubicles to men's (of approximately 3:1). Where possible, urinals should be provided for men (see Appendix 3).

4. ***Communal toilets:*** for a displaced population where there are no existing toilets, it is not always possible to provide one toilet per 20 people immediately. In such cases, a figure of 50 people per toilet can be used, decreasing to 20 as soon as possible, and changing the sharing arrangements accordingly. Any communal toilet must have a system in place, developed with the community, to ensure that it is maintained and kept clean. In some circumstances, space limitations make it impossible to meet this figure. In this case, while advocating strongly for extra space to be made available, it should be remembered that the primary aim is to provide and maintain an environment free from human faeces.

5. ***Shared facilities:*** where one toilet is shared by four or five families it is generally better kept, cleaner and therefore regularly used when the families have been consulted about its siting and design and have the

responsibility and the means to clean and maintain it. It is important to organise access to shared facilities by working with the intended users to decide who will have access to the toilet and how it will be cleaned and maintained. Efforts should be made to provide people living with HIV/AIDS with easy access to a toilet as they frequently suffer from chronic diarrhoea and reduced mobility.

6. ***Children's faeces:*** particular attention should be given to the disposal of children's faeces, which are commonly more dangerous than those of adults, as the level of excreta-related infection among children is frequently higher and children lack antibodies. Parents or care givers need to be involved, and facilities should be designed with children in mind. It may be necessary to provide parents or care givers with information about safe disposal of infant faeces and nappy (diaper) laundering practices.

Excreta disposal standard 2: design, construction and use of toilets

Toilets are sited, designed, constructed and maintained in such a way as to be comfortable, hygienic and safe to use.

HP/
Wat San

Key indicators (to be read in conjunction with the guidance notes)

● Users (especially women) have been consulted and approve of the siting and design of the toilet (see guidance notes 1-3).

● Toilets are designed, built and located to have the following features:

– they are designed in such a way that they can be used by all sections of the population, including children, older people, pregnant women and physically and mentally disabled people (see guidance note 1);

– they are sited in such a way as to minimise threats to users, especially women and girls, throughout the day and night (see guidance note 2);

– they are sufficiently easy to keep clean to invite use and do not present a health hazard;

– they provide a degree of privacy in line with the norms of the users;

– they allow for the disposal of women's sanitary protection, or provide women with the necessary privacy for washing and drying sanitary protection cloths (see guidance note 4);

– they minimise fly and mosquito breeding (see guidance note 7).

● All toilets constructed that use water for flushing and/or a hygienic seal have an adequate and regular supply of water (see guidance notes 1 and 3).

● Pit latrines and soakaways (for most soils) are at least 30 metres from any groundwater source and the bottom of any latrine is at least 1.5 metres above the water table. Drainage or spillage from defecation systems must not run towards any surface water source or shallow groundwater source (see guidance note 5).

● People wash their hands after defecation and before eating and food preparation (see guidance note 6).

● People are provided with tools and materials for constructing, maintaining and cleaning their own toilets if appropriate (see guidance note 7).

Guidance notes

1. ***Acceptable facilities:*** successful excreta disposal programmes are based on an understanding of people's varied needs as well as on the participation of the users. It may not be possible to make all toilets acceptable to all groups and special toilets may need to be constructed for children, older people and disabled people e.g. potties, or toilets with lower seats or hand rails. The type of toilet constructed should depend on the preferences and cultural habits of the intended users, the existing infrastructure, the ready availability of water (for flushing and water seals), ground conditions and the availability of construction materials.

2. **Safe facilities:** inappropriate siting of toilets may make women and girls more vulnerable to attack, especially during the night, and ways must be found to ensure that women feel, and are, safe using the toilets provided. Where possible, communal toilets should be provided with lighting or families provided with torches. The input of the community should be sought with regard to ways of enhancing the safety of users.

3. **Anal cleansing:** water should be provided for people who use it. For other people it may be necessary to provide toilet paper or other material for anal cleansing. Users should be consulted on the most culturally appropriate cleansing materials and on their safe disposal.

4. **Menstruation:** women and girls who menstruate should have access to suitable materials for the absorption and disposal of menstrual blood. Women should be consulted on what is culturally appropriate (see Non-food items standard 2 on page 232).

5. **Distance of defecation systems from water sources:** the distances given above may be increased for fissured rocks and limestone, or decreased for fine soils. In disasters, groundwater pollution may not be an immediate concern if the groundwater is not consumed. In flooded or high water table environments, it may be necessary to build elevated toilets or septic tanks to contain excreta and prevent it contaminating the environment.

6. **Hand washing:** the importance of hand washing after defecation and before eating and preparing food, to prevent the spread of disease, cannot be over-estimated. Users should have the means to wash their hands after defecation with soap or an alternative (such as ash), and should be encouraged to do so. There should be a constant source of water near the toilet for this purpose.

7. **Hygienic toilets:** if toilets are not kept clean they may become a focus for disease transmission and people will prefer not to use them. They are more likely to be kept clean if users have a sense of ownership. This is encouraged by promotional activities, having toilets close to where people sleep and involving users in decisions about their design and construction, rules on proper operation, maintenance, monitoring and use. Flies and mosquitoes are discouraged by keeping the toilet clean, having a water seal, Ventilated Improved Pit (VIP) latrine design or simply by the correct use of a lid on a squat hole.

HP/ Wat San

4 Vector Control

A vector is a disease-carrying agent and vector-borne diseases are a major cause of sickness and death in many disaster situations. Mosquitoes are the vector responsible for malaria transmission, which is one of the leading causes of morbidity and mortality. Mosquitoes also transmit other diseases, such as yellow fever and dengue haemorrhagic fever. Non-biting or synanthropic flies, such as the house fly, the blow fly and the flesh fly, play an important role in the transmission of diarrhoeal disease. Biting flies, bed bugs and fleas are a painful nuisance and in some cases transmit significant diseases such as murine typhus and plague. Ticks transmit relapsing fever and human body lice transmit typhus and relapsing fever. Rats and mice can transmit diseases such as leptospirosis; and a specific species of rat is responsible for transmission of Lassa fever. These rodents can also be hosts for other vectors e.g. fleas, which may transmit plague and murine typhus.

Vector-borne diseases can be controlled through a variety of initiatives, including appropriate site selection and shelter provision, appropriate water supply, excreta disposal, solid waste management and drainage, the provision of health services (including community mobilisation and health promotion), the use of chemical controls, family and individual protection and the effective protection of food stores. Although the nature of vector-borne disease is often complex and addressing vector-related problems may demand specialist attention, there is much that can be done to help prevent the spread of such diseases with simple and effective measures, once the disease, its vector and their interaction with the population have been identified.

Vector control standard 1: individual and family protection

All disaster-affected people have the knowledge and the means to protect themselves from disease and nuisance vectors that are likely to represent a significant risk to health or well-being.

Key indicators (to be read in conjunction with the guidance notes)

● All populations at risk from vector-borne disease understand the modes of transmission and possible methods of prevention (see guidance notes 1-5).

● All populations have access to shelters that do not harbour or encourage the growth of vector populations and are protected by appropriate vector control measures.

● People avoid exposure to mosquitoes during peak biting times by using all non-harmful means available to them. Special attention is paid to protection of high-risk groups such as pregnant and feeding mothers, babies, infants, older people and the sick (see guidance note 3).

● People with treated mosquito nets use them effectively (see guidance note 3).

● Control of human body lice is carried out where louse-borne typhus or relapsing fever is a threat (see guidance note 4).

● Bedding and clothing are aired and washed regularly (see guidance note 4).

● Food is protected at all times from contamination by vectors such as flies, insects and rodents.

Guidance notes

1. ***Defining vector-borne disease risk:*** decisions about vector control interventions should be based on an assessment of potential disease risk,

HP/ Wat San

as well as on clinical evidence of a vector-borne disease problem. Factors influencing this risk include:

– immunity status of the population, including previous exposure, nutritional stress and other stresses. Movement of people (e.g. refugees, IDPs) from a non-endemic to an endemic area is a common cause of epidemics;

– pathogen type and prevalence, in both vectors and humans;

– vector species, behaviours and ecology;

– vector numbers (season, breeding sites, etc.);

– increased exposure to vectors: proximity, settlement pattern, shelter type, existing individual protection and avoidance measures.

2. ***Indicators for vector control programmes:*** commonly used indicators for measuring the impact of vector control activities are vector-borne disease incidence rates (from epidemiological data, community-based data and proxy indicators, depending on the response) and parasite counts (using rapid diagnostic kits or microscopy).

3. ***Individual malaria protection measures:*** if there is a significant risk of malaria, the systematic and timely provision of protection measures, such as insecticide-treated materials, i.e. tents, curtains and bednets, is recommended. Impregnated bednets have the added advantage of giving some protection against body and head lice, fleas, ticks, cockroaches and bedbugs. Long-sleeved clothing, household fumigants, coils, aerosol sprays and repellents are other protection methods that can be used against mosquitoes. It is vital to ensure that users understand the importance of protection and how to use the tools correctly so that the protection measures are effective. Where resources are scarce, they should be directed at individuals and groups most at risk, such as children under five years old, non-immunes and pregnant women.

4. ***Individual protection measures for other vectors:*** good personal hygiene and regular washing of clothes and bedding is the most effective protection against body lice. Infestations can be controlled by personal treatment (powdering), mass laundering or delousing campaigns and by treatment protocols as newly displaced people arrive in a settlement. A

clean household environment, together with good waste disposal and good food storage, will deter rats and other rodents from entering houses or shelters.

5. ***Water-borne diseases:*** people should be informed of health risks and should avoid entering water bodies where there is a known risk of contracting diseases such as schistosomiasis, Guinea worm or leptospirosis (transmitted by exposure to mammalian urine, especially that of rats: see Appendix 4). Agencies may need to work with the community to find alternative sources of water or ensure that water for all uses is appropriately treated.

Vector control standard 2: physical, environmental and chemical protection measures

The numbers of disease vectors that pose a risk to people's health and nuisance vectors that pose a risk to people's well-being are kept to an acceptable level.

HP/ Wat San

Key indicators (to be read in conjunction with the guidance notes)

● Displaced populations are settled in locations that minimise their exposure to mosquitoes (see guidance note 1).

● Vector breeding and resting sites are modified where practicable (see guidance notes 2-4).

● Intensive fly control is carried out in high-density settlements when there is a risk or the presence of a diarrhoea epidemic.

● The population density of mosquitoes is kept low enough to avoid the risk of excessive transmission levels and infection (see guidance note 4).

● People infected with malaria are diagnosed early and receive treatment (see guidance note 5).

Guidance notes

1. **Site selection** is important in minimising the exposure of the population to the risk of vector-borne disease; this should be one of the key factors when considering possible sites. With regard to malaria control, for example, camps should be located 1-2km upwind from large breeding sites, such as swamps or lakes, whenever an additional clean water source can be provided (see Shelter and settlement standards 1-2 on pages 211-218).

2. **Environmental and chemical vector control:** there are a number of basic environmental engineering measures that can be taken to reduce the opportunities for vector breeding. These include the proper disposal of human and animal excreta (see Excreta Disposal section), proper disposal of refuse to control flies and rodents (see Solid Waste Management section), and drainage of standing water to control mosquitoes (see Drainage section). Such priority environmental health measures will have some impact on the population density of some vectors. It may not be possible to have sufficient impact on all the breeding, feeding and resting sites within a settlement or near it, even in the longer term, and localised chemical control measures or individual protection measures may be needed. For example, space spraying may reduce the numbers of adult flies and prevent a diarrhoea epidemic, or may help to minimise the disease burden if employed during an epidemic.

3. **Designing a response:** vector control programmes may have no impact on disease if they target the wrong vector, use ineffective methods, or target the right vector in the wrong place or at the wrong time. Control programmes should initially aim to address the following three objectives: 1) to reduce the vector population density; 2) to reduce the human-vector contact; and 3) to reduce the vector breeding sites. Poorly executed programmes can be counter-productive. Detailed study, and often expert advice, are needed and should be sought from national and international health organisations, while local advice should be sought on local disease patterns, breeding sites, seasonal variations in vector numbers and incidence of diseases, etc.

4. **Environmental mosquito control:** environmental control aims primarily at eliminating mosquito breeding sites. The three main species of mosquitoes responsible for transmitting disease are *Culex* (filariasis),

Anopheles (malaria and filariasis) and *Aedes* (yellow fever and dengue). *Culex* mosquitoes breed in stagnant water loaded with organic matter such as latrines, *Anopheles* in relatively unpolluted surface water such as puddles, slow-flowing streams and wells, and *Aedes* in water receptacles such as bottles, buckets, tyres, etc. Examples of environmental mosquito control include good drainage, properly functioning VIP latrines, keeping lids on the squatting hole of pit latrines and on water containers, and keeping wells covered and/or treating them with a larvicide (e.g. for areas where dengue fever is endemic).

5. **Malaria treatment:** malaria control strategies that aim to reduce the mosquito population density by eliminating breeding sites, reducing the mosquito daily survival rate and restricting the human biting habit should be carried out simultaneously with early diagnosis and treatment with effective anti-malarials. Campaigns to encourage early diagnosis and treatment should be initiated and sustained. In the context of an integrated approach, active case finding by trained outreach workers and treatment with effective anti-malarials is more likely to reduce the malaria burden than passive case finding through centralised health services (see Control of communicable diseases standard 5 on page 281).

HP/
Wat San

Vector control standard 3: chemical control safety

Chemical vector control measures are carried out in a manner that ensures that staff, the people affected by the disaster and the local environment are adequately protected, and avoids creating resistance to the substances used.

Key indicators (to be read in conjunction with the guidance notes)

● Personnel are protected by the provision of training, protective clothing, use of bathing facilities, supervision and a restriction on the number of hours spent handling chemicals.

● The choice, quality, transport and storage of chemicals used for vector control, the application equipment and the disposal of the substances follow international norms, and can be accounted for at all times (see guidance note 1).

● Communities are informed about the potential risks of the substances used in chemical vector control and about the schedule for application. They are protected during and after the application of poisons or pesticides, according to internationally agreed procedures (see guidance note 1).

Guidance note

1. *National and international protocols:* there are clear international protocols and norms, published by WHO, for both the choice and the application of chemicals in vector control, which should be adhered to at all times. Vector control measures should address two principal concerns: efficacy and safety. If national norms with regard to the choice of chemicals fall short of international standards, resulting in little or no impact or endangering health and safety, then the agency should consult and lobby the relevant national authority for permission to adhere to the international standards.

5 Solid Waste Management

If organic solid waste is not disposed of, major risks are incurred of fly and rat breeding (see Vector Control section) and surface water pollution. Uncollected and accumulating solid waste and the debris left after a natural disaster or conflict may also create a depressing and ugly environment, discouraging efforts to improve other aspects of environmental health. Solid waste often blocks drainage channels and leads to environmental health problems associated with stagnant and polluted surface water.

Solid waste management standard 1: collection and disposal

People have an environment that is acceptably uncontaminated by solid waste, including medical waste, and have the means to dispose of their domestic waste conveniently and effectively.

Key indicators (to be read in conjunction with the guidance notes)

- People from the affected population are involved in the design and implementation of the solid waste programme.

- Household waste is put in containers daily for regular collection, burnt or buried in a specified refuse pit.

- All households have access to a refuse container and/or are no more than 100 metres from a communal refuse pit.

- At least one 100-litre refuse container is available per 10 families, where domestic refuse is not buried on-site.

● Refuse is removed from the settlement before it becomes a nuisance or a health risk (see guidance notes 1, 2 and 6).

● Medical wastes are separated and disposed of separately and there is a correctly designed, constructed and operated pit, or incinerator with a deep ash pit, within the boundaries of each health facility (see guidance notes 3 and 6).

● There are no contaminated or dangerous medical wastes (needles, glass, dressings, drugs, etc.) at any time in living areas or public spaces (see guidance note 3).

● There are clearly marked and appropriately fenced refuse pits, bins or specified areas at public places, such as markets and slaughtering areas, with a regular collection system in place (see guidance note 4).

● Final disposal of solid waste is carried out in such a place and in such a way as to avoid creating health and environmental problems for the local and affected populations (see guidance notes 5-6).

Guidance notes

1. ***Burial of waste:*** if waste is to be buried on-site in either household or communal pits, it should be covered at least weekly with a thin layer of soil to prevent it attracting vectors such as flies and rodents and becoming their breeding ground. If children's faeces/nappies are being disposed of they should be covered with earth directly afterwards. Disposal sites should be fenced off to prevent accidents and access by children and animals; care should be taken to prevent any leachate contaminating the ground water.

2. ***Refuse type and quantity:*** refuse in settlements varies widely in composition and quantity, according to the amount and type of economic activity, the staple foods consumed and local practices of recycling and/or waste disposal. The extent to which solid waste has an impact on people's health should be assessed and appropriate action taken if necessary. Recycling of solid waste within the community should be encouraged, provided it presents no significant health risk. Distribution of commodities that produce a large amount of solid waste from packaging or processing on-site should be avoided.

3. **Medical waste:** poor management of health-care waste exposes the community, health-care workers and waste handlers to infections, toxic effects and injuries. In a disaster situation the most hazardous types of waste are likely to be infectious sharps and non-sharps (wound dressings, blood-stained cloth and organic matter such as placentas, etc.). The different types of waste should be separated at source. Non-infectious waste (paper, plastic wrappings, food waste, etc.) can be disposed of as solid waste. Contaminated sharps, especially used needles and syringes, should be placed in a safety box directly after use. Safety boxes and other infectious waste can be disposed of on-site by burial, incineration or other safe methods.

4. **Market waste:** most market waste can be treated in the same way as domestic refuse. Slaughterhouse waste may need special treatment and special facilities to deal with the liquid wastes produced, and to ensure that slaughtering is carried out in hygienic conditions and in compliance with local laws. Slaughter waste can often be disposed of in a large pit with a hole cover next to the abattoir. Blood, etc. can be run from the abattoir into the pit through a slab-covered channel (reducing fly access to the pit). Water should be made available for cleaning purposes.

5. **Controlled tipping/sanitary landfill:** large-scale disposal of waste should be carried out off-site through either controlled tipping or sanitary landfill. This method is dependent upon sufficient space and access to mechanical equipment. Ideally waste that is tipped should be covered with soil at the end of each day to prevent scavenging and vector breeding.

6. **Staff welfare:** all solid waste management staff who collect, transport or dispose of waste should be provided with protective clothing, at minimum gloves and ideally overalls, boots and protective masks. Water and soap should be available for hand and face washing. Staff who come into contact with medical waste should be informed of the correct methods of storage, transport and disposal and the risks associated with improper management of the waste.

HP/
Wat San

6 Drainage

Surface water in or near emergency settlements may come from household and water point wastewater, leaking toilets and sewers, rainwater or rising floodwater. The main health risks associated with surface water are contamination of water supplies and the living environment, damage to toilets and dwellings, vector breeding and drowning. Rainwater and rising floodwaters can worsen the drainage situation in a settlement and further increase the risk of contamination. A proper drainage plan, addressing stormwater drainage through site planning and wastewater disposal using small-scale, on-site drainage, should be implemented to reduce potential health risks to the population. This section addresses small-scale drainage problems and activities. Large-scale drainage is generally determined by site selection and development (see Shelter, Settlement and Non-Food Items, chapter 4 on page 203).

Drainage standard 1: drainage works

People have an environment in which the health and other risks posed by water erosion and standing water, including stormwater, floodwater, domestic wastewater and wastewater from medical facilities, are minimised.

Key indicators (to be read in conjunction with the guidance notes)

● Areas around dwellings and water points are kept free of standing wastewater, and stormwater drains are kept clear (see guidance notes 1, 2, 4 and 5).

● Shelters, paths and water and sanitation facilities are not flooded or eroded by water (see guidance notes 2-4).

● Water point drainage is well planned, built and maintained. This includes drainage from washing and bathing areas as well as water collection points (see guidance notes 2 and 4).

● Drainage waters do not pollute existing surface or groundwater sources or cause erosion (see guidance note 5).

● Sufficient numbers of appropriate tools are provided for small drainage works and maintenance where necessary (see guidance note 4).

Guidance notes

1. *Site selection and planning:* the most effective way to control drainage problems is in the choice of site and the layout of the settlement (see Shelter and settlement standards 1-4 on pages 211-224).

2. *Wastewater:* sullage or domestic wastewater is classified as sewage when mixed with human excreta. Unless the settlement is sited where there is an existing sewerage system, domestic wastewater should not be allowed to mix with human waste. Sewage is difficult and more expensive to treat than domestic wastewater. At water points and washing and bathing areas, the creation of small gardens to utilise wastewater should be encouraged. Special attention needs to be paid to prevent wastewater from washing and bathing areas contaminating water sources.

3. *Drainage and excreta disposal:* special care is needed to protect toilets and sewers from flooding in order to avoid structural damage and leakage.

4. *Promotion:* it is essential to involve the affected population in providing small-scale drainage works as they often have good knowledge of the natural flow of drainage water and of where channels should be. Also, if they understand the health and physical risks involved and have assisted in the construction of the drainage system, they are more likely to maintain it (see Vector Control section). Technical support and tools may then be needed.

5. *On-site disposal:* where possible, and if favourable soil conditions exist, drainage from water points and washing areas should be on-site rather than via open channels, which are difficult to maintain and often clog. Simple and cheap techniques such as soak pits can be used for on-site

HP/
Wat San

disposal of wastewater. Where off-site disposal is the only possibility, channels are preferable to pipes. Channels should be designed both to provide flow velocity for dry-weather sullage and to carry stormwater. Where the slope is more than 5%, engineering techniques must be applied to prevent excessive erosion. Drainage of residuals from any water treatment processes should be carefully controlled so that people cannot use such water and it does not contaminate surface or groundwater sources.

Appendix 1

Water Supply and Sanitation Initial Needs Assessment Checklist

This list of questions is primarily for use to assess needs, identify indigenous resources and describe local conditions. It does not include questions to determine external resources needed in addition to those immediately and locally available.

1 General

- How many people are affected and where are they? Disaggregate the data as far as possible by sex, age, disability etc.

- What are people's likely movements? What are the security factors for the people affected and for potential relief responses?

- What are the current or threatened water- and sanitation-related diseases? What are the extent and expected evolution of problems?

- Who are the key people to consult or contact?

- Who are the vulnerable people in the population and why?

- Is there equal access for all to existing facilities?

- What special security risks exist for women and girls?

- What water and sanitation practices were the population accustomed to before the emergency?

2 Water supply

- What is the current water source and who are the present users?

- How much water is available per person per day?

- What is the daily/weekly frequency of the water supply?

- Is the water available at the source sufficient for short-term and longer-term needs for all groups in the population?

● Are water collection points close enough to where people live? Are they safe?

● Is the current water supply reliable? How long will it last?

● Do people have enough water containers of the appropriate size and type?

● Is the water source contaminated or at risk of contamination (microbiological or chemical/radiological)?

● Is treatment necessary? Is treatment possible? What treatment is necessary?

● Is disinfection necessary, even if the supply is not contaminated?

● Are there alternative sources nearby?

● What traditional beliefs and practices relate to the collection, storage and use of water?

● Are there any obstacles to using available supplies?

● Is it possible to move the population if water sources are inadequate?

● Is it possible to tanker water if water sources are inadequate?

● What are the key hygiene issues related to water supply?

● Do people have the means to use water hygienically?

3 Excreta disposal

● What is the current defecation practice? If it is open defecation, is there a designated area? Is the area secure?

● What are current beliefs and practices, including gender-specific practices, concerning excreta disposal?

● Are there any existing facilities? If so, are they used, are they sufficient and are they operating successfully? Can they be extended or adapted?

● Is the current defecation practice a threat to water supplies (surface or ground water) or living areas?

● Do people wash their hands after defecation and before food preparation and eating? Are soap or other cleansing materials available?

● Are people familiar with the construction and use of toilets?

● What local materials are available for constructing toilets?

● Are people prepared to use pit latrines, defecation fields, trenches, etc.?

● Is there sufficient space for defecation fields, pit latrines, toilets, etc.?

● What is the slope of the terrain?

● What is the level of the groundwater table?

● Are soil conditions suitable for on-site excreta disposal?

● Do current excreta disposal arrangements encourage vectors?

● Are there materials or water available for anal cleansing? How do people normally dispose of these materials?

● How do women manage issues related to menstruation? Are there appropriate materials or facilities available for this?

4 Vector-borne disease

● What are the vector-borne disease risks and how serious are these risks?

● What traditional beliefs and practices relate to vectors and vector-borne disease? Are any of these either useful or harmful?

● If vector-borne disease risks are high, do people at risk have access to individual protection?

● Is it possible to make changes to the local environment (by drainage, scrub clearance, excreta disposal, refuse disposal, etc.) to discourage vector breeding?

● Is it necessary to control vectors by chemical means? What programmes, regulations and resources exist for vector control and the use of chemicals?

● What information and safety precautions need to be provided to households?

5 Solid waste disposal

● Is solid waste a problem?

● How do people dispose of their waste? What type and quantity of solid waste is produced?

● Can solid waste be disposed of on-site, or does it need to be collected and disposed of off-site?

● What is the normal practice of solid waste disposal for the affected population? (compost/refuse pits? collection system? bins?)

● Are there medical facilities and activities producing waste? How is this being disposed of? Who is responsible?

6 Drainage

● Is there a drainage problem (e.g. flooding of dwellings or toilets, vector breeding sites, polluted water contaminating living areas or water supplies)?

● Is the soil prone to waterlogging?

● Do people have the means to protect their dwellings and toilets from local flooding?

Appendix 2

Planning Guidelines for Minimum Water Quantities for Institutions and Other Uses

Health centres and hospitals	5 litres/out-patient 40-60 litres/in-patient/day Additional quantities may be needed for laundry equipment, flushing toilets, etc.
Cholera centres	60 litres/patient/day 15 litres/carer/day
Therapeutic feeding centres	30 litres/in-patient/day 15 litres/carer/day
Schools	3 litres/pupil/day for drinking and hand washing (use for toilets not included: see below)
Mosques	2-5 litres/person/day for washing and drinking
Public toilets	1-2 litres/user/day for hand washing 2-8 litres/cubicle/day for toilet cleaning
All flushing toilets	20-40 litres/user/day for conventional flushing toilets connected to a sewer 3-5 litres/user/day for pour-flush toilets
Anal washing	1-2 litres/person/day
Livestock	20-30 litres/large or medium animal/day 5 litres/small animal/day
Small-scale irrigation	3-6mm/m²/day, but can vary considerably

HP/ Wat San

Appendix 3

Planning Guidelines for Minimum Numbers of Toilets at Public Places and Institutions in Disaster Situations

Institution	Short term	Long term
Market areas	1 toilet to 50 stalls	1 toilet to 20 stalls
Hospitals/medical centres	1 toilet to 20 beds or 50 out-patients	1 toilet to 10 beds or 20 out-patients
Feeding centres	1 toilet to 50 adults 1 toilet to 20 children	1 toilet to 20 adults 1 toilet to 10 children
Reception/transit centres	1 toilet per 50 people 3:1 female to male	
Schools	1 toilet to 30 girls 1 toilet to 60 boys	1 toilet to 30 girls 1 toilet to 60 boys
Offices		1 toilet to 20 staff

Source: *adapted from Harvey, Baghri and Reed (2002)*

Appendix 4

Water- and Excreta-Related Diseases and Transmission Mechanisms

Water-borne or water-washed	Cholera, shigellosis, diarrhoea, salmonellosis, etc. Typhoid, paratyphoid, etc. Amoebic dysentery, giardiasis Hepatitis A, poliomyelitis, rotavirus diarrhoea	Faecal-oral bacterial Faecal-oral non-bacterial	Water contamination Poor sanitation Poor personal hygiene Crop contamination
Water-washed or water-scarce	Skin and eye infections Louse-borne typhus and louse-borne relapsing fever		Inadequate water Poor personal hygiene
Excreta-related helminths	Roundworm, hookworm, whipworm, etc.	Soil-transmitted helminths	Open defecation Ground contamination
Beef and pork tape worms	Taeniasis	Man-animal	Half-cooked meat Ground contamination
Water-based	Schistosomiasis, Guinea worm, clonorchiasis, etc.	Long stay in infected water	Water contamination
Water-related insect vectors	Malaria, dengue, sleeping sickness, filariasis, etc.	Biting by mosquitoes, flies	Bite near water Breed in water
Excreta-related insect vectors	Diarrhoea and dysentery	Transmitted by flies and cockroaches	Dirty environment

Appendix 5

References

Thanks to the Forced Migration Online programme of the Refugee Studies Centre at the University of Oxford, many of these documents have received copyright permission and are posted on a special Sphere link at: http://www.forcedmigration.org

International legal instruments

The Right to Water (article 11 and 12 of the International Covenant on Economic, Social and Cultural Rights), CESCR General Comment 15, 26 November 2002, U.N. Doc. E/C.12/2002/11, Committee on Economic, Social and Cultural Rights.

United Nations Treaty Collection: http://untreaty.un.org

University of Minnesota Human Rights Library: http://www1.umn.edu/humanrts

http://www.who.int/water_sanitation_health/Documents/righttowater/righttowater.htm

General

Adams, J (1999), *Managing Water Supply and Sanitation in Emergencies*. Oxfam GB.

Cairncross, S and Feachem, R (1993), *Environmental Health Engineering in the Tropics: An Introductory Text (Second Edition)*. John Wiley & Sons Ltd, Chichester, UK.

Davis, J and Lambert, R (2002), *Engineering in Emergencies: A Practical Guide for Relief Workers. Second Edition*. RedR/IT Publications, London.

Drouarty, E and Vouillamoz, JM (1999), *Alimentation en eau des populations menacées*. Hermann, Paris.

International Research Centre (Netherlands) website: http://www.irc.nl/publications

MSF (1994), *Public Health Engineering in Emergency Situations. First Edition.* Médecins Sans Frontières, Paris.

UNHCR (1999), *Handbook for Emergencies. Second Edition.* UNHCR. Geneva. http://www.unhcr.ch/

Water, Engineering and Development Centre (WEDEC), Loughborough University, UK. http://www.lboro.ac.uk

WHO Health Library for Disasters: http://www.helid.desastres.net

WHO Water, Sanitation, Health Programme: http://www.who.int/water_sanitation_health

Sanitary surveys

ARGOSS manual: http://www.bgs.ac.uk

Gender

Gender and Water Alliance: http://www.genderandwateralliance.org

Islamic Global Health Network, Islamic Supercourse Lectures. *On Health Promotion, Child Health and Islam.* http://www.pitt.edu

WCRWC/UNICEF (1998), *The Gender Dimensions of Internal Displacement.* Women's Commission for Refugee Women and Children. New York.

Hygiene promotion

Almedom, A, Blumenthal, U and Manderson, L (1997), *Hygiene Evaluation Procedures: Approaches and Methods for Assessing Water- and Sanitation-Related Hygiene Practices.* International Nutrition Foundation for Developing Countries. Available from Intermediate Technology Publications, Southampton Row, London WC1, UK.

Benenson, AS, ed. (1995), *Control of Communicable Diseases Manual,*

16th Edition. American Public Health Association.

Ferron, S, Morgan, J and O'Reilly, M (2000), *Hygiene Promotion: A Practical Manual for Relief and Development.* Oxfam GB.

Water supply

FAO: http://www.fao.org

House, S and Reed, R (1997), *Emergency Water Sources: Guidelines for Selection and Treatment.* WEDEC, Loughborough University, UK.

Water quality

WHO (2003), *Guidelines for Drinking Water Quality. Third Edition.* Geneva.

Excreta disposal

Harvey, PA, Baghri, S and Reed, RA (2002), *Emergency Sanitation, Assessment and Programme Design.* WEDEC, Loughborough University, UK.

Pickford, J (1995), *Low Cost Sanitation: A Survey of Practical Experience.* IT Publications, London.

Vector control

Hunter, P (1997), *Waterborne Disease: Epidemiology and Ecology.* John Wiley & Sons Ltd, Chichester, UK.

Lacarin, CJ and Reed, RA (1999), *Emergency Vector Control Using Chemicals.* WEDEC, Loughborough, UK.

Thomson, M (1995), *Disease Prevention Through Vector Control: Guidelines for Relief Organisations.* Oxfam GB.

UNHCR (1997), *Vector and Pest Control in Refugee Situations.* UNHCR, Geneva.

Warrell, D and Gilles, H, eds. (2002), *Essential Malariology. Fourth*

Edition. Arnold, London.

WHO, *Chemical methods for the control of vectors and pests of public health importance.* http://www.who.int

WHO Pesticide Evaluation Scheme (WHOPES), *Guidelines for the purchase of pesticides for use in public health.* http://www.who.int.

Solid waste

Design of landfill sites: http://www.lifewater.org

The International Solid Waste Association: http://www.iswa.org

Medical waste

Prüss, A, Giroult, E, Rushbrook, P, eds. (1999), *Safe Management of Health-Care Wastes.* WHO, Geneva.

WHO (2000), *Aide-Memoire: Safe Health-Care Waste Management.* Geneva.

WHO: http://www.healthcarewaste.org

WHO: http://www.injectionsafety.org

Drainage

Environmental Protection Agency (EPA) (1980), *Design Manual: On-Site Wastewater Treatment and Disposal Systems,* Report EPA-600/2-78-173. Cincinnati.

HP/
Wat San

Notes

Notes

HP/
Wat San

Notes

Chapter 3:
Minimum Standards in Food Security, Nutrition and Food Aid

How to use this chapter

This chapter is divided into four sections: 1) Food Security and Nutrition Assessment and Analysis standards, 2) Food Security standards, 3) Nutrition standards and 4) Food Aid standards. While the Food Security and Nutrition standards are a practical expression of the right to food, the Food Aid standards are more operationally focused. The Food Aid standards can contribute towards the achievement of both the Food Security and Nutrition standards.

Each of the sections contains the following:

● *the minimum standards:* these are qualitative in nature and specify the minimum levels to be attained in the provision of food security, nutrition and food aid responses;

● *key indicators:* these are 'signals' that show whether the standard has been attained. They provide a way of measuring and communicating the impact, or result, of programmes as well as the process, or methods, used. The indicators may be qualitative or quantitative;

● *guidance notes:* these include specific points to consider when applying the standards and indicators in different situations, guidance on tackling practical difficulties, and advice on priority issues. They may also include critical issues relating to the standards or indicators, and describe dilemmas, controversies or gaps in current knowledge.

Appendices at the end of the chapter include checklists for assessments, examples of food security responses, guidance on measuring acute malnutrition and determining the public health significance of micronutrient deficiency, nutritional requirements and a select list of references, which point to sources of information on both general issues and specific technical issues relating to this chapter.

Contents

Food

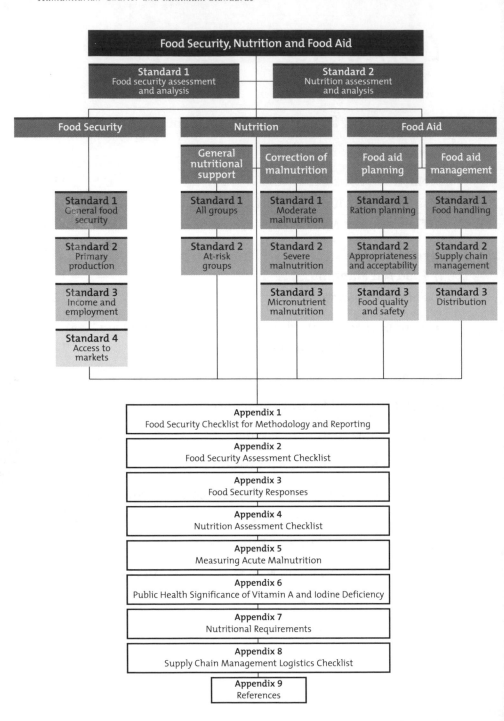

Introduction

Links to international legal instruments

The Minimum Standards in Food Security, Nutrition and Food Aid are a practical expression of the principles and rights embodied in the Humanitarian Charter. The Humanitarian Charter is concerned with the most basic requirements for sustaining the lives and dignity of those affected by calamity or conflict, as reflected in the body of international human rights, humanitarian and refugee law.

Everyone has the right to adequate food. This right is recognised in international legal instruments and includes the right to be free from hunger. Key aspects of the right to adequate food include:

● the availability of food in a quantity and of a quality sufficient to satisfy the dietary needs of individuals, free from adverse substances and acceptable within a given culture;

● the accessibility of such food in ways that are sustainable and do not interfere with the enjoyment of other human rights.

States and non-state actors have responsibilities in fulfilling the right to food. There are many situations in which the non-fulfilment of these obligations and violations of international law – including, for example, the deliberate starvation of populations or destruction of their livelihoods as a war strategy – have devastating effects on food security and nutrition. In times of armed conflict, it is prohibited for combatants to attack or destroy foodstuffs, agricultural areas for the production of foodstuffs, crops or livestock. In these situations, humanitarian actors can help to realise the rights of affected populations: for example, by providing food assistance in ways that respect national law and international human rights obligations.

The Minimum Standards in this chapter are not a full expression of the Right to Adequate Food. However, the Sphere standards reflect the core content of the Right to Food and contribute to the progressive realisation of this right globally.

Food

The importance of food security, nutrition and food aid in disasters

Access to food and the maintenance of adequate nutritional status are critical determinants of people's survival in a disaster. Malnutrition can be the most serious public health problem and may be a leading cause of death, whether directly or indirectly. The resilience of livelihoods and people's subsequent food security determine their health and nutrition in the short term and their future survival and well-being. Food aid can be important in protecting and providing for food security and nutrition, as part of a combination of measures.

The food security standards are less detailed than the nutrition or the food aid standards, largely because food security is a diverse field with a limited body of best practice in disaster situations.

For this chapter the following definitions are used:

● **food security** exists when all people, at all times, have physical and economic access to sufficient, safe and nutritious food for a healthy and active life (World Food Summit Plan of Action, paragraph 1, 1996);

● **livelihoods** comprise the capabilities, assets (including both material and social resources) and activities required for a means of living linked to survival and future well-being. *Livelihood strategies* are the practical means or activities through which people access food or income to buy food, while *coping strategies* are temporary responses to food insecurity.

● **malnutrition** encompasses a range of conditions, including acute malnutrition, chronic malnutrition and micronutrient deficiencies. Acute malnutrition refers to wasting (thinness) and/or nutritional oedema, while chronic malnutrition refers to stunting (shortness). Stunting and wasting are two forms of growth failure. In this chapter we refer only to acute malnutrition and micronutrient deficiency.

As women usually assume overall responsibility for food in the household and because they are the major recipients of food aid, it is important to encourage their participation in the design and implementation of programmes wherever possible.

Links to other chapters

Many of the standards in the other sector chapters are relevant to this chapter. Progress in achieving standards in one area often influences and even determines progress in other areas. For an intervention to be effective, close coordination and collaboration are required with other sectors. Coordination with local authorities and other responding agencies is also necessary to ensure that needs are met, that efforts are not duplicated, and that the quality of food security, nutrition and food aid responses is optimised.

For example, requirements for cooking utensils, fuel and water for food consumption, and for the maintenance of public health, are addressed in the standards for Water, Sanitation and Hygiene Promotion, Health Services and Shelter, Settlement and Non-Food Items. These requirements have a direct impact on the ability of households to access food and the maintenance of adequate nutritional status. Reference to specific standards or guidance notes in other technical chapters is made where relevant.

Links to the standards common to all sectors

The process by which a response is developed and implemented is critical to its effectiveness. This chapter should be utilised in conjunction with the standards common to all sectors, which cover participation, initial assessment, response, targeting, monitoring, evaluation, aid worker competencies and responsibilities, and the supervision, management and support of personnel (see chapter 1, page 21). In particular, in any response the participation of disaster-affected people – including the vulnerable groups outlined below – should be maximised to ensure its appropriateness and quality.

Food

Vulnerabilities and capacities of disaster-affected populations

The groups most frequently at risk in emergencies are women, children, older people, disabled people and people living with HIV/AIDS (PLWH/A). In certain contexts, people may also become vulnerable by reason of ethnic origin, religious or political affiliation, or displacement. This is not an exhaustive list, but it includes those most frequently identified. Specific vulnerabilities influence people's ability to cope and survive in a disaster, and those most at risk should be identified in each context.

Throughout the handbook, the term 'vulnerable groups' refers to all these groups. When any one group is at risk, it is likely that others will also be threatened. Therefore, whenever vulnerable groups are mentioned, users are strongly urged to consider all those listed here. Special care must be taken to protect and provide for all affected groups in a non-discriminatory manner and according to their specific needs. However, it should also be remembered that disaster-affected populations possess, and acquire, skills and capacities of their own to cope, and that these should be recognised and supported.

1 Food Security and Nutrition Assessment and Analysis

These two standards follow on from the common Initial assessment (see page 29) and Participation (see page 28) standards, and both apply wherever nutrition and food security interventions are planned or are advocated. These assessments are in-depth and require considerable time and resources to undertake properly. In an acute crisis and for immediate response, a rapid assessment may be sufficient to decide whether or not immediate assistance is required, and if so what provisions should be made. Assessment checklists are provided in Appendices 1-2, pages 172-176.

Assessment and analysis standard 1: food security

Where people are at risk of food insecurity, programme decisions are based on a demonstrated understanding of how they normally access food, the impact of the disaster on current and future food security, and hence the most appropriate response.

Key indicators (to be read in conjunction with the guidance notes)

● Assessments and analyses examine food security in relevant geographic locations and livelihood groupings, distinguishing between seasons, and over time, to identify and prioritise needs (see guidance note 1).

Food

● The assessment demonstrates understanding of the broader social, economic and political policies, institutions and processes that affect food security (see guidance note 2).

● The assessment includes an investigation and analysis of coping strategies (see guidance note 3).

● Where possible, the assessment builds upon local capacities, including both formal and informal institutions (see guidance note 4).

● The methodology used is comprehensively described in the assessment report and is seen to adhere to widely accepted principles (see guidance note 5).

● Use is made of existing secondary data, and the collection of new primary data in the field is focused on additional information essential for decision-making (see guidance note 6).

● Recommended food security responses are designed to support, protect and promote livelihood strategies, while also meeting immediate needs (see guidance note 7).

● The impact of food insecurity on the population's nutritional status is considered (see guidance note 8).

Guidance notes

1. **Scope of analysis:** food security varies according to people's livelihoods, their location, their social status, the time of year and the nature of the disaster and associated responses. The focus of the assessment will reflect how the affected population acquired food and income before the disaster, and how the disaster has affected this. For example, in urban and peri-urban areas, the focus may be on reviewing the market supply of food, while in rural areas it will usually be on food production. Where people have been displaced, the food security of the host population must also be taken into account. Food security assessments may be undertaken when planning to phase out a programme as well as prior to starting one. In either case, they should be coordinated among all concerned parties to minimise duplication of effort. Assessments gathering new information should complement secondary data from existing information sources.

2. **Context:** food insecurity may be the result of wider macro-economic and structural socio-political factors e.g. national and international policies, processes or institutions that affect people's access to nutritionally adequate food. This is usually defined as chronic food insecurity, in that it is a long-term condition resulting from structural vulnerabilities, but it may be aggravated by the impact of a disaster.

3. **Coping strategies:** assessment and analysis should consider the different types of coping strategy, who is applying them and how well they work. While strategies vary, there are nonetheless distinct stages of coping. Early coping strategies are not necessarily abnormal, are reversible and cause no lasting damage e.g. collection of wild foods, selling non-essential assets or sending a family member to work elsewhere. Later strategies, sometimes called crisis strategies, may permanently undermine future food security e.g. sale of land, distress migration of whole families or deforestation. Some coping strategies employed by women and girls tend to expose them to higher risk of HIV infection e.g. prostitution and illicit relationships, or sexual violence as they travel to unsafe areas. Increased migration generally may increase risk of HIV transmission. Coping strategies may also affect the environment e.g. over-exploitation of commonly owned natural resources. It is important that food security is protected and supported before all non-damaging options are exhausted.

4. **Local capacities:** participation of the community and appropriate local institutions at all stages of assessment and planning is vital. Programmes should be based on need and tailored to the particular local context. In areas subject to recurrent natural disasters or long-running conflicts there may be local early warning and emergency response systems or networks. Communities which have previously experienced drought or floods may have their own contingency plans. It is important that such local capacities are supported.

5. **Methodology:** it is important to consider carefully the coverage of assessments and sampling procedures, even if informal. The process documented in the report should be both logical and transparent, and should reflect recognised procedures for food security assessment. Methodological approaches need to be coordinated among agencies and with the government to ensure that information and analyses are complementary and

Food

consistent, so that information can be compared over time. Multi-agency assessments are usually preferable. The triangulation of different sources and types of food security information is vital in order to arrive at a consistent conclusion across different sources e.g. crop assessments, satellite images, household assessments etc. A checklist of the main areas to be considered in an assessment is given in Appendix 1. A checklist for reviewing methodology is provided in Appendix 2.

6. **Sources of information:** in many situations a wealth of secondary information exists about the situation pre-disaster, including the normal availability of food, the access that different groups normally have to food, the groups that are most food-insecure, and the effects of previous crises on food availability and the access of different groups. Effective use of secondary information enables the gathering of primary data during the assessment to be focused on what is essential in the new situation.

7. **Long-term planning:** while meeting immediate needs and preserving productive assets will always be the priority during the initial stages of a crisis, responses must always be planned with the longer term in mind. This requires technical expertise in a range of sectors, as well as abilities to work closely with members of the community, including representatives from all groups. Participation of community members at all stages of assessment and programme planning is vital, not least for their perspectives of long-term possibilities and risks. Recommendations must be based on a sound and demonstrated understanding by appropriately qualified and experienced personnel. The assessment team should include relevant sectoral experts, including e.g. agriculturalists, agro-economists, veterinarians, social scientists, and water and sanitation or other appropriate experts (see Participation standard on page 28).

8. **Food insecurity and nutritional status:** food insecurity is one of three underlying causes of malnutrition, and therefore wherever there is food insecurity there is risk of malnutrition, including micronutrient deficiencies. Consideration of the impact of food insecurity on the nutrition situation is an essential part of food security assessment. However, it should not be assumed that food insecurity is the sole cause of malnutrition, without considering possible health and care causal factors.

Assessment and analysis standard 2: nutrition

Where people are at risk of malnutrition, programme decisions are based on a demonstrated understanding of the causes, type, degree and extent of malnutrition, and the most appropriate response.

Key indicators (to be read in conjunction with the guidance notes)

● Before conducting an anthropometric survey, information on the underlying causes of malnutrition (food, health and care) is analysed and reported, highlighting the nature and severity of the problem(s) and those groups with the greatest nutritional and support needs (see guidance note 1 and General nutrition support standard 2 on page 140).

● The opinions of the community and other local stakeholders on the causes of malnutrition are considered (see guidance note 1).

● Anthropometric surveys are conducted only where information and analysis is needed to inform programme decision-making (see guidance note 2).

● International anthropometric survey guidelines, and national guidelines consistent with these, are adhered to for determining the type, degree and extent of malnutrition (see guidance note 3).

● Where anthropometric surveys are conducted among children under five years, international weight-for-height reference values are used for reporting malnutrition in Z scores and percentage of the median for planning purposes (see guidance note 3).

● Micronutrient deficiencies to which the population is at risk are determined (see guidance note 4).

● Responses recommended after nutrition assessment build upon and complement local capacities in a coordinated manner.

Food

Guidance notes

1. ***Underlying causes:*** the immediate causes of malnutrition are disease and/or inadequate food intake (which in turn result from food insecurity), a poor public health or social and care environment, or inadequate access to health services at household and community levels. These underlying causes are influenced by other basic causes including human, structural, natural and economic resources, the political, cultural and security context, the formal and informal infrastructure, and population movements (forced or unforced) and constraints on movement. An understanding of the causes of malnutrition in each specific context is an essential prerequisite for any nutrition programme. Information on the causes of malnutrition can be gathered from primary or secondary sources, including existing health and nutrition profiles, research reports, early warning information, health centre records, food security reports and community welfare groups, and can comprise both quantitative and qualitative information. A nutrition assessment checklist can be found in Appendix 4.

2. ***Decision-making*** should rely on an understanding of all three possible underlying causes of malnutrition as well as results from anthropometric surveys. In an acute crisis, however, decisions to implement general food distribution need not await the results of anthropometric surveys, as these can take up to three weeks. It should, however, be possible to use anthropometric survey findings to inform decisions on responses aimed at correcting malnutrition.

3. ***Anthropometric surveys*** provide an estimate of the prevalence of malnutrition. The most widely accepted practice is to assess malnutrition levels in children aged 6-59 months as a proxy for the population as a whole. However, other groups may be affected to a greater extent or face greater nutritional risk. When this is the case, the situation of these groups should be assessed, although measurement can be problematic (see Appendix 5). International guidelines stipulate that a representative sample is used for surveys; adherence to national guidelines can promote coordination and comparability of reporting. Where representative data are available on trends in nutritional status, these are preferable to a single prevalence figure. Immunisation coverage rates can also usefully be

gathered during an anthropometric survey, as can retrospective mortality data, using a different sampling frame. Reports should always describe the probable causes of malnutrition, and nutritional oedema should be reported separately.

4. ***Micronutrient deficiencies:*** if the population is known to have been vitamin A-, iodine- or iron-deficient prior to the disaster, it can be assumed that this will remain a problem during the disaster. When analysis of the health and food security situations suggests a risk of micronutrient deficiency, steps to improve the quantification of specific deficiencies should be taken (see also General nutrition support standard 1 on page 137 and Correction of malnutrition standard 3 on page 152).

Food

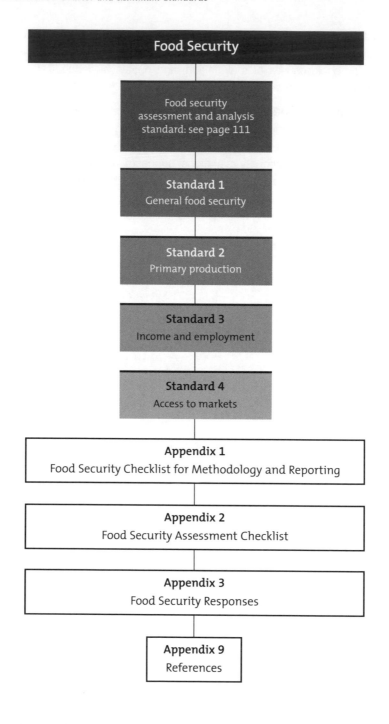

2 Minimum Standards in Food Security

Food security includes access to food (including affordability), adequacy of food supply or availability, and the stability of supply and access over time. It also covers the quality, variety and safety of food, and the consumption and biological utilisation of food.

The resilience of people's livelihoods, and their vulnerability to food insecurity, is largely determined by the resources available to them, and how these have been affected by disaster. These resources include economic and financial property (such as cash, credit, savings and investments) and also include physical, natural, human and social capital. For people affected by disaster, the preservation, recovery and development of the resources necessary for their food security and future livelihoods is usually a priority.

In conflict situations, insecurity and the threat of conflict may seriously restrict livelihood activities and access to markets. Households may suffer direct loss of assets, either abandoned as a result of flight or destroyed or commandeered by warring parties.

The first food security standard, following on from the food security assessment and analysis standard on page 111, is a general standard that applies to all aspects of food security programming in disasters, including issues relating to survival and preservation of assets. The remaining three standards relate to primary production, income generation and employment, and access to markets, including goods and services. Appendix 3 describes a range of food security responses.

There is some obvious overlap between the food security standards, as food security responses usually have multiple objectives, relating to different aspects of food security and hence are covered by more than one standard (including also standards in the water, health and shelter sectors). In addition, a balance of programmes is required to achieve all standards in food security. Disaster response should support and/or complement existing government services in terms of structure, design and long-term sustainability.

Food security standard 1: general food security

People have access to adequate and appropriate food and non-food items in a manner that ensures their survival, prevents erosion of assets and upholds their dignity.

Key indicators (to be read in conjunction with the guidance notes)

● Where people's lives are at risk through lack of food, responses prioritise meeting their immediate food needs (see guidance note 1).

● In all disaster contexts, measures are taken to support, protect and promote food security. This includes preserving productive assets or recovering those lost as the result of disaster (see guidance note 2).

● Responses that protect and support food security are based on sound analysis, in consultation with the disaster-affected community.

● Responses take account of people's coping strategies, their benefits and any associated risks and costs (see guidance note 3).

● Transition and exit strategies are developed for all food security responses to disaster, and are publicised and applied as appropriate (see guidance note 4).

● When a response supports the development of new or alternative livelihood strategies, all groups have access to appropriate support, including necessary knowledge, skills and services (see guidance note 5).

● Food security responses have the least possible degradative effect on the environment (see guidance note 6).

● Numbers of beneficiaries are monitored to determine the level of acceptance and access by different groups in the population and to ensure overall coverage of the affected population without discrimination (see guidance note 7).

● The effects of responses on the local economy, social networks, livelihoods and the environment are monitored, in addition to ongoing monitoring linked to programme objectives (see guidance note 8).

Guidance notes

1. ***Prioritising life-saving responses:*** although food distribution is the most common response to acute food insecurity in disasters, other types of response may also help people meet their immediate food needs. Examples include sales of subsidised food (when people have some purchasing power but supplies are lacking); improving purchasing power through employment programmes (including food-for-work); and destocking initiatives or cash distributions. Especially in urban areas, the priority may be to re-establish normal market arrangements and revitalise economic activities that provide employment. Such strategies may be more appropriate than food distribution because they uphold dignity, support livelihoods and thereby reduce future vulnerability. Agencies have a responsibility to take into account what others are doing to ensure that the combined response provides complementary inputs and services. General food distributions should be introduced only when absolutely necessary and should be discontinued as soon as possible. General free food distribution may not be appropriate when:

   − adequate supplies of food are available in the area (and the need is to address obstacles to access);

   − a localised lack of food availability can be addressed by support of market systems;

   − local attitudes or policies are against free food handouts.

2. ***Support, protection and promotion of food security:*** appropriate measures to support food security can include a wide range of responses

Food Security

and advocacy (see Appendix 3). Although in the short term it may not be feasible to achieve food security based entirely on people's own livelihood strategies, existing strategies that contribute to household food security and preserve dignity should be protected and supported wherever possible. Food security responses do not necessarily seek a complete recovery of assets lost as a result of disaster, but seek to prevent further erosion and to promote a process of recovery.

3. *Risks associated with coping strategies:* many coping strategies carry costs or incur risks that may increase vulnerability. For example:

 – cutbacks in amounts of food eaten or in the quality of diets lead to declining health and nutritional status;

 – cutbacks in expenditure on school fees and health care undermine human capital;

 – prostitution and external relationships to secure food undermine dignity, and risk social exclusion and HIV infection or other sexually transmitted diseases;

 – sale of household assets may reduce the future productive capacity of the household;

 – failure to repay loans risks losing future access to credit;

 – over-use of natural resources reduces the availability of natural capital (e.g. excessive fishing, collection of firewood etc);

 – travel to insecure areas to work or to gather food or fuel exposes people (especially women and children) to attack;

 – producing or trading illicit goods risks arrest and imprisonment;

 – separation of families and mothers from children risks poor standards of child care and malnutrition.

These progressive and debilitating effects must be recognised and early interventions undertaken to discourage such strategies and prevent asset loss. Certain coping strategies may also undermine dignity, where people are forced to engage in socially demeaning or unacceptable activities. However, in many societies certain strategies (such as sending a family member to work elsewhere during hard times) are a well-established tradition.

4. ***Exit and transition strategies:*** such strategies must be considered from the outset of a programme, particularly where the response may have long-term implications e.g. the provision of free services which would normally be paid for, such as access to credit or veterinary services. Before closing the programme or transiting to a new phase, there should be evidence that the situation has improved.

5. ***Access to knowledge, skills and services:*** structures that provide relevant services should be designed and planned together with the users, so that they are appropriate and adequately maintained, where possible beyond the life of the project. Some groups have very specific needs e.g. children orphaned as a result of AIDS may miss out on the information and skills transfer that takes place within families.

6. ***Environmental impact:*** as far as possible, the natural resource base for production and livelihoods of the affected population – and of host populations – should be preserved. Impact on the surrounding environment should be considered during assessment and the planning of any response. For example, people living in camps require cooking fuel, which may lead rapidly to local deforestation. The distribution of foodstuffs which have long cooking times, such as certain beans, will require more cooking fuel, thus also potentially affecting the environment (see Food aid planning standard 2 on page 158). Where possible, responses should aim to preserve the environment from further degradation. For example, destocking programmes reduce the pressure of animal grazing on pasture during a drought, making more feed available for surviving livestock.

7. ***Coverage, access and acceptability:*** beneficiaries and their characteristics should be described and their numbers estimated before determining the level of participation of different groups (paying particular attention to vulnerable groups). Participation is partly determined by ease of access and the acceptability of activities to participants. Even though some food security responses are targeted at the economically active, they should nevertheless be non-discriminatory and seek to provide access for vulnerable groups, as well as protecting dependents, including children. Various constraints, including capacity to work, workload at home, responsibilities for caring for children, the chronically ill or disabled, and restricted physical access, may limit the participation of women, people with disabilities and older people. Overcoming these constraints

Food Security

involves identifying activities that are within the capacity of these groups or setting up appropriate support structures. Targeting mechanisms based on self-selection should normally be established with full consultation with all groups in the community (see Targeting standard on page 35).

8. ***Monitoring:*** as well as routine monitoring (see Monitoring and Evaluation standards on pages 37-40), it is also necessary to monitor the wider food security situation in order to assess the continued relevance of the programme, determine when to phase out specific activities or to introduce modifications or new projects as needed, and to identify any need for advocacy. Local and regional food security information systems, including famine early warning systems, are important sources of information.

Food security standard 2: primary production

Primary production mechanisms are protected and supported.

Key indicators (to be read in conjunction with the guidance notes)

● Interventions to support primary production are based on a demonstrated understanding of the viability of production systems, including access to and availability of necessary inputs and services (see guidance note 1).

● New technologies are introduced only where their implications for local production systems, cultural practices and environment are understood and accepted by food producers (see guidance note 2).

● Where possible, a range of inputs is provided in order to give producers more flexibility in managing production, processing and distribution and in reducing risks (see guidance note 3).

● Productive plant, animal or fisheries inputs are delivered in time, are locally acceptable and conform to appropriate quality norms (see guidance notes 4-5).

● The introduction of inputs and services does not exacerbate vulnerability or increase risk, e.g. by increasing competition for scarce natural resources or by damaging existing social networks (see guidance note 6).

- Inputs and services are purchased locally whenever possible, unless this would adversely affect local producers, markets or consumers (see guidance note 7).

- Food producers, processors and distributors receiving project inputs make appropriate use of them (see guidance notes 8-9).

- Responses understand the need for complementary inputs and services and provide these where appropriate.

Guidance notes

1. ***Viability of primary production:*** to be viable, food production strategies must have a reasonable chance of developing adequately and succeeding. This may be influenced by a wide range of factors including:

   - access to sufficient natural resources (farmland, pasture, water, rivers, lakes, coastal waters, etc.). The ecological balance should not be endangered, e.g. by over-exploitation of marginal lands, over-fishing, or pollution of water, especially in peri-urban areas;

   - levels of skills and capacities, which may be limited where communities are seriously affected by disease, or where education and training may be barred to some groups;

   - labour availability in relation to existing patterns of production and the timing of key agricultural activities;

   - availability of inputs and the nature and coverage of related services (financial, veterinary, agricultural extension), which may be provided by government institutions and/or other bodies;

   - the legality of specific activities or the affected groups' right to work e.g. controls on the collection of firewood or restrictions on rights of refugees to undertake paid work;

   - security because of armed conflict, destruction of transport infrastructure, landmines, threat of attack or banditry.

   Production should not adversely affect the access of other groups to life-sustaining natural resources such as water.

Food
Security

2. ***Technological development:*** 'new' technologies may include improved crop varieties or livestock species, new tools or fertilisers. As far as possible, food production activities should follow existing patterns and/or be linked with national development plans. New technologies should only be introduced during a disaster if they have previously been tested in the local area and are known to be appropriate. When introduced, new technologies should be accompanied by appropriate community consultations, provision of information, training and other relevant support. The capacity of extension services within local government departments, NGOs and others to facilitate this should be assessed and if necessary reinforced.

3. ***Improving choice:*** examples of interventions that offer producers greater choice include cash inputs or credit in lieu of, or to complement, productive inputs, and seed fairs that provide farmers with the opportunity to select seed of their choice. Production should not have negative nutritional implications, such as the replacement of food crops by cash crops. The provision of animal fodder during drought can provide a more direct human nutrition benefit to pastoralists than the provision of food assistance.

4. ***Timeliness and acceptability:*** examples of productive inputs include seeds, tools, fertiliser, livestock, fishing equipment, hunting implements, loans and credit facilities, market information, transport facilities, etc. The provision of agricultural inputs and veterinary services must be timed to coincide with the relevant agricultural and animal husbandry seasons; e.g. the provision of seeds and tools must precede the planting season. Emergency destocking of livestock during a drought should take place before excess livestock mortality occurs, while restocking should start when recovery is well assured, e.g. following the next rains.

5. ***Seeds:*** priority should be given to local seed, so that farmers can use their own criteria to establish quality. Local varieties should be approved by farmers and local agricultural staff. Seeds should be adaptable to local conditions and be resistant to disease. Seeds originating from outside the region need to be adequately certified and checked for appropriateness to local conditions. Hybrid seeds may be appropriate where farmers are familiar with them and have experience growing them. This can only be determined through consultation with the community. When seeds are provided free of charge, farmers may prefer hybrid seeds to local varieties

because these are otherwise costly to purchase. Government policies regarding hybrid seeds should also be complied with before distribution. Genetically modified (GMO) seeds should not be distributed unless they have been approved by the national or other ruling authorities.

6. ***Impact on rural livelihoods:*** primary food production may not be viable if there is a shortage of vital natural resources. Promoting production that requires increased or changed access to locally available natural resources may heighten tensions within the local population, as well as further restricting access to water and other essential needs. Care should be taken with the provision of financial resources, in the form of either grants or loans, since these may also increase the risk of local insecurity (see Food security standard 3, guidance note 5 on page 130). In addition, the free provision of inputs may disturb traditional mechanisms for social support and redistribution.

7. ***Local purchase of inputs:*** inputs and services for food production, such as livestock health services, seed, etc., should be obtained through existing in-country supply systems where possible. However, before embarking on local purchases the risk should be considered of project purchases distorting the market e.g. raising prices of scarce items.

8. ***Monitoring usage:*** indicators of the process and the outputs from food production, processing and distribution may be estimated e.g. area planted, quantity of seed planted per hectare, yield, number of offspring, etc. It is important to determine how producers use the project inputs i.e. verifying that seeds are indeed planted, and that tools, fertilisers, nets and fishing gear are used as intended. The quality of the inputs should also be reviewed in terms of their acceptability and producer preferences. Important for evaluation is consideration of how the project has affected food available to the household e.g. household food stocks, the quantity and quality of food consumed, or the amount of food traded or given away. Where the project aims to increase production of a specific food type, such as animal or fish products or protein-rich legumes, the households' use of these products should be investigated. The results of this type of analysis may be cross-validated with nutritional surveys (provided health and care determinants of nutritional status are also considered).

Food
Security

9. ***Unforeseen or negative effects of inputs:*** for example, the effect of changes in labour patterns in subsequent agricultural seasons, the effect of responses on alternative and existing coping strategies (e.g. diversion of labour), labour patterns of women and effect on child care, school attendance and effect on education, risks taken in order to access land and other essential resources.

Food security standard 3: income and employment

Where income generation and employment are feasible livelihood strategies, people have access to appropriate income-earning opportunities, which generate fair remuneration and contribute towards food security without jeopardising the resources on which livelihoods are based.

Key indicators (to be read in conjunction with the guidance notes)

● Project decisions about timing, work activities, type of remuneration and the technical feasibility of implementation are based on a demonstrated understanding of local human resource capacities, a market and economic analysis, and an analysis of demand and supply for relevant skills and training needs (see guidance notes 1-2).

● Responses providing job or income opportunities are technically feasible and all necessary inputs are available on time. Where possible, responses contribute to the food security of others and preserve or restore the environment.

● The level of remuneration is appropriate, and payments for waged labour are prompt, regular and timely. In situations of acute food insecurity, payments may be made in advance (see guidance note 3).

● Procedures are in place to provide a safe, secure working environment (see guidance note 4).

● Projects involving large sums of cash include measures to avoid diversion and/or insecurity (see guidance note 5).

● Responses providing labour opportunities protect and support household caring responsibilities, and do not negatively affect the local environment or interfere with regular livelihood activities (see guidance note 6).

● The household management and use of remuneration (cash or food), grants or loans are understood and seen to be contributing towards the food security of all household members (see guidance note 7).

Guidance notes

1. ***Appropriateness of initiatives:*** project activities should make maximum use of local human resources in project design and the identification of appropriate activities. As far as possible, food-for-work (FFW) and cash-for-work (CFW) activities should be selected by, and planned with, the participating groups themselves. Where there are large numbers of displaced people (refugees or IDPs), employment opportunities should not be at the expense of the local host population. In some circumstances, employment opportunities should be made available to both groups. Understanding household management and use of cash is important in deciding whether and in what form microfinance services could support food security (see also Food security standard 2).

2. ***Type of remuneration:*** remuneration may be in cash or in food, or a combination of both, and should enable food-insecure households to meet their needs. Rather than payment, remuneration may often take the form of an incentive provided to help people to undertake tasks that are of direct benefit to themselves. FFW may be preferred to CFW where markets are weak or unregulated, or where little food is available. FFW may also be appropriate where women are more likely to control the use of food than of cash. CFW is preferred where trade and markets can assure the local availability of food, and secure systems for dispersal of cash are available. People's purchasing needs, and the impact of giving either cash or food on other basic needs (school attendance, access to health services, social obligations) should be considered. The type and level of remuneration should be decided on a case-by-case basis, taking account of the above and the availability of cash and food resources.

Food Security

3. *Payments:* levels of remuneration should take account of the needs of the food-insecure households and of local labour rates. There are no universally accepted guidelines for setting levels of remuneration, but where remuneration is in kind and provided as an income transfer, the resale value of the food on local markets must be considered. The net gain to individuals in income through participation in the programme activities should be greater than if they had spent their time on other activities. This applies to FFW, CFW and also credit, business start-ups, etc. Income-earning opportunities should enhance the range of income sources, and not take the place of existing sources. Remuneration should not have a negative impact on local labour markets e.g. by causing wage rate inflation, diverting labour from other activities or undermining essential public services.

4. *Risk in the work environment:* a high-risk working environment should be avoided, by introducing practical procedures for minimising risk or treating injuries e.g. briefings, first aid kits, protective clothing where necessary. This should include risk of HIV exposure, and measures should be taken to minimise this.

5. *Risk of insecurity and diversion:* handing out cash, e.g. in the distribution of loans or payment of remuneration for work done, introduces security concerns for both programme staff and the recipients. A balance has to be achieved between security risks to both groups, and a range of options should be reviewed. For ease of access and safety of recipients, the point of distribution should be as close as possible to their homes, i.e. decentralised, though this may jeopardise the safety of programme staff. If a high level of corruption or diversion of funds is suspected, FFW may be preferable to CFW.

6. *Caring responsibilities and livelihoods:* participation in income-earning opportunities should not undermine child care or other caring responsibilities as this could increase the risk of malnutrition. Programmes may need to consider employing care providers or providing care facilities (see General nutrition support standard 2 on page 140). Responses should not adversely affect access to other opportunities, such as other employment or education, or divert household resources from productive activities already in place.

7. **Use of remuneration:** fair remuneration means that the income generated contributes a significant proportion of the resources necessary for food security. The household management of cash or food inputs (including intra-household distribution and end uses) must be understood, as the way cash is given may either defuse or exacerbate existing tensions, and thereby affect food security and the nutrition of household members. Responses that generate income and employment often have multiple food security objectives, including community-level resources that affect food security. For example, repairing roads may improve access to markets and access to health care, while repairing or constructing water-harvesting and irrigation systems may improve productivity.

Food security standard 4: access to markets

People's safe access to market goods and services as producers, consumers and traders is protected and promoted.

Key indicators (to be read in conjunction with the guidance notes)

● Food security responses are based on a demonstrated understanding of local markets and economic systems, which informs their design and, where necessary, leads to advocacy for system improvement and policy change (see guidance notes 1-2).

● Producers and consumers have economic and physical access to operating markets, which have a regular supply of basic items, including food at affordable prices (see guidance note 3).

● Adverse effects of food security responses, including food purchases and distribution, on local markets and market suppliers are minimised where possible (see guidance note 4).

● There is increased information and local awareness of market prices and availability, of how markets function and the policies that govern this (see guidance note 5).

● Basic food items and other essential commodities are available (see guidance note 6).

Food
Security

● The negative consequences of extreme seasonal or other abnormal price fluctuations are minimised (see guidance note 7).

Guidance notes

1. **Market analysis:** the types of market – local, regional, national – and how they are linked to each other should be reviewed. Consideration should be given to access to functioning markets for all affected groups, including vulnerable groups. Responses that remunerate in food, or provide inputs, such as seeds, agricultural tools, shelter materials, etc., should be preceded by a market analysis in relation to the commodity supplied. Local purchase of any surpluses will support local producers. Imports are likely to reduce local prices. Where inputs such as seeds may not be available on the open market, despite still being accessible to farmers through their own seed supply networks and systems, consideration should be given to the effect of external inputs on such systems.

2. **Advocacy:** markets operate in the wider national and global economies, which influence local market conditions. For example, governmental policies, including pricing and trade policies, influence access and availability. Although actions at this level are beyond the scope of disaster response, analysis of these factors is necessary as there may be opportunities for a joint agency approach, or advocacy to government and other bodies to improve the situation.

3. **Market demand and supply:** economic access to markets is influenced by purchasing power, market prices and availability. Affordability depends on the terms of trade between basic needs (including food, essential agricultural inputs such as seeds, tools, health care, etc.) and income sources (cash crops, livestock, wages, etc). Erosion of assets occurs when deterioration in terms of trade forces people to sell assets (often at low prices) in order to buy basic needs (at inflated prices). Access to markets may also be influenced by the political and security environment, and by cultural or religious considerations, which restrict access by certain groups (such as minorities).

4. **Impact of interventions:** local procurement of food, seeds or other commodities may cause local inflation to the disadvantage of consumers but to the benefit of local producers. Conversely, imported food aid may drive prices down and act as a disincentive to local food production,

increasing the numbers who are food-insecure. Those responsible for procurement should monitor and take account of these effects. Food distribution also affects the purchasing power of beneficiaries, as it is a form of income transfer. Some commodities are easier to sell for a good price than others, e.g. oil versus blended food. The 'purchasing power' associated with a given food or food basket will influence whether it is eaten or sold by the beneficiary household. An understanding of household sales and purchases is important in determining the wider impact of food distribution programmes (see also Food aid management standard 3).

5. ***Transparent market policies:*** local producers and consumers need to be aware of market pricing controls and other policies that influence supply and demand. These may include state pricing and taxation policies, policies influencing movement of commodities across regional boundaries, or local schemes to facilitate trade with neighbouring areas (although in many conflict situations clear policies on these issues may not necessarily exist).

6. ***Essential food items:*** selection of food items for market monitoring depends on local food habits and therefore must be locally determined. The principles of planning nutritionally adequate rations should be applied to deciding what food items are essential in a particular context (see General nutrition support standard 1 on page 137 and Food aid planning standard 1 on page 157).

7. ***Abnormally extreme seasonal price fluctuations*** may adversely affect poor agricultural producers, who have to sell their produce when prices are at their lowest (i.e. after harvest). Conversely, consumers who have little disposable income cannot afford to invest in food stocks, depending instead on small but frequent purchases. They are therefore forced to buy even when prices are high (e.g. during drought). Examples of interventions which can minimise these effects include improved transport systems, diversified food production and cash or food transfers at critical times.

Food Security

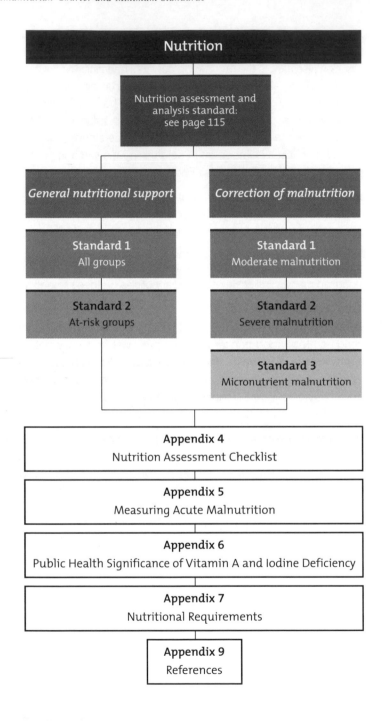

3 Minimum Standards in Nutrition

The immediate causes of malnutrition are disease and/or inadequate food intake, which in turn result from inadequate food, health or care at household or community levels.

The aim of preventive programmes is to ensure that the causes of malnutrition identified in the assessment are addressed. This includes ensuring that people have safe access to food of adequate quality and quantity, and have the means to prepare and consume it safely; ensuring that people's living environment, their access to, and the quality of health services (both preventive and curative) minimise their risk of disease; and ensuring that an environment exists in which care can be provided to nutritionally vulnerable members of the population. Care includes the provision within households and the community of time, attention and support to meet the physical, mental and social needs of household members. The protection of the social and care environment is addressed through the Food Aid and Food Security standards, while nutritional care and support for groups of the population that may be at increased risk are addressed in the Nutrition standards.

Programmes aiming to correct malnutrition may include special feeding programmes, medical treatment and/or supportive care for malnourished individuals. Feeding programmes should only be implemented when anthropometric surveys have been conducted or are planned. They should always be complemented by preventive measures.

The first two standards in this section deal with the nutritional issues relating to programmes that prevent malnutrition and should be used alongside the Food Aid and Food Security standards. The last three standards concern programmes that correct malnutrition.

Responses to prevent and correct malnutrition require the achievement of minimum standards both in this chapter and those in other chapters: health services, water supply and sanitation, and shelter. They also require the common standards detailed in chapter 1 to be achieved (see page 21). In other words, in order for the nutrition of all groups to be protected and supported, in a manner that ensures their survival and upholds their dignity, it is not sufficient to achieve only the standards in this section of the handbook.

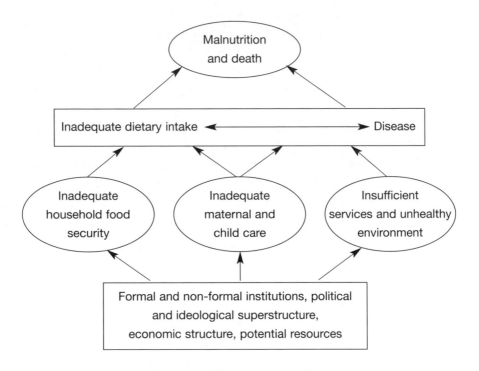

Conceptual framework showing the causes of malnutrition

i) General Nutrition Support

This section considers the nutritional resources and services required to meet the needs of both the general population and specific groups that may be at increased nutritional risk. Until these needs are met, any response aimed at the correction of malnutrition is likely to have a limited impact, since those who recover will return to a context of inadequate nutritional support and are therefore likely to deteriorate again.

Where populations require food aid to meet some or all of their nutritional needs, General nutrition support standard 1 should be used alongside Food aid planning standards 1-2 on pages 157-160 and Non-food items standards 3-4 on pages 233-236. General nutrition support standard 2 focuses on at-risk groups. However, those who are vulnerable to a disaster vary according to the context and so the specific groups at risk should be identified in each situation.

General nutrition support standard 1: all groups

The nutritional needs of the population are met.

Key indicators (to be read in conjunction with the guidance notes)

- There is access to a range of foods – staple (cereal or tuber), pulses (or animal products) and fat sources – that meet nutritional requirements (see guidance note 1).

- There is access to vitamin A-, C- and iron-rich or fortified foods or appropriate supplements (see guidance notes 2, 3, 5 and 6).

- There is access to iodised salt for the majority (>90%) of households (see guidance notes 2, 3 and 6).

- There is access to additional sources of niacin (e.g. pulses, nuts, dried fish) if the staple is maize or sorghum (see guidance notes 2-3).

- There is access to additional sources of thiamine (e.g. pulses, nuts, eggs) if the staple is polished rice (see guidance notes 2-3).

Nutrition

- There is access to adequate sources of riboflavin where people are dependent on a very limited diet (see guidance notes 2-3).

- Levels of moderate and severe malnutrition are stable at, or declining to, acceptable levels (see guidance note 4).

- There are no cases of scurvy, pellagra, beri-beri or riboflavin deficiency (see guidance note 5).

- Rates of xerophthalmia and iodine deficiency disorders are not of public health significance (see guidance note 6).

Guidance notes

1. ***Nutritional requirements:*** the following estimates for average population requirements should be used, with the figures adjusted for each population as described in Appendix 7.

   - 2,100 kcals per person per day

   - 10-12% of total energy provided by protein

   - 17% of total energy provided by fat

   - adequate micronutrient intake through fresh or fortified foods.

   It should be noted that these are the requirements for food aid provision only if the population is entirely dependent on food aid to meet its nutritional requirements. In situations where people can meet some of their nutritional needs themselves, food aid provision should be adjusted accordingly, based on the assessment. For planning food rations, see Food aid planning standard 1 on page 157.

2. ***Preventing micronutrient diseases:*** if these indicators are met, then deterioration of the micronutrient status of the population should be prevented, provided adequate public health measures are in place to prevent diseases such as measles, malaria and parasitic infection (see Control of communicable diseases standards on page 273). Possible options for the prevention of micronutrient deficiencies include food security measures to promote access to nutritious foods (see Food security standards 2-3 on pages 124-131); improving the nutritional quality of the ration through fortification or inclusion of blended foods or locally purchased commodities to provide nutrients otherwise missing;

and/or medicinal supplementation. Micronutrient losses which can occur during transport, storage, processing and cooking should be taken into account. Exceptionally, where nutrient-rich foods are available locally, increasing the quantity of food in any general ration to allow more food exchanges may be considered, but cost-effectiveness and impact on markets must be taken into account.

3. ***Monitoring access to micronutrients:*** the indicators measure the quality of the diet but do not quantify nutrient availability. Measuring the quantity of nutrient intake would impose unrealistic requirements for information collection. Indicators can be measured using information from various sources gathered by different techniques. These might include monitoring food availability and use at the household level; assessing food prices and food availability on the markets; assessing the nutrient content of any distributed food; examining food aid distribution plans and records; assessing any contribution of wild foods; and conducting food security assessments. Household-level analysis will not determine individual access to food. Intra-household food allocation may not always be equitable and vulnerable groups may be particularly affected, but this is not practical to measure. Distribution mechanisms (see Food aid management standard 3 on page 168), the choice of food aid commodities and discussion with the affected population could contribute to improved intra-household allocation.

4. ***Interpreting levels of malnutrition:*** trends in malnutrition might be indicated by health centre records, repeat anthropometric surveys, nutritional surveillance, screening or reports from the community. It may be expensive to set up systems to monitor malnutrition rates over large areas or long periods of time, and technical expertise is required. The relative cost of such a system should be judged against the scale of resourcing. A combination of complementary information systems, e.g. both surveillance and intermittent surveys, may be the most effective use of resources. Wherever possible, local institutions and communities should participate in monitoring activities, interpretation of findings and the planning of any response. Determining whether levels of malnutrition are acceptable requires analysis of the situation in the light of the reference population, morbidity and mortality rates (see Health systems and infrastructure standard 1, guidance note 3 on page 260), seasonal fluctuations, pre-emergency levels of malnutrition and the underlying causes of malnutrition.

Nutrition

5. ***Epidemic micronutrient deficiencies:*** four micronutrient deficiencies – scurvy (vitamin C), pellagra (niacin), beri-beri (thiamine) and riboflavin – have been highlighted, as these are the most commonly observed deficiencies to result from inadequate access to micronutrients in food aid-dependent populations and are usually avoidable in a disaster situation. If individuals with any of these deficiencies present at health centres, for example, it is likely to be as a result of restricted access to certain types of food and probably indicative of a population-wide problem. As such, deficiencies should be tackled by population-wide interventions as well as individual treatment (see Correction of malnutrition standard 3 on page 152). In any context where there is clear evidence that these micronutrient deficiencies are an endemic problem, their levels should be reduced at least to pre-disaster levels.

6. ***Endemic micronutrient deficiencies:*** tackling micronutrient deficiencies within the initial phase of a disaster is complicated by difficulties in identifying them. The exceptions are xerophthalmia (vitamin A) and goitre (iodine) for which clear 'field-friendly' identification criteria are available. These deficiencies can also be tackled by population-level interventions, e.g. high-dose vitamin A supplementation for children and post-partum women, salt iodisation and public awareness campaigns. See Appendix 6 for definitions of their public health significance.

General nutrition support standard 2: at-risk groups

The nutritional and support needs of identified at-risk groups are met.

Key indicators (to be read in conjunction with the guidance notes)

- Infants under six months are exclusively breastfed or, in exceptional cases, have access to an adequate amount of an appropriate breast milk substitute (see guidance notes 1-2).

- Children aged 6-24 months have access to nutritious, energy-dense complementary foods (see guidance note 3).

- Pregnant and breastfeeding women have access to additional nutrients and support (see guidance note 4).

- Specific attention is paid to the protection, promotion and support of the care and nutrition of adolescent girls (see guidance note 4).

- Appropriate nutritional information, education and training is given to relevant professionals, care givers and organisations on infant and child feeding practices (see guidance notes 1-4 and 8).

- Older people's access to appropriate nutritious foods and nutritional support is protected, promoted and supported (see guidance note 5).

- Families with chronically ill members, including people living with HIV/AIDS, and members with specific disabilities have access to appropriate nutritious food and adequate nutritional support (see guidance notes 6-8).

- Community-based systems are in place to ensure appropriate care of vulnerable individuals (see guidance note 8).

Guidance notes

1. *Infant feeding:* exclusive breastfeeding is the healthiest way to feed a baby under six months. Babies who are exclusively breastfed receive no prelactates, water, teas or complementary foods. Rates of exclusive breastfeeding are typically low and so it is important to promote and support breastfeeding, especially when hygiene and care practices have broken down and the risk of infection is high. There are exceptional cases where a baby cannot be exclusively breastfed (such as where the mother has died or the baby is already fully artificially fed). In these cases adequate amounts of an appropriate breast milk substitute should be used, judged according to the Codex Alimentarius standards, and relactation encouraged where possible. Breast milk substitutes can be dangerous because of the difficulties involved in safe preparation. Feeding bottles should never be used, as they are unhygienic. Professionals should be trained in providing adequate protection, promotion and support for breastfeeding, including relactation. If infant formula is distributed, care givers will need advice and support on its safe use. Procurement and distribution must adhere to the International Code of Marketing of Breastmilk Substitutes and relevant World Health Assembly resolutions.

Nutrition

2. **HIV and infant feeding:** if voluntary and confidential testing for HIV/AIDS is not possible, all mothers should be supported to breastfeed. Alternatives to breast milk are too risky to offer if a woman does not know her status. If a woman has been tested and knows she is HIV-positive, replacement feeding is recommended if it can be done in a way that is acceptable, feasible, affordable, sustainable and safe. HIV-positive mothers who choose not to breastfeed should be provided with specific guidance and support for at least the first two years of the child's life to ensure adequate feeding.

3. **Young child feeding:** breastfeeding should continue for at least the first two years of life. At the age of six months, young children require energy-dense foods in addition to breast milk; it is recommended that 30% of the energy content of their diet comes from fat sources. Where children aged 6-24 months do not have access to breast milk, foods must be sufficient to meet all their nutritional requirements. Efforts should be made to provide households with the means and skills to prepare appropriate complementary foods for children under 24 months. This may be through the provision of specific food commodities or of utensils, fuel and water. When measles or other immunisation is carried out, it is usual practice to provide a vitamin A supplement to all children aged 6-59 months. Low birth-weight infants and young children can also benefit from iron supplementation, though compliance with daily protocols is very difficult to maintain.

4. **Pregnant and breastfeeding women:** the risks associated with inadequate nutrient intakes for pregnant and breastfeeding women include pregnancy complications, maternal mortality, low birth weight and impaired breastfeeding performance. The average planning figures for general rations take into account the additional needs of pregnant and breastfeeding women. When the general ration is inadequate, supplementary feeding to prevent nutritional deterioration may be necessary. Low body weight at conception is strongly associated with low birth weight which means that, where they exist, mechanisms for providing nutritional support to adolescent girls should be used. Pregnant and breastfeeding women should receive daily supplements of iron and folic acid but as with children, compliance can be problematic. It is therefore important to ensure that steps are taken to reduce the prevalence of iron deficiency through a diversified diet (see General

nutrition support standard 1). Post-partum women should also receive vitamin A within six weeks of delivery.

5. ***Older people*** can be particularly affected by disasters. Nutritional risk factors which reduce access to food and can increase nutrient requirements include disease and disability, psychosocial stress, cold and poverty. These factors can be exacerbated when normal support networks, either formal or informal, are disrupted. While the average planning figures for general rations take into account the nutritional requirements of older people, special attention should be paid to their nutritional and care needs. Specifically:

   – older people should be able to easily access food sources (including relief food);

   – foods should be easy to prepare and consume;

   – foods should meet the additional protein and micronutrient requirements of older people.

   Older people are often important care givers to other household members and may need specific support in fulfilling this function.

6. ***People living with HIV/AIDS (PLWH/A)*** may face greater risk of malnutrition, because of a number of factors. These include reduced food intake due to appetite loss or difficulties in eating; poor absorption of nutrients due to diarrhoea; parasites or damage to intestinal cells; changes in metabolism; and chronic infections and illness. There is evidence to show that the energy requirements of PLWH/A increase according to the stage of the infection. Micronutrients are particularly important in preserving immune function and promoting survival. PLWH/A need to ensure that they keep as well nourished and healthy as possible to delay the onset of AIDS. Milling and fortification of food aid or provision of fortified, blended foods are possible strategies for improving their access to an adequate diet and in some situations it may be appropriate to increase the overall size of any food ration (see Targeting standard on page 35).

7. ***Disabled people*** may face a range of nutritional risks which can be further exacerbated by the environment in which they are living. Nutritional risks include difficulties in chewing and swallowing, leading to reduced food intake and choking; inappropriate position/posture when feeding;

Nutrition

reduced mobility affecting food access and access to sunlight (affecting vitamin D status); discrimination affecting food access; and constipation, particularly affecting individuals with cerebral palsy. Disabled individuals may be at particular risk of being separated from immediate family members (and usual care givers) in a disaster. Efforts should be made to determine and reduce these risks by ensuring physical access to food (including relief food), developing mechanisms for feeding support (e.g. provision of spoons and straws, developing systems for home visiting or outreach) and access to energy-dense foods.

8. **Community-based care:** care givers and those they are caring for may have specific nutritional needs: e.g. they may have less time to access food because they are ill/caring for the ill; they may have a greater need to maintain hygienic practices which may be compromised; they may have fewer assets to exchange for food due to the costs of treatment or funerals; and they may face social stigma and reduced access to community support mechanisms. The availability of care givers may have changed as a consequence of the disaster e.g. due to family break-up or death, children and older people can become the main care givers. It is important that care givers be supported and not undermined in the care of vulnerable groups; this includes feeding, hygiene, health and psychosocial support and protection. Existing social networks can be used to provide training to selected community members to take on responsibilities in these areas.

ii) Correction of Malnutrition

Malnutrition, including micronutrient deficiency, is associated with increased risk of morbidity and mortality for affected individuals. Therefore, when rates of malnutrition are high, it is necessary to ensure access to services which correct as well as prevent malnutrition. The impact of these services will be considerably reduced if appropriate general support for the population is not in place – for example, if there is a failure in the general food pipeline, or acute food insecurity, or if supplementary feeding without general support is being done for security reasons. In these instances, advocacy for general nutritional support should be a key element of the programme (see Response standard on page 33).

There are many ways to address moderate malnutrition, for example through the improvement of the general food ration, improving food security, improving access to health care and to sanitation and potable water. In disasters, targeted supplementary feeding is often the primary strategy for correction of moderate malnutrition and prevention of severe malnutrition (standard 1). In some instances, rates of malnutrition may be so high that it may be inefficient to target the moderately malnourished and all individuals meeting certain at-risk criteria (e.g. those aged 6-59 months) may be eligible. This is known as blanket supplementary feeding.

Severe malnutrition is corrected through therapeutic care which can be delivered through a variety of approaches, including 24-hour in-patient care, day care and home-based care (standard 2). The provision of in-patient care relies on other standards being achieved, such as the provision of functioning water and sanitation facilities (see Water, Sanitation and Hygiene Promotion, page 51). The correction of micronutrient deficiencies (standard 3) relies on the achievement of standards in health systems and infrastructure and control of communicable diseases (see Health Services, page 249).

Correction of malnutrition standard 1: moderate malnutrition

Moderate malnutrition is addressed.

Nutrition

Key indicators (to be read in conjunction with the guidance notes)

● From the outset, clearly defined and agreed objectives and criteria for set-up and closure of the programme are established (see guidance note 1).

● Coverage is >50% in rural areas, >70% in urban areas and >90% in a camp situation (see guidance note 2).

● More than 90% of the target population is within <1 day's return walk (including time for treatment) of the distribution centre for dry ration supplementary feeding programmes and no more than 1 hour's walk for on-site supplementary feeding programmes (see guidance note 2).

● The proportion of exits from targeted supplementary feeding programmes who have died is <3%, recovered is >75% and defaulted is <15% (see guidance note 3).

● Admission of individuals is based on assessment against internationally accepted anthropometric criteria (see guidance note 4 and Appendix 5).

● Targeted supplementary feeding programmes are linked to any existing health structure and protocols are followed to identify health problems and refer accordingly (see guidance note 5).

● Supplementary feeding is based on the distribution of dry take-home rations unless there is a clear rationale for on-site feeding (see guidance note 6).

● Monitoring systems are in place (see guidance note 7).

Guidance notes

1. ***Design of targeted supplementary feeding:*** programme design must be based on an understanding of the complexity and dynamics of the nutrition situation. Targeted supplementary feeding programmes should only be implemented when anthropometric surveys have been conducted or are planned and if the underlying causes of moderate malnutrition are being addressed simultaneously. Targeted supplementary feeding programmes may be implemented in the short term, before General nutrition support standard 1 is met. The purpose of the programme should be clearly communicated and discussed with the target population (see Participation standard on page 28).

2. ***Coverage*** is calculated in relation to the target population, defined at the start of the programme, and can be estimated as part of an anthropometric survey. It can be affected by the acceptability of the programme, location of distribution points, security for staff and those requiring treatment, waiting times, service quality and the extent of home visiting. Distribution centres

should be close to the targeted population, to reduce the risks and costs associated with travelling long distances with young children and the risk of people being displaced to them. Affected communities should be involved in deciding where to locate distribution centres. The final decision should be based on wide consultation and on non-discrimination.

3. **Exit indicators:** exits from a feeding programme are those individuals no longer registered. The total of exited individuals is made up of those who have defaulted, recovered (including those who are referred) and died.

Proportion of exits defaulted =
number of defaulters in the programme x 100%
number of exits

Proportion of exits died =
number of deaths in the programme x 100%
number of exits

Proportion of exits recovered =
number of individuals successfully discharged in the programme x 100%
number of exits.

4. **Admission criteria:** individuals other than those who meet anthropometric criteria defining malnutrition may also benefit from supplementary feeding e.g. people living with HIV/AIDS or TB or those who have a disability. Monitoring systems will need to be adjusted if these individuals are included. In situations where emergency feeding programmes are overwhelmed with the numbers of individuals eligible for treatment, this may not be the best way to address the needs of these individuals, who will also remain at risk beyond the duration of the disaster. It may be better to identify alternative mechanisms for providing longer-term nutritional support e.g. through community home-based support or TB treatment centres.

5. **Health inputs:** targeted supplementary feeding programmes should include appropriate medical protocols such as the provision of anti-helminths, vitamin A supplementation and immunisations, but delivery of these services should take into account the capacity of existing health services. In areas where there is a high prevalence of particular diseases (e.g. HIV/AIDS), the quality and quantity of the supplementary food should be given special consideration.

Nutrition

6. **On-site feeding:** dry take-home rations, distributed on a weekly or bi-weekly basis, are preferred to on-site feeding but their size should take into account household sharing. On-site feeding may be considered only where security is a concern. Where fuel, water or cooking utensils are in short supply, such as in populations which are displaced or on the move, distributions of ready-to-eat foods may be considered in the short term, provided they do not disrupt traditional feeding patterns. For take-home feeding, clear information should be given on how to prepare supplementary food in a hygienic manner, how and when it should be consumed and the importance of continued breastfeeding for children under 24 months of age (see Food aid management standard 3 on page 168).

7. **Monitoring systems:** systems should monitor community participation, acceptability of the programme (a good measure of this is the rate of defaulting), rates of readmission, the quantity and quality of food being provided, programme coverage, admission and discharge rates and external factors such as morbidity patterns, levels of malnutrition in the population, level of food insecurity in households and in the community, and the capacity of existing systems for service delivery. Individual causes of readmission, defaulting and failure to recover should be investigated on an ongoing basis.

Correction of malnutrition standard 2: severe malnutrition

Severe malnutrition is addressed.

Key indicators (to be read in conjunction with the guidance notes)

- From the outset, clearly defined and agreed criteria for set-up and closure of the programme are established (see guidance note 1).

- Coverage is >50% in rural areas, >70% in urban areas and >90% in camp situations (see guidance note 2).

- The proportion of exits from therapeutic care who have died is <10%, recovered is >75% and defaulted is <15% (see guidance notes 3-5).

- Discharge criteria include non-anthropometric indices such as good appetite and the absence of diarrhoea, fever, parasitic infestation and other untreated illness (see guidance note 4).

- Mean weight gain is >8g per kg per person per day (see guidance note 6).

- Nutritional and medical care is provided according to internationally recognised therapeutic care protocols (see guidance note 7).

- As much attention is attached to breastfeeding and psychosocial support, hygiene and community outreach as to clinical care (see guidance note 8).

- There should be a minimum of one feeding assistant for 10 in-patients.

- Constraints to caring for malnourished individuals and affected family members should be identified and addressed (see guidance note 9).

Guidance notes

1. *Starting therapeutic care:* factors which should be taken into account in the opening of centres for the treatment of severe malnutrition are the numbers and geographical spread of affected individuals; the security situation; recommended criteria for setting up and for closing centres; and the capacity of existing health structures. Therapeutic feeding programmes should not undermine the capacity of health systems, nor allow governments to abdicate their responsibilities for providing services. Wherever possible, programmes should aim to build on and strengthen existing capacity to treat severe malnutrition. The purpose of the programme should be clearly communicated and discussed with the target population (see Participation standard on page 28). A therapeutic care programme should only be started if there is a plan in place for remaining patients, at the end of the programme, to complete their treatment.

2. *Coverage* is calculated according to the target population and can be estimated as part of an anthropometric survey. It can be affected by the acceptability of the programme, location of treatment centres, security for staff and those requiring treatment, waiting times and service quality.

Nutrition

3. **Exit indicators:** the time needed to achieve the exit indicators for a therapeutic feeding programme is 1-2 months. Exits from a feeding programme are those no longer registered. The population of exited individuals is made up those who have defaulted, recovered (including those who are referred) and died (see previous standard, guidance note 3 for how to calculate exit indicators). Mortality rates should be interpreted in the light of coverage rates and the severity of malnutrition treated. The extent to which mortality rates are affected in situations where a high proportion of admissions are HIV-positive is unknown; for this reason, the figures have not been adjusted for these situations.

4. **Recovery rates:** a discharged individual must be free from medical complications and have achieved and maintained sufficient weight gain (e.g. for two consecutive weighings). Established protocols suggest discharge criteria which should be adhered to, in order to avoid the risks associated with premature exit from the programme. Protocols also define limits for the mean length of stay for patients in therapeutic feeding, aimed at avoiding prolonged recovery periods (e.g. typical lengths of stay may be 30-40 days). HIV/AIDS and TB may result in some malnourished individuals failing to recover. Options for longer-term treatment or care should be considered in conjunction with health services and other social and community support (see Control of communicable disease standards 3 and 6, pages 277 and 283). Causes of readmission, defaulting and failure to respond should be investigated and documented on an ongoing basis. Individuals should be followed up wherever possible after discharge and referred for supplementary feeding where possible.

5. **Default rates** can be high when the programme is not accessible to the population. Accessibility may be affected by the distance of the treatment point from the community, an ongoing armed conflict, a lack of security, the level of support offered to the care giver of the individual treated, the number of care givers who are left at home to look after other dependants (this may be very few in situations of high HIV/AIDS prevalence), and the quality of the care provided. A defaulter from a therapeutic feeding programme is an individual who has not attended for a defined period of time (e.g. for more than 48 hours for in-patients).

6. **Weight gain:** similar rates of weight gain can be achieved in both adults and children when they are given similar diets. Average rates of weight

gain, however, may mask situations where individual patients are not improving and are not being discharged. Lower rates may be more acceptable in out-patient programmes because the risks and demands on the community, e.g. in terms of time, can be much lower. Mean weight gain is calculated as follows: (weight on exit (g) minus weight on admission (g))/(weight on admission (kg)) x duration of treatment (days).

7. **Protocols:** internationally accepted protocols, including definitions of failure to respond, are found in the references in Appendix 9. In order to implement treatment protocols, clinical staff require special training (see Health systems and infrastructure standards, page 258). Individuals admitted for therapeutic care who are tested or suspected to be HIV-positive should have equal access to care if they meet the criteria for admission. This is also applicable to TB cases. PLWH/A who do not meet admission criteria often require nutritional support, but this is not best offered in the context of treatment for severe malnutrition in disasters. These individuals and their families should be supported through a range of services including community home-based care, TB treatment centres and prevention programmes aimed at mother-to child-transmission.

8. **Breastfeeding and psychosocial support:** breastfeeding mothers require special attention to support lactation and optimal infant and young child feeding. A breastfeeding corner may be set up for this purpose. Emotional and physical stimulation through play is important for severely malnourished children during the rehabilitation period. Care givers of severely malnourished children often require social and psychosocial support to bring their children for treatment. This may be achieved through outreach and mobilisation programmes (see General nutrition support standard 2).

9. **Carers:** all carers of severely malnourished individuals should be enabled to feed and care for them during treatment through the provision of advice, demonstrations and health and nutrition information. Programme staff should be aware that discussions with care givers may expose individual human rights violations (e.g. deliberate starvation of populations by warring parties) and they should be trained in procedures for dealing with such situations.

Nutrition

Correction of malnutrition standard 3: micronutrient malnutrition

Micronutrient deficiencies are addressed.

Key indicators (to be read in conjunction with the guidance notes)

● All clinical cases of deficiency diseases are treated according to WHO micronutrient supplementation protocols (see guidance note 1).

● Procedures are established to respond efficiently to micronutrient deficiencies to which the population may be at risk (see guidance note 2).

● Health staff are trained in how to identify and treat micronutrient deficiencies to which the population is most at risk (see guidance note 2).

Guidance notes

1. ***Diagnosis and treatment:*** diagnosis of some micronutrient deficiencies is possible through simple clinical examination. Indicators of these deficiencies can then be incorporated into health or nutritional surveillance systems, although careful training of staff is required to ensure that assessment is accurate. Other micronutrient deficiencies cannot be identified without biochemical examination. In such instances, case definition is problematic and in emergencies can often only be determined through the response to supplementation by individuals who present themselves to health staff. Treatment of micronutrient deficiencies or those at risk of deficiency due to disease should take place in the health system and within feeding programmes.

2. ***Preparedness:*** strategies for the prevention of micronutrient deficiencies are given in General nutrition support standard 1. Prevention can also be achieved through the reduction of the incidence of diseases such as acute respiratory infection, measles, parasitic infection, malaria and diarrhoea that deplete micronutrient stores (see Control of communicable diseases

standards on page 273). Treatment of deficiencies will involve active case finding and the development of case definitions and protocols for treatment.

Nutrition

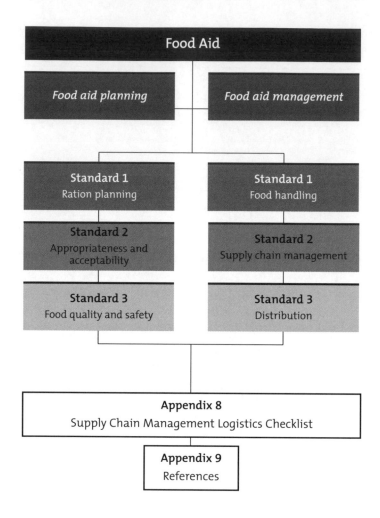

4 Minimum Standards
in Food Aid

If a community's normal means of accessing food is compromised by disaster (for example, through loss of crops due to natural disaster, deliberate starvation by a party to an armed conflict, commandeering of food by soldiers, or forced or non-forced displacement), a food aid response may be required to sustain life, protect or restore people's self-reliance, and reduce the need for them to adopt potentially damaging coping strategies.

Whenever analysis determines that food aid is an appropriate response, this should be undertaken in a manner that meets short-term needs but also, as far as possible, contributes to restoring long-term food security. The following should be taken into account.

● General (free) distributions are introduced only when absolutely necessary, targeted to those who need the food most, and discontinued as soon as possible.

● Dry rations for home preparation are provided wherever possible. Mass feeding (the provision of cooked food that is eaten on the spot) is organised only for an initial short period following a major sudden disaster or population movement when people do not have the means to cook for themselves, or in a situation of insecurity when the distribution of dry rations could put recipients at risk.

● Food assistance to refugees and IDPs is based on assessment of their situation and needs, not on their status as refugees or IDPs.

● Food commodities are imported only when there is an in-country deficit or no practical possibility of moving available surpluses into the disaster-affected area.

Food Aid

● Where there is a risk of food aid being commandeered or used by combatants in an armed conflict, measures are put in place to avoid it fuelling the conflict.

Arrangements for food aid distribution must be particularly robust and accountable in view of the high value and high volume involved in most disaster relief programmes. Delivery and distribution systems should be monitored at all stages, including at the community level. Programme evaluation should be carried out regularly, and findings disseminated to and discussed with all stakeholders, including the affected population.

The six Food Aid standards are divided into two sub-categories. Food Aid Planning covers ration planning, appropriateness and acceptability of food, and food quality and safety. Food Aid Management deals with food handling, supply chain management and distribution. Appendix 8 at the end of the chapter provides a logistics checklist for supply chain management purposes.

i) Food Aid Planning

Initial assessment and analysis of an emergency situation should identify people's own food and income sources, as well as any threats to those sources. It should determine whether food aid is required and, if so, the type and quantity needed to ensure that people are able to maintain an adequate nutritional status. When it is determined that free distribution of food is necessary, an appropriate general ration must be established to enable households to meet their nutritional needs, taking account of the food they are able to provide for themselves without adopting damaging coping strategies (see Food security analysis standard 1, guidance note 3 on page 113 and Food security standard 1, guidance note 3 on page 122).

When it is determined that a supplementary feeding programme (SFP) is needed, an appropriate supplementary ration must be established. In such cases, the SFP ration is in addition to any general ration to which individuals are entitled (see Correction of malnutrition standard 1, guidance note 1 on page 147).

In all cases, the commodities provided must be carefully chosen, in consultation with the affected population. They must be of good quality, safe to consume, and appropriate and acceptable to recipients.

Food aid planning standard 1: ration planning

Rations for general food distributions are designed to bridge the gap between the affected population's requirements and their own food resources.

Key indicators (to be read in conjunction with the guidance notes)

● Rations for general distribution are designed on the basis of the standard initial planning requirements for energy, protein, fat and micronutrients, adjusted as necessary to the local situation (see guidance note 1; see also General nutrition support standards on pages 137-144 and Appendix 7).

● The ration distributed reduces or eliminates the need for disaster-affected people to adopt damaging coping strategies.

● When relevant, the economic transfer value of the ration is calculated and is appropriate to the local situation (see guidance note 2).

Guidance notes

1. *Nutritional requirements:* where people are displaced and have no access to any food at all, the distributed ration should meet their total nutritional requirement. However, most disaster-affected populations are able to obtain some food by their own means. Rations should then be planned to make up the difference between the nutritional requirement and what people can provide for themselves. Thus, if the standard requirement is 2,100 kcals/person/day and the assessment determines that people within the target population can, on average, acquire 500 kcals/person/day from their own efforts or resources, the ration should be designed to provide 2,100 – 500 = 1,600 kcals/person/day. Similar calculations should be made for fat and protein. Agreed estimates must

Food Aid

be established for the average quantities of food to which people have access (see Food security assessment standard on page 111).

2. ***Economic context:*** where little or no other food is available and people can be expected to consume all (or almost all) of any food distributed, the ration should be designed strictly on the basis of nutritional criteria, taking into account issues of acceptability and cost-effectiveness. Where other foods are available and beneficiaries may be expected to trade some of their ration to obtain them, the ration's transfer value becomes relevant. The transfer value is the local market value of the ration i.e. what it would cost to buy the same quantities of the same items on the local market.

Food aid planning standard 2: appropriateness and acceptability

The food items provided are appropriate and acceptable to recipients and can be used efficiently at the household level.

Key indicators (to be read in conjunction with the guidance notes)

● People are consulted during assessment or programme design on the acceptability, familiarity and appropriateness of food items, and results are factored into programme decisions on the choice of commodities (see guidance note 1).

● When an unfamiliar food is distributed, instructions on its preparation in a locally palatable manner, with minimum nutrient loss, are provided to women and other people who prepare food, preferably in the local language (see guidance note 1).

● People's ability to access cooking fuel and water, and the duration of cooking times and requirements for soaking, are considered when selecting commodities for distribution (see guidance note 2).

● When a whole grain cereal is distributed, recipients either have the means to mill or process it in a traditional home-based manner or have access to adequate milling/processing facilities reasonably close to their dwellings (see guidance note 3).

● People have access to culturally important items, including condiments (see guidance note 4).

● There is no distribution of free or subsidised milk powder or of liquid milk as a single commodity (see guidance note 5).

Guidance notes

1. *Familiarity and acceptability:* while nutritional value is the primary consideration when choosing commodities for a food basket, the foods distributed should be familiar to the recipients and consistent with their religious and cultural traditions, including any food taboos for pregnant or breastfeeding women. In assessment reports and requests to donors, the reasons for the choice of particular commodities or the exclusion of others should be explained. When there are acute survival needs and there is no access to cooking facilities, ready-to-eat foods must be provided. In these circumstances there may sometimes be no practical alternative to providing unfamiliar items. Only in such instances should special 'emergency rations' be considered.

2. *Fuel requirements:* when assessing food requirements, a fuel assessment should also be undertaken to ensure that recipients are able to cook food sufficiently to avoid adverse effects to their health, and without degradation of the environment through excessive collection of fuel wood. When necessary, appropriate fuel should be provided or a wood harvesting programme established that is supervised for the safety of women and children, who are the main gatherers of firewood. In general, items should be provided that do not require long cooking times or the use of large quantities of water. The provision of milled grain or of grain mills will reduce cooking times and the amount of fuel required.

3. *Grain processing:* milling is a particular concern for maize, as milled whole maize has a shelf life of only 6-8 weeks. Milling should therefore take place shortly before consumption. Where household-level grinding is part of the recipients' tradition, whole grain can be distributed. Whole grain has the advantage of a longer shelf life and may have a higher economic value for recipients. Alternatively, facilities for low-extraction commercial milling can be provided: this removes the germ, oil and enzymes, which cause rancidity. This greatly increases the shelf life of the grain, although at the

Food Aid

same time it reduces its protein content. National laws relating to the import and distribution of whole grain should be complied with.

4. ***Culturally important items:*** the assessment should 1) identify culturally important condiments and other food items that are an essential part of daily food habits; and 2) determine the access people have to these items. The food basket should be designed accordingly, especially where people will be dependent on distributed rations for an extended period.

5. ***Milk:*** powdered milk, or liquid milk distributed as a single commodity (this includes milk intended for mixing with tea), should not be included in a general food distribution or a take-home supplementary feeding programme, as its indiscriminate use may give rise to serious health hazards. This is especially relevant in the case of young children, for whom the risks of inappropriate dilution and germ contamination are very high (see General nutrition support standard 2 on page 140).

Food aid planning standard 3: food quality and safety

Food distributed is of appropriate quality and is fit for human consumption.

Key indicators (to be read in conjunction with the guidance notes)

● Food commodities conform to national (recipient country) and other internationally accepted standards (see guidance notes 1-2).

● All imported packaged food has a minimum six-month shelf life on arrival in the country and is distributed before the expiry date or well within the 'best before' period (see guidance note 1).

● There are no verifiable complaints about the quality of food distributed (see guidance note 3).

● Food packaging is sturdy, convenient for handling, storage and distribution, and is not a hazard for the environment (see guidance note 4).

● Food packages are labelled in an appropriate language with, for packaged foods, the date of production, the 'best before' date and details of the nutrient content.

● Storage conditions are adequate and appropriate, stores are properly managed and routine checks on food quality are carried out in all locations (see guidance note 5).

Guidance notes

1. ***Food quality:*** foods must conform to the food standards of the recipient government and/or the Codex Alimentarius standards with regard to quality, packaging, labelling, shelf life, etc. Samples should be systematically checked at the point of delivery by the supplier to ensure their quality is appropriate. Whenever possible, commodities purchased (either locally or imported), should be accompanied by phytosanitary certificates or other inspection certificates that confirm their fitness for human consumption. Random sample testing should be carried out on in-country stocks to ensure their continued fitness for consumption. When large quantities are involved or there are doubts and could be disputes about quality, independent quality surveyors should inspect the consignment. Information on the age and quality of particular food consignments may be obtained from supplier certificates, quality control inspection reports, package labels, warehouse reports, etc.

2. ***Genetically modified foods:*** national regulations concerning the receipt and use of genetically modified foods must be understood and respected. External food aid should take such regulations into account when any food aid programme is being planned.

3. ***Complaints:*** recipients' complaints about food quality should be followed up promptly and handled in a transparent and fair manner.

4. ***Packaging:*** if possible, packaging should allow direct distribution of goods, without the need for repacking.

5. ***Storage areas*** should be dry and hygienic, adequately protected from climatic conditions and uncontaminated by chemical or other residues. They should also be secured, as far as possible, against pests such as insects and rodents. See also Food aid management standard 2 on page 165.

Food Aid

ii) Food Aid Management

The goal of food aid management is to deliver food to those people who need it most. Generally speaking, this involves delivering the right goods, to the right location, in the right condition, at the right time and for the right price, with minimal handling loss.

The weight and volume of food aid required to sustain a large population severely affected by disaster may amount to thousands of tonnes. The physical movement of food commodities to points of distribution may involve an extensive network of purchasers, forwarding agents, transporters and receivers, and multiple handling and transfers from one mode of transport to another. These networks, or supply chains, are put together using a series of contracts and agreements, which define roles and responsibilities, and establish liabilities and rights to compensation, among the contracting parties. All of this requires proper and transparent procedures that contribute towards establishing accountability.

Setting up and managing the supply chain entails cooperation among donors, the recipient government, humanitarian actors, local authorities, various service providers and local community organisations engaged in the food aid programme. Each party will have specific roles and responsibilities as a link, or series of links, in the supply chain. As a chain is only as strong as its weakest link, all parties involved in food aid logistics share responsibility for maintaining the flow of sufficient commodities to meet distribution targets and schedules.

Equity in the distribution process is of primary importance and the involvement of people from the disaster-affected population in decision-making and implementation is essential. People should be informed about the quantity and type of food rations to be distributed, and they should feel assured that the distribution process is fair and that they receive what has been promised. Any differences between rations provided to different groups must be explained and understood.

Food aid management standard 1: food handling

Food is stored, prepared and consumed in a safe and appropriate manner at both household and community levels.

Key indicators (to be read in conjunction with the guidance notes)

● There are no adverse health effects resulting from inappropriate food handling or preparation at any distribution site (see guidance note 1).

● Recipients of food aid are informed about and understand the importance of food hygiene (see guidance note 1).

● There are no complaints concerning difficulties in storing, preparing, cooking or consuming the food distributed (see guidance note 2).

● Every household has access to appropriate cooking utensils, fuel and hygiene materials (see guidance notes 3-4).

● Individuals who cannot prepare food or cannot feed themselves have access to a carer who prepares appropriate food in a timely manner and administers feeding where necessary (see guidance notes 4-5).

● Where food is distributed in cooked form, staff have received training in safe storage, handling of commodities and the preparation of food and understand the potential health hazards caused by improper practices.

Guidance notes

1. *Food hygiene:* changed circumstances may disrupt people's normal hygiene practices. It may therefore be necessary to promote food hygiene and actively support measures compatible with local conditions and disease patterns e.g. stressing the importance of washing hands before handling food, avoiding contamination of water, taking pest control

Food Aid

measures, etc. People should be informed about how to store food safely at the household level, and care givers should be provided with information on the optimal use of household resources for child feeding and safe methods for food preparation (see Hygiene promotion standard on page 59).

2. ***Sources of information*** may include programme monitoring systems, focus group discussions with recipients and rapid household surveys.

3. ***Household items and fuel:*** each household should have access to at least one cooking pot, water storage containers with a capacity of 40 litres, 250g of soap per person per month, and adequate fuel for food preparation. If access to cooking fuel is limited, foods requiring a short cooking time should be distributed. If this is not possible, then external sources of fuel supply should be established to bridge the gap (see Water supply standard 3 on page 69 and Non-food items standards 2-4 on pages 232-236).

4. ***Access to grinding mills*** and other processing facilities, and access to clean water, are very important in that they enable people to prepare food in the best form of their choice and also save time for other productive activities. Care givers spending excessive amounts of time waiting for these services could otherwise be preparing food, feeding children or engaging in other tasks that have a positive effect on nutritional outcomes and/or long-term self-reliance. Household-level food processing (including grinding) can reduce the time (as well as the quantities of water and fuel) required for cooking.

5. ***Special needs:*** although not an exhaustive list, those who require assistance with feeding usually include young children, older people, disabled people and people living with HIV/AIDS. See General nutrition support standard 2 on page 140.

Food aid management standard 2: supply chain management

Food aid resources (commodities and support funds) are well managed, using transparent and responsive systems.

Key indicators (to be read in conjunction with the guidance notes)

● Food aid resources reach the intended beneficiaries.

● An assessment is made of local supply chain management (SCM) capabilities and logistics infrastructure and a co-ordinated, efficient SCM system is established, using local capacity where this is feasible (see guidance notes 1-2).

● The assessment considers the availability of locally sourced food commodities (see guidance note 3).

● The award of contracts for SCM services is transparent, fair and open (see guidance note 4).

● Staff at all levels of the SCM system are adequately trained and observe procedures relating to food quality and safety (see guidance note 5).

● Appropriate inventory accounting, reporting and financial systems are in place to ensure accountability at all levels of the SCM system (see guidance notes 6-7).

● Care is taken to minimise losses, including through theft, and all losses are accounted for (see guidance notes 8-10).

● The food pipeline is monitored and maintained in such a way that any interruption to distribution is avoided (see guidance note 11).

● Information on the performance of the supply chain is provided to all stakeholders on a regular basis (see guidance note 12).

Food Aid

Guidance notes

1. ***Supply chain management (SCM)*** is an integrated approach to food aid logistics. Starting with the choice of commodity, it includes sourcing,

procurement, quality assurance, packaging, shipping, transportation, warehousing, inventory management, insurance, etc. The chain involves many different players, and it is important that their activities are coordinated. Appropriate management and monitoring practices should be adopted to ensure that all commodities are safeguarded until distribution to recipient households.

2. **Using local services:** an assessment should be made of the availability and reliability of local capability before sourcing from outside the area. Reputable local or regional transporters and freight forwarders can be contracted to provide logistics services. Such organisations have valuable knowledge of local regulations, procedures and facilities, and can help to ensure compliance with the laws of the host country as well as expediting delivery operations.

3. **Local sourcing vs. importation:** the local availability of food commodities, and the implications for local production and market systems of food being either sourced locally or imported, should be assessed (see Food security assessment and analysis standard on page 111; Food security standard 2 on page 124; and Food security standard 4 on page 131). Where a number of different organisations are involved in supplying food, local sourcing including purchases of commodities should be co-ordinated as far as possible. Other in-country sources of food commodities may include loans or reallocations from existing food aid programmes or national grain reserves, and loans from, or swaps with, commercial suppliers.

4. **Impartiality:** fair and transparent contracting procedures are essential in order to avoid any suspicion of favouritism or corruption. Food aid packaging should not carry any messages that are politically or religiously motivated or divisive in nature.

5. **Skills and training:** experienced SCM practitioners and food aid managers should be mobilised to set up the SCM system and train staff. Particular types of relevant expertise include contracts management, transportation and warehouse management, inventory management, pipeline analysis and information management, shipment tracking, import management, etc. When training is carried out, it should include the staff of partner organisations.

6. ***Reporting:*** most food aid donors have specific reporting requirements; supply chain managers should be aware of these requirements and establish systems that meet them as well as day-to-day management needs. This includes reporting promptly any delays or deviations in the supply chain. Pipeline information and other SCM reports should be shared in a transparent manner.

7. ***Documentation:*** a sufficient stock of documentation and forms (waybills, stock ledgers, reporting forms, etc.) should be available at all locations where food aid is received, stored, and/or dispatched in order to maintain a documented audit trail of transactions.

8. ***Warehousing:*** dedicated (food-only) warehouses are preferable to shared facilities. When selecting a warehouse, it should be established that no hazardous goods have previously been stored there and there is no danger of contamination. Other factors to consider include security, capacity, ease of access, solidity (of roof, walls, doors and floor) and absence of any threat of flooding.

9. ***Disposal of commodities unfit for human consumption:*** damaged commodities should be inspected by qualified inspectors, such as medical doctors, public health laboratories etc., to certify them as fit or unfit for human consumption. Methods of disposal of unfit commodities may include sale for animal feed, burial or incineration. In the case of disposal for animal feed, certification must be obtained to certify the commodity's fitness for this purpose. In all cases it must be ensured that unfit commodities do not re-enter the human or animal food supply chain and that their disposal does not cause harm to the environment or contaminate water sources in the vicinity.

10. ***Threats to the supply chain:*** in a situation of armed conflict, there is a danger of food aid being looted or requisitioned by warring parties, and the security of transport routes and warehouses should be taken into consideration. In all disaster situations, there is the potential for loss through theft at all levels of the supply chain, and control systems must be established and supervised at all storage, hand-over and distribution points to minimise this risk. Internal control systems should ensure division of duties/responsibilities to reduce the risk of collusion. Stocks should be regularly checked to detect any diversion of food. If diversion is detected,

Food Aid

measures should be taken not only to ensure the integrity of the supply chain, but also to analyse and address the broader political and security implications (e.g. the possibility of diverted stocks fuelling an armed conflict).

11. **Pipeline analysis:** regular pipeline analysis should be carried out and relevant information on stock levels, expected arrivals, distributions, etc. shared among all those involved in the supply chain. The regular tracking and forecasting of stock levels along the supply chain should highlight anticipated shortfalls or problems in time for solutions to be found.

12. **Providing information:** the use of local media or traditional methods of news dissemination should be considered as a way of keeping people informed about food supplies and operations. This reinforces transparency. Women's groups may be enlisted to help provide information about food aid programmes to the community.

Food aid management standard 3: distribution

The method of food distribution is responsive, transparent, equitable and appropriate to local conditions.

Key indicators (to be read in conjunction with the guidance notes)

● Recipients of food aid are identified and targeted on the basis of need, by means of an assessment carried out through consultation with stakeholders, including community groups (see guidance notes 1-2).

● Efficient and equitable distribution methods are designed in consultation with local groups and partner organisations, and involve the various recipient groups (see guidance notes 1-3).

● The point of distribution is as close as possible to recipients' homes to ensure easy access and safety (see guidance notes 4-5).

● Recipients are informed well in advance of the quality and quantity of the food ration and the distribution plan (see guidance notes 6-7).

● The performance and effectiveness of the food aid programme are properly monitored and evaluated (see guidance note 8).

Guidance notes

1. ***Targeting:*** food aid should be targeted to meet the needs of the most vulnerable in the community, without discrimination on the basis of gender, disability, religious or ethnic background, etc. The selection of distribution agents should be based on their impartiality, capacity and accountability. Distribution agents may include local elders, locally elected relief committees, local institutions, local NGOs, or government or international NGOs (see Participation and Initial assessment standards on pages 28-33 and Targeting standard on page 35).

2. ***Registration:*** formal registration of households receiving food aid should be carried out as soon as is feasible, and updated as necessary. Lists developed by local authorities and community-generated family lists may be useful, and the involvement of women from the affected population in this process is to be encouraged. Women should have the right to be registered in their own names if they wish. Care should be taken to ensure that female or adolescent-headed households and other vulnerable individuals are not omitted from distribution lists. If registration is not possible in the initial stages of the emergency, it should be completed as soon as the situation has stabilised. This is especially important when food aid may be required for lengthy periods.

3. ***Distribution methods:*** most distribution methods evolve over time. In the initial stages, general distributions based on family lists or population estimates provided by local communities may be the only feasible method. Any system should be monitored closely to ensure that food is reaching the intended recipients, and that the system is fair and equitable. Particular emphasis should be given to the accessibility of the programme to vulnerable groups. However, attempts to target vulnerable groups should not add to any stigma already experienced by these groups. This may be a particular issue in populations with large number of people living with HIV/AIDS (see Participation, Targeting, Monitoring and Evaluation standards in chapter 1).

4. ***Distribution points*** should be established where they are safe and most convenient for the recipients, not merely on the basis of logistic convenience for the distributing agency. The frequency of distribution and the number of distribution points should take into account the time spent by recipients

Food Aid

travelling to/from centres, and the practicalities and cost of transporting commodities. Recipients should not be made to walk long distances to collect rations, and distributions should be scheduled at convenient times to minimise disruption to everyday activities. Waiting areas and potable water should be provided at distribution points (see Correction of malnutrition standards 1-2 on pages 145-152).

5. ***Minimising security risks:*** food is a valuable commodity and its distribution can create security risks, including both the risk of diversion and the potential for violence. When food is in short supply, tensions can run high when deliveries are made. Women, children, elderly people and people with disabilities may be unable to obtain their entitlement, or may have it taken from them by force. The risks must be assessed in advance and steps taken to minimise them. These should include adequate supervision of distributions and guarding of distribution points, including the involvement of local police where appropriate. Measures to prevent, monitor and respond to gender-based violence or sexual exploitation associated with food distribution may also be necessary.

6. ***Dissemination of information:*** recipients should be informed about

   – the quantity and type of ration to be distributed and the reasons for any differences from established norms;

   – the distribution plan (day, time, location, frequency) and deviation, if any, due to outside circumstances;

   – the nutritional quality of the food and, if needed, special attention required to protect its nutritional value; and

   – the requirements for the safe handling and use of the food commodities.

7. ***Changes to the programme:*** changes in the food basket or ration levels caused by insufficient availability of food must be discussed with the recipients, through distribution committees or community leaders, and a course of action should be jointly developed. The distribution committee should inform the population of changes and the reasons behind them, how long changes will continue and when the distribution of normal rations will be resumed. It is essential to communicate clearly what people should receive. For example, ration quantities should be displayed

prominently at distribution sites, written in the local language and/or drawn pictorially, so that people are aware of their entitlements.

8. ***Monitoring and evaluation*** of food aid distribution should be carried out at all levels of the supply chain. At distribution points, random weighing should be carried out of rations collected by households to measure the accuracy and equity of distribution management, and exit interviews should be conducted. At community level, random visits to households receiving food aid can help to ascertain the acceptability and usefulness of the ration, and also to identify people who meet the selection criteria but who are not receiving food aid. Such visits can also ascertain if extra food is being received and where it is coming from (e.g. as a result of commandeering, recruitment or exploitation, sexual or otherwise). The wider effects on the food distribution system should also be considered. These may include implications for the agricultural cycle, agricultural activities, market conditions and availability of agricultural inputs.

Food Aid

Appendix 1

Food Security Checklist for Methodology and Reporting

Food security assessments should:

1. include a clear description of the methodology

   – overall design and objectives

   – background and number of assessors (whether they are working individually or in pairs)

   – selection of key informants (are they representative of all groups?)

   – composition of focus or other discussion groups

   – criteria for selecting informants

   – timeframe of the assessment

   – framework for analysis and methodological tools, including PRA tools and techniques;

2. be based on a qualitative approach, including review of secondary sources of quantitative information;

3. use terms correctly e.g. purposive sampling, key informant, focus group, terms for specific techniques;

4. involve local institutions as partners in the assessment process, unless inappropriate e.g. in some conflict situations;

5. employ an appropriate range of PRA tools and techniques (which are applied in sequence to analyse and triangulate findings);

6. involve a representative range of affected population groups or livelihood groupings;

7. describe the limitations or practical constraints of the assessment;

8. describe the coverage of the assessment, including its geographic spread, the range of livelihood groups included and other relevant stratification of the population (e.g. gender, ethnicity, tribal group, etc.);

9. include interviews with representatives of relevant government ministries and public services, traditional leaders, representatives of key civil society organisations (religious groups, local NGOs, advocacy or pressure groups, farmers' or pastoralists' associations, women's groups) and representatives of each of the livelihood groups under consideration.

The assessment report findings should cover:

1. the recent history of food security and relevant policies prior to the current situation;

2. a description of the different livelihood groups and their food security situation prior to the disaster;

3. food security pre-disaster for different livelihood groups;

4. the impact of the disaster on the food system and food security for different livelihood groups;

5. identification of particularly vulnerable livelihood groups or those vulnerable to food insecurity in the present situation;

6. suggested interventions, including means of implementation, advocacy and any additional assessments required;

7. the precise nature, purpose and duration of any food aid response, if a response is considered appropriate. Food aid responses should be justified on the basis of the above data and analysis.

Food

Appendix 2

Food Security Assessment Checklist

Food security assessments often broadly categorise the affected population into livelihood groupings, according to their sources of, and strategies for obtaining, income or food. This may also include a breakdown of the population according to wealth groups or strata. It is important to compare the prevailing situation with the history of food security pre-disaster. So-called 'average years' may be considered as a baseline. The specific roles and vulnerabilities of women and men, and the implications for household food security should be considered. Consideration of intra-household food security differences may also be important.

This checklist covers the broad areas that are usually considered in a food security assessment. Additional information must also be collected on the wider context of the disaster (e.g. its political context, population numbers and movements, etc.) and possibly in relation to other relevant sectors (nutrition, health, water and shelter). The checklist must be adapted to suit the local context and the objectives of the assessment. More detailed checklists are available in, for example, the Field Operations Guide of USAID (1998).

Food security of livelihood groups

1. Are there groups in the community who share the same livelihood strategies? How can these be categorised according to their main sources of food or income?

Food security pre-disaster (baseline)

2. How did the different livelihood groups acquire food or income before the disaster? For an average year in the recent past, what were their sources of food and income?

3. How did these different sources of food and income vary between seasons in a normal year? (Constructing a seasonal calendar may be useful.)

4. Looking back over the past 5 or 10 years, how has food security varied from year to year? (Constructing a timeline or history of good and bad years may be useful.)

5. What kind of assets, savings or other reserves are owned by the different livelihood groups (e.g. food stocks, cash savings, livestock holdings, investments, credit, unclaimed debt, etc.)?

6. Over a period of a week or a month, what do household expenditures include, and what proportion is spent on each item?

7. Who is responsible for management of cash in the household, and on what is cash spent?

8. How accessible is the nearest market for obtaining basic goods? (Consider distance, security, ease of mobility, availability of market information, etc.)

9. What is the availability and price of essential goods, including food?

10. Prior to the disaster, what were the average terms of trade between essential sources of income and food, e.g. wages to food, livestock to food, etc.?

Food security during disaster

11. How has the disaster affected the different sources of food and income for each of the livelihood groups identified?

12. How has it affected the usual seasonal patterns of food security for the different groups?

13. How has it affected access to markets, market availability and prices of essential goods?

14. For different livelihood groups, what are the different coping strategies and what proportion of people are engaged in them?

15. How has this changed as compared with the pre-disaster situation?

16. Which group or population is most affected?

17. What are the short- and medium-term effects of coping strategies on people's financial and other assets?

Food

18. For all livelihood groups, and all vulnerable groups, what are the effects of coping strategies on their health, general well-being and dignity? Are there risks associated with coping strategies?

Appendix 3

Food Security Responses

The range of interventions possible to support, protect and promote food security in emergencies is wide. The list below is not exhaustive. Each intervention must be designed to suit the local context and strategy for supporting food security, and therefore is unique in its objectives and design. It is important to consider a range of responses and programming options based on analysis and consideration of expressed needs. 'Off-the-shelf' interventions that do not take account of local priorities rarely work. The responses are categorised into three groups, which relate to the Food Security standards 2-4:

● primary production

● income and employment

● access to market goods and services.

General food distribution provides free food assistance directly to households and thus is of great importance in ensuring food security in the short term.

Primary production

● *Distribution of seeds, tools and fertiliser:* provided to encourage agricultural production, as starter packs to returnees, or to diversify crops. Often combined with agricultural extension services and possibly technical training.

● *Seed vouchers and fairs:* based on the provision of seed vouchers to potential buyers. Organising a seed fair to bring together potential sellers stimulates local seed procurement systems while allowing buyers access to a wide range of seeds.

● *Local agricultural extension services*

● *Training and education in relevant skills*

Food

- *Livestock interventions:* can include animal health measures; emergency destocking; restocking of livestock; distribution of livestock fodder and nutritional supplementation; livestock refuges; and provision of alternative water sources.

- *Distribution of fish nets and gear, or hunting implements*

- *Promotion of food processing*

Income and employment

- *Cash-for-work (CFW)* provides food-insecure households with opportunities for paid work.

- *Food-for-work (FFW)* provides food-insecure households with opportunities for paid work that at the same time produce outputs of benefit to themselves and the community.

- *Food-for-recovery (FFR):* a less structured form of food-for-work. Activities can contribute to initial recovery and should not require outside technical supervision.

- *Income generating schemes* allow people to diversify their sources of income in small-scale, self-employment business schemes. These include support of people in the management, supervision and implementation of their businesses.

Access to market goods and services

- *Market and infrastructure support:* includes transportation to allow producers to take advantage of distant markets.

- *Destocking:* provides herders with a good price for their livestock in times of drought, when there is pressure on water supplies and grazing and market prices of livestock are falling.

- *Fair price shops:* sale of basic items at controlled or subsidised prices, or in exchange for vouchers or goods in kind.

- *Food or cash vouchers:* for exchange in shops for food and other goods.

- *Support and technical assistance to government services:* including agricultural extension services and veterinary services.

- *Microfinance projects:* including e.g. the provision of credit and methods for saving assets, which may involve grants, loans, cattle banks, cooperative savings accounts, etc.

See also the Food Security references in Appendix 9.

Food

Appendix 4

Nutrition Assessment Checklist

Below are sample questions for assessments examining the underlying causes of malnutrition, the level of nutritional risk and possibilities for response. The questions are based on the conceptual framework of the causes of malnutrition (see page 136). The information is likely to be available from a variety of sources and gathering it will require a variety of assessment tools, including key informant interviews, observation and review of secondary data (see also Initial assessment and Participation standards on pages 28-33).

1. What information on the **nutritional situation** exists?

   a) Have any nutrition surveys been conducted?

   b) Are there any data from mother and child health clinics?

   c) Are there any data from existing supplementary or therapeutic feeding centres?

   d) What information exists on the nutritional situation of the affected population prior to the current crisis (even if people are no longer in the same place)?

2. What is the **risk of malnutrition related to poor public health?**

   a) Are there any reports of disease outbreaks which may affect nutritional status, such as measles or acute diarrhoeal disease? Is there a risk that these outbreaks will occur? (See Control of communicable diseases standards on page 273.)

   b) What is the estimated measles vaccination coverage of the affected population? (See Control of communicable diseases standard 2 on page 275.)

   c) Is Vitamin A routinely given in measles vaccination? What is the estimated Vitamin A supplement coverage?

d) Has anyone estimated mortality rates (either crude or under five)? What are they and what method has been used? (see Health systems and infrastructure standard 1 on page 259).

e) Is there, or will there be, a significant decline in ambient temperature likely to affect the prevalence of acute respiratory infection or the energy requirements of the affected population?

f) Is there a high prevalence of HIV/AIDS, and are people already vulnerable to malnutrition due to poverty or ill health?

g) Have people been in water or wet clothes for long periods of time?

3. What is the **risk of malnutrition related to inadequate care?**

a) Is there a change in work patterns (e.g. due to migration, displacement or armed conflict) which means that roles and responsibilities in the household have changed?

b) Is there a change in the normal composition of households? Are there large numbers of separated children?

c) Has the normal care environment been disrupted (e.g. through displacement), affecting access to secondary carers, access to foods for children, access to water, etc?

d) What are the normal infant feeding practices? Are mothers bottle feeding their babies or using manufactured complementary foods? If so, is there an infrastructure that can support safe bottle feeding?

e) Is there evidence of donations of baby foods and milks, bottles and teats or requests for donations?

f) In pastoral communities, have the herds been away from young children for long? Has access to milk changed from normal?

g) Has HIV/AIDS affected caring practices at household level?

4. What is the **risk of malnutrition related to reduced food access?** See Appendix 2 for food security assessment checklist.

Food

5. What formal and informal **local structures** are currently in place through which potential interventions could be channelled?

   a) What is the capacity of the Ministry of Health, religious organisations, HIV/AIDS community support groups, infant feeding support groups, or NGOs with a long- or short-term presence in the area?

   b) What is available in the food pipeline?

   c) Is the population likely to move (for pasture/assistance/work) in the near future?

6. What **nutrition intervention or community-based support was already in place** before the current disaster, organised by local communities, individuals, NGOs, government organisations, UN agencies, religious organisations, etc.? What are the nutrition policies (past, ongoing and lapsed), the planned long-term nutrition responses, and programmes that are being implemented or planned in response to the current situation?

Appendix 5

Measuring Acute Malnutrition

Children under five years

The table below shows the commonly used indicators of different grades of malnutrition among children aged 6-59 months. Weight for height (WFH) indicators should be taken from the NCHS/CDC reference data. The WFH Z score is the preferred indicator for reporting anthropometric survey results and WFH percentage of the median is preferred to determine eligibility for treatment. Mid Upper Arm Circumference (MUAC) should not be used alone in anthropometric surveys, but it is one of the best predictors of mortality, partly because it is biased towards younger children. It is, therefore, often used as part of a two-stage screening for admission to feeding programmes. The cut-offs commonly used are <12.5cm: total malnutrition and <11.0cm: severe malnutrition, among children aged 12-59 months.

	Total* malnutrition	Moderate malnutrition	Severe malnutrition
Children 6.0-59.9 mths	• <-2Z scores WFH *or* 80% median WFH *and/or* nutritional oedema	• -3 to <-2 Z scores WFH *or* 70% to <80% median WFH	• <-3Z scores WFH or <70% median WFH *and/or* nutritional oedema

* sometimes known as global malnutrition

There are no agreed anthropometric cut-offs for malnutrition in infants below six months, apart from the presence of nutritional oedema. The NCHS/CDC growth references are of limited use since they are drawn from a population of babies fed artificially, whereas breastfed babies grow at a different rate. This means that malnutrition will tend to be overestimated in this age group. It is important to assess infant feeding practices, particularly access to breast milk, and any medical conditions in order to determine whether malnutrition in this age group may be a problem.

Food

Other age groups: older children, adolescents, adults and older people

There are no internationally accepted definitions of acute malnutrition in other age groups. This is partly because ethnic differences in growth start to become apparent after the age of five years, meaning that it is impractical to use a single reference population to compare all ethnic groups. A further reason is that, in most circumstances, information on the nutritional status of the group aged 6-59 months is sufficient for planners to make their decisions, and thus there has been little impetus to undertake research into malnutrition in other age groups.

However, in major nutritional emergencies, it may be necessary to include older children, adolescents, adults or older people in nutrition assessments or nutritional programmes. Surveys of age groups other than children aged 6-59 months should only be undertaken if:

- a thorough contextual analysis of the situation is undertaken. This should include an analysis of the causes of malnutrition. Only if the results of this analysis suggest that the nutritional status of young children does not reflect the nutritional status of the general population should a nutrition survey for another age group be considered;

- technical expertise is available to ensure quality of data collection, adequate analysis and correct presentation and interpretation of results;

- the resource and/or opportunity costs of including other age groups in a survey have been considered;

- clear and well-documented objectives for the survey are formulated.

Research on defining the most suitable indicators of malnutrition for people aged more than 59 months is currently being undertaken, and this information is liable to change in the next few years.

Older children (5-9.9 years)

In the absence of alternative measures of nutritional status in older children, use of the NCHS/CDC references is recommended to determine WFH Z score and percentage of the median and the same cut-offs as for younger children should be applied (see table above). As for younger children, nutritional oedema should be assessed.

Adolescents (10-19.9 years)

There is no clear, tested, agreed definition of malnutrition in adolescents. Guidance on assessment can be found in the list of references in Appendix 9.

Adults (20-59.9 years)

There is no agreed definition of acute malnutrition in adults, but evidence suggests that cut-offs for severe malnutrition could be lower than a Body Mass Index (BMI) of 16. Surveys of adult malnutrition should aim to gather data on weight, height, sitting height and MUAC measurements. These data can be used to calculate BMI. BMI should be adjusted for Cormic index (the ratio of sitting height to standing height) to make comparisons between populations. Such adjustment can substantially change the apparent prevalence of undernutrition in adults and may have important programmatic ramifications. MUAC measurements should always be taken. If immediate results are needed or resources are severely limited, surveys may be based on MUAC measurements alone.

Because the interpretation of anthropometric results is complicated by the lack of validated functional outcome data and benchmarks for determining the meaning of the result, such results must be interpreted along with detailed contextual information. Guidance on assessment can be found in the references.

For screening individuals for nutritional care admission and discharge, criteria should include a combination of anthropometric indices, clinical signs and social factors (e.g. access to food, presence of carers, shelter, etc). Note that oedema in adults can be caused by a variety of reasons other than malnutrition, and clinicians should assess adult oedema to exclude other causes. Individual agencies should decide on the indicator to determine eligibility for care, taking into account the

Food

known shortcomings of BMI, the lack of information on MUAC and the programme implications of their use. Interim definitions of adult malnutrition for screening for treatment can be found in the references.

MUAC may be used as a screening tool for pregnant women (e.g. as a criterion for entry into a feeding programme). Given their additional nutritional needs, pregnant women may be at greater risk than other groups in the population (see General nutrition support standard 2 on page 140). MUAC does not change significantly through pregnancy. MUAC <20.7 cm (severe risk) and <23.0cm (moderate risk) have been shown to carry a risk of growth retardation of the foetus. The risk is likely to vary according to the population.

Older people

There is currently no agreed definition of malnutrition in older people and yet this group may be at risk of malnutrition in emergencies. WHO suggests that the BMI thresholds for adults may be appropriate for older people aged 60-69 years, but these are subject to the same problems as in younger adults. In addition, accuracy of measurement is problematic because of spinal curvature (stooping) and compression of the vertebrae. Arm span or demi-span can be used instead of height, but the multiplication factor to calculate height varies according to the population. MUAC may be a useful tool for measuring malnutrition in older people but research on appropriate cut-offs is currently still in progress.

Disabled people

No guidelines currently exist for the measurement of individuals with physical disabilities and thus they are often excluded from anthropometric surveys. Visual assessment is necessary. MUAC measurements may be misleading in cases where upper arm muscle might build up to aid mobility. There are alternatives to standard measures of height, including length, arm span, demi-span or lower leg length. It is necessary to consult the latest research findings to determine the most appropriate way of measuring disabled individuals for whom standard weight, height and MUAC measurement is not appropriate.

Appendix 6

Measures of the Public Health Significance of Vitamin A and Iodine Deficiency

Indicators of vitamin A deficiency (xerophthalmia) in children aged 6-71 months

(prevalence of one or more indicators signifies a public health problem)

Indicator	Minimum prevalence
Night blindness (present at 24-71 mths)	> 1%
Bitot spots	> 0.5%
Corneal xerosis/ulceration/keratomalacia	> 0.01%
Corneal scars	> 0.05%

Indicators of iodine deficiency (goitre)

The indicators shown in the table below are those that may be possible to measure in a disaster. The prevalence of at least one and, more definitely, two indicators signifies a public health problem. These indicators of iodine deficiency may be problematic: biochemical indicators may not be possible to measure in many emergency contexts, and clinical assessment risks high levels of inaccuracy. Nevertheless, while assessment of urinary iodine is necessary to obtain a full picture of iodine status, a rough indication of the severity of the situation can be obtained by clinical examination of a valid sample of children aged 6-12 years.

Food

Indicator	Target population	Severity of public health problem (prevalence)		
		Mild	Moderate	Severe
Total goitre rate (% of population)	school-age children*	5-19.9	20-29.9	>=30.0
Median urinary iodine level (µg/l)	school-age children*	50-99	20-49	<20

*preferably children aged 6-12 years

Appendix 7

Nutritional Requirements

The following figures can be used for planning purposes in the initial stage of a disaster:

Nutrient	Mean population requirements
Energy	2,100 kcals
Protein	10-12% total energy (52g-63g), but <15%
Fat	17% of total energy (40g)
Vitamin A	1.666 IU (or 0.5mg retinol equivalents)
Thiamine (B1)	0.9mg (or 0.4mg per 1,000 kcal intake)
Riboflavin (B2)	1.4mg (or 0.6mg per 1,000 kcal intake)
Folic acid	160 µg
Niacin (B3)	12.0mg (or 6.6mg per 1,000 kcal intake)
Vitamin B12	0.9 µg
Vitamin C	28.0mg
Vitamin D	3.2 - 3.8 µg calciferol
Iron	22mg (low bio-availability ie 5-9%)
Iodine	150 µg
Magnesium*	201 mg
Zinc*	12.3 mg
Selenium*	27.6 µg
Vitamin E*	8.0 mg alpha-TE
Vitamin K*	48.2 µg
Biotin*	25.3 µg
Pantothenate*	4.6 µg

Reference: WHO, 2000, *Management of Nutrition in Major Emergencies*

*provisional requirements. Reference: FAO/WHO, 2002 *Human Vitamin and Mineral Requirements*. Report of a joint FAO/WHO expert consultation, Bangkok, Thailand. FAO, Rome.

Food

There are two important points to consider before using the requirements listed above. Firstly, the mean per capita requirements for population groups incorporate the requirements of all age groups and both sexes. They are therefore not specific to any single age or sex group and should not be used as requirements for an individual. Secondly, these requirements are based on a particular population profile, as follows:

Group	% of population
0-4 years:	12
5-9 years:	12
10-14 years:	11
15-19 years:	10
20-59 years:	49
60+ years:	7
Pregnant:	2.5
Breastfeeding:	2.5
Male/female:	51/49

As the demographic structure of different populations varies, this will affect the nutritional requirements of the population concerned. For example, if 26% of a refugee population is aged under five, and the population consists of 50% males and 50% females, the energy requirement is reduced to 1,940 kcals.

Energy and protein requirements should be adjusted for the following factors:

- the demographic structure of the population, in particular the percentage of those under five years old and the percentage of females (this may change in populations affected by HIV/AIDS);

- mean adult weights and actual, usual or desirable body weights. Requirements will increase if the mean body weight for adult males exceeds 60kg and the mean body weight for adult females exceeds 52kg;

– activity levels to maintain productive life. Requirements will increase if activity levels exceed light (ie 1.55 x Basal Metabolic Rate for men and 1.56 x Basal Metabolic Rate for women);

– average ambient temperature and shelter and clothing capacities. Requirements will increase if the mean ambient temperature is less than 20°C;

– the nutritional and health status of the population. Requirements will increase if the population is malnourished and has extra requirements for catch-up growth. HIV/AIDS prevalence may affect average population requirements (see General nutrition support standard 2 on page 140). Whether general rations should be adjusted to meet these needs will depend on current international recommendations.

If it is not possible to incorporate this kind of information into the initial assessment, the figures in the table above may be used as a minimum in the first instance.

Food

Appendix 8

Supply Chain Management Logistics Checklist

1. Purchase contracts provide for delivery-linked payments, the return of damaged goods and penalties for any deviations in fulfilment of the contract, other than in situations of force majeure.

2. Transporters and handling agents assume total liability for food commodities in their care and reimburse any losses.

3. Storage facilities are safe and clean, and protect food commodities from damage and/or loss.

4. Steps are taken at all levels to minimise commodity losses.

5. All losses are identified and accounted for.

6. Commodities in damaged containers are salvaged as far as possible.

7. Commodities are inspected at regular intervals and any suspect commodities are tested. Unfit items are certified and disposed of in accordance with clearly defined procedures and national public health regulations. Recycling of unfit commodities into the market is avoided.

8. Physical inventory counts are undertaken periodically by knowledgeable persons in the area of inventory management not associated with the project under review, and are reconciled with stock balances.

9. Summary inventory reports are compiled at regular intervals and made available to all stakeholders.

10. Waybills properly document all commodity transactions.

11. Stock ledgers provide details of all receipts, issues and balances.

12. Auditing, including process management auditing, is carried out at all levels of the supply chain.

13. Vehicles used to carry food commodities are in good running order;

cargo spaces have no protruding edges that may damage packaging and are adequately protected from bad weather (e.g. by tarpaulins).

14. Vehicles do not carry other commercial and/or hazardous materials along with food commodities.

15. Vehicles have not carried hazardous materials in the past and there are no residues.

Sources: WFP, *Emergency Field Operations Pocketbook* (2002) and CARE, *Food Resource Management* handbook.

Appendix 9

References

Thanks to the Forced Migration Online programme of the Refugee Studies Centre at the University of Oxford, many of these documents have received copyright permission and are posted on a special Sphere link at: http://www.forcedmigration.org

International legal instruments

The Right to Adequate Food (Article 11 of the International Covenant on Economic, Social and Cultural Rights), CESCR General Comment 12, 12 May 1999. U.N. Doc E/C. 12/1999/5. United National Economic and Social Council (1999). http://www.unhchr.ch

Cotula, L and Vidar, M (2003), *The Right to Adequate Food in Emergencies*. FAO Legislative Study 77. Food and Agriculture Organisation of the UN. Rome. http://www.fao.org/righttofood

Pejic, J (2001), *The Right to Food in Situations of Armed Conflict: The Legal Framework*. International Review of the Red Cross, vol 83, no 844, p1097. Geneva. http://www.icrc.org

United Nations (2002), Report by the Special Rapporteur on the Right to Food, Mr. Jean Ziegler, submitted in accordance with Commission on Human Rights resolution 2001/25, UN document E/CN. 4/2002/58. http://www.righttofood.org

United Nations General Assembly (2001), *Preliminary Report of the Special Rapporteur of the Commission on Human Rights on the Right to Food*. Jean Ziegler. http://www.righttofood.org

Food security assessment

CARE (forthcoming), *Program Guidelines for Conditions of Chronic Vulnerability*. CARE East/Central Africa Regional Management Unit. Nairobi.

Frieze, J (forthcoming), *Food Security Assessment Guidelines*. Oxfam GB. Oxford.

Longley, C, Dominguez, C, Saide, MA and Leonardo, WJ (2002), *Do Farmers Need Relief Seed? A Methodology for Assessing Seed Systems. Disasters*, 26, 343-355. http://www.blackwellpublishing.com/journal

Mourey, A (1999), *Assessing and Monitoring the Nutritional Situation*. ICRC. Geneva.

Seaman, J, Clark, P, Boudreau, T and Holt, J (2000), *The Household Economy Approach: A Resource Manual for Practitioners. Development Manual 6*. Save the Children. London.

USAID (1998), *Field Operations Guide (FOG) for Disaster Assessment and Response*. U.S. Agency for International Development/Bureau for Humanitarian Response/Office of Foreign Disaster Assistance. http://www.info.usaid.gov/ofda

WFP (2000), *Food and Nutrition Handbook*. World Food Programme of the United Nations. Rome.

WFP (2002), *Emergency Field Operations Pocketbook*. World Food Programme of the United Nations. Rome.

Food security information systems

Famine Early Warning Systems Network (FEWS NET): http://www.fews.net

Food Insecurity and Vulnerability Information and Mapping Systems (FIVIMS): http://www.fivims.net/index.jsp

Global Information and Early Warning System on Food and Agriculture (GIEWS), Food and Agriculture Organisation of the United Nations. http://www.fao.org

Anthropometric assessment

Collins, S, Duffield, A and Myatt, M (2000), *Adults: Assessment of Nutritional Status in Emergency-Affected Populations*. Geneva. http://www.unsystem.org/scn/archives/adults/index.htm

Food

UN ACC Sub Committee on Nutrition (2001), *Assessment of Adult Undernutrition in Emergencies.* Report of an SCN working group on emergencies special meeting in *SCN News* 22, pp49-51. Geneva. http://www.unsystem.org/scn/publications

Woodruff, B and Duffield, A (2000), *Adolescents: Assessment of Nutritional Status in Emergency-Affected Populations.* Geneva. http://www.unsystem.org/scn/archives/adolescents/index.htm

Young, H and Jaspars, S (1995), *Nutrition Matters.* Intermediate Technology Publications. London.

Methods for measuring nutritional status and mortality: http://www.smartindicators.org

Food security interventions

Alidri, P, Doorn, J v., El-Soghbi, M, Houtart, M, Larson, D, Nagarajan, G and Tsilikounas, C (2002), *Introduction to Microfinance in Conflict-Affected Communities.* International Labour Office and UNHCR. Geneva. http://www.ilo.org

CRS (2002), *Seed Vouchers and Fairs: A Manual for Seed-Based Agricultural Recovery in Africa.* Catholic Relief Services, in collaboration with Overseas Development Institute and the International Crops Research Institute for the Semi-Arid Tropics.

Lumsden, S and Naylor, E (forthcoming), *Cash-For-Work Programming. A Practical Guide.* Oxfam GB. Oxford.

Powers, L (2002), *Livestock Interventions: Important Principles,* OFDA. Office of US Foreign Disaster Assistance, USAID. Washington. http://www.usaid.gov

Remington, T, Maroko, J, Walsh, S, Omanga, P and Charles, E (2002), *Getting Off the Seeds-and-Tools Treadmill with CRS Seed Vouchers and Fairs. Disasters,* 26, 316-328. http://www.blackwellpublishing.com/journal

General emergency nutrition manuals

Prudhon, C (2002), *Assessment and Treatment of Malnutrition in Emergency Situations*. Paris.

UNHCR/UNICEF/WFP/WHO (2002), *Food and Nutrition Needs in Emergencies*. Geneva.

WFP (2000), *Food and Nutrition Handbook*. Rome

WHO (2000), *The Management of Nutrition in Major Emergencies*. Geneva. http://www.who.int

At-risk groups

FAO/WHO (2002), *Living Well with HIV/AIDS. A Manual on Nutritional Care and Support for People Living with HIV/AIDS*. Rome http://www.fao.org

HelpAge International (2001), *Addressing the Nutritional Needs of Older People in Emergency Situations in Africa:* Ideas for Action. Nairobi. http://www.helpage.org/publications

Piwoz, E and Preble, E (2000), *HIV/AIDS and Nutrition: a Review of the Literature and Recommendations for Nutritional Care and Support in Sub-Saharan Africa*. USAID Washington. http://www.aed.org.

Winstock, A (1994), *The Practical Management of Eating and Drinking Difficulties in Children*. Winslow Press. Bicester, UK.

Infant and young child feeding

Ad Hoc Group on Infant Feeding in Emergencies (1999), *Infant Feeding in Emergencies: Policy, Strategy and Practice*. http://www.ennonline.net

FAO/WHO (1994, under revision), Codex Standard for Infant Formula, *Codex STAN 72-1981 (amended 1983, 1985, 1987) Codex Alimentarius, Volume 4: Foods for Special Dietary Uses, Second Edition*. Rome. http: www.codexalimentarius.net

Food

Interagency Working Group on Infant and Young Child Feeding in Emergencies (2001), *Infant Feeding in Emergencies Operational Guidance.* London. http://www.ennonline.net

WHO/UNICEF/LINKAGES/IBFAN/ENN (2001), *Infant Feeding in Emergencies: Module 1 for Emergency Relief Staff (Revision 1).* http://www.ennonline.net

WHO (1981), *The International Code of Marketing of Breast-Milk Substitutes.* The full code and relevant World Health Assembly Resolutions at: http://www.ibfan.org/english/resource/who/fullcode.html

Therapeutic feeding

WHO (1999), *Management of Severe Malnutrition: A Manual for Physicians and Other Senior Health Workers.* Geneva. http://www.who.int/nut

Micronutrient deficiencies

ICCIDD/UNICEF/WHO (2001), *Assessment of Iodine Deficiency Disorders and Monitoring Their Elimination: A Guide for Programme Managers, Second Edition.* Geneva. http://www.who.int/nut

UNICEF/UNU/WHO (2001), *Iron Deficiency Anaemia: Assessment, Prevention and Control. A Guide for Programme Managers.* Geneva. http://www.who.int/nut

WHO (1997), *Vitamin A Supplements: A Guide to Their Use in the Treatment and Prevention of Vitamin A Deficiency and Xeropthalmia. Second Edition.* Geneva. http://www.who.int/nut

WHO (2000), *Pellagra and Its Prevention and Control in Major Emergencies.* Geneva. http://www.who.int/nut

WHO (1999), *Scurvy and Its Prevention and Control in Major Emergencies.* Geneva. http://www.who.int/nut

WHO (1999), *Thiamine Deficiency and Its Prevention and Control in Major Emergencies.* Geneva. http://www.who.int/nut

Food aid

Jaspars S, and Young, H (1995), *General Food Distribution in Emergencies: From Nutritional Needs to Political Priorities. Good Practice Review 3*. Relief and Rehabilitation Network, Overseas Development Institute. London.

OMNI (1994), *Micronutrient Fortification and Enrichment of PL480 Title II Commodities*.

UNHCR, UNICEF, WFP, WHO, (2002), *Food and Nutrition Needs in Emergencies*. United Nations High Commissioner for Refugees, United Nations Children's Fund, World Food Programme, World Health Organisation. Geneva.

WFP (2002), *Emergency Field Operations Pocketbook*. Rome.

WFP (2000), *Food and Nutrition Handbook*. World Food Programme. Rome.

Food

Notes

Notes

Notes

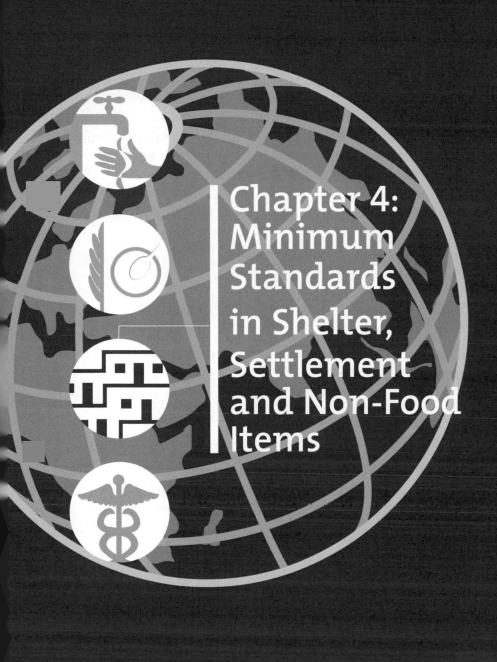

Chapter 4:
Minimum
Standards
in Shelter,
Settlement
and Non-Food
Items

How to use this chapter

This chapter is divided into two sections, comprising 1) Shelter and Settlement and 2) Non-Food Items: Clothing, Bedding and Household Items. Both sections provide general standards for use in any of several response scenarios, such as the return to and repair of damaged dwellings, accommodation with host families, mass shelter in existing buildings and structures, and temporary planned or self-settled camps. Both sections contain the following:

● *the minimum standards:* these are qualitative in nature and specify the minimum levels to be attained in shelter, settlement and non-food item responses;

● *key indicators:* these are 'signals' that show whether the standard has been attained. They provide a way of measuring and communicating the impact, or result, of programmes as well as the process, or methods, used. The indicators may be qualitative or quantitative;

● *guidance notes:* these include specific points to consider when applying the standard and indicators in different situations, guidance on tackling practical difficulties, and advice on priority issues. They may also include critical issues relating to the standard or indicators, and describe dilemmas, controversies or gaps in current knowledge.

A needs assessment checklist is included as Appendix 1. A list of references, detailing further sources of information that offer select 'how to' guidance, is included as Appendix 2.

Contents

Shelter

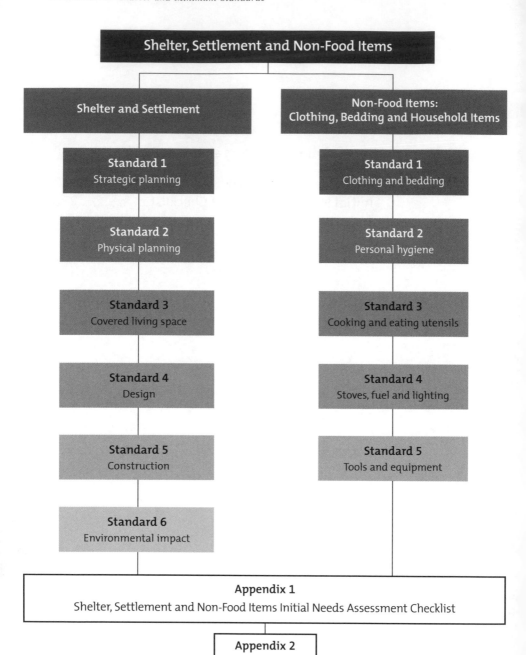

Shelter, Settlement and Non-Food Items

Shelter and Settlement

Standard 1
Strategic planning

Standard 2
Physical planning

Standard 3
Covered living space

Standard 4
Design

Standard 5
Construction

Standard 6
Environmental impact

**Non-Food Items:
Clothing, Bedding and Household Items**

Standard 1
Clothing and bedding

Standard 2
Personal hygiene

Standard 3
Cooking and eating utensils

Standard 4
Stoves, fuel and lighting

Standard 5
Tools and equipment

Appendix 1
Shelter, Settlement and Non-Food Items Initial Needs Assessment Checklist

Appendix 2
References

Introduction

Links to international legal instruments

The Minimum Standards in Shelter, Settlement and Non-Food Items are a practical expression of the principles and rights embodied in the Humanitarian Charter. The Humanitarian Charter is concerned with the most basic requirements for sustaining the lives and dignity of those affected by calamity or conflict, as reflected in the body of international human rights, humanitarian and refugee law. In humanitarian response, shelter and settlement are familiar terms that fall within the scope of the right to housing, which is enshrined in human rights law.

Everyone has the right to adequate housing. This right is recognised in international legal instruments and includes the right to live in security, peace and dignity, and with security of tenure. Key aspects of the right to housing include the availability of services, facilities, materials and infrastructure; affordability; habitability; accessibility; location; and cultural appropriateness. The right to housing also extends to goods and services, such as sustainable access to natural and common resources; safe drinking water; energy for cooking, heating and lighting; sanitation and washing facilities; means of food storage; refuse disposal; site drainage; and emergency services. People should have adequate space and protection from cold, damp, heat, rain, wind or other threats to health, structural hazards and disease vectors. The appropriate siting of settlements and housing should provide access to health-care services, schools, child-care centres and other social facilities and to livelihood opportunities. The way housing is constructed, the building materials used and the policies supporting these must appropriately enable the expression of cultural identity and diversity of housing.

The right to housing is inextricably related to other human rights, including that of protection against forced eviction, harassment and other threats to physical safety and well-being, the right of everyone to be protected against arbitrary displacement from their home or place of habitual residence, and the prohibition of indiscriminate armed attacks on civilian objects.

Shelter

The Minimum Standards in this chapter are not a full expression of the Right to Housing. However, the Sphere standards reflect the core content of the Right to Housing and contribute to the progressive realisation of this right globally.

The importance of shelter, settlement and non-food items in disasters

Shelter is a critical determinant for survival in the initial stages of a disaster. Beyond survival, shelter is necessary to provide security and personal safety, protection from the climate and enhanced resistance to ill health and disease. It is also important for human dignity and to sustain family and community life as far as possible in difficult circumstances.

Shelter and associated settlement and non-food item responses should support communal coping strategies, incorporating as much self-sufficiency and self-management into the process as possible. Any such responses should also minimise the long-term adverse impact on the environment, whilst maximising opportunities for the affected communities to maintain or establish livelihood support activities.

The most individual level of response to the need for shelter and the maintenance of health, privacy and dignity is the provision of clothing, blankets and bedding. People also require basic goods and supplies to meet their personal hygiene needs, to prepare and eat food, and to provide necessary levels of thermal comfort. Disaster-affected households and those displaced from their dwellings often possess only what they can salvage or carry, and the provision of appropriate non-food items may be required to meet essential needs.

The type of response required to meet the needs of people and households affected by a disaster is determined by key factors including the nature and scale of the disaster and the resulting loss of shelter, the climatic conditions and the local environment, the political and security situation, the context (rural or urban) and the ability of the community to cope. Consideration must also be given to the rights and needs of those who are secondarily affected by the disaster, such as any host community. Any response should be informed by the steps taken by the affected households in the initial aftermath of the disaster, using their own skills and material resources to provide temporary shelter or to begin the construction of new, longer-term dwellings. Shelter responses should enable affected households to incrementally upgrade from emergency to durable shelter solutions within a reasonably short time and with regard to the constraints on acquiring the additional resources required.

Involving women in shelter and settlement programmes can help ensure that they and all members of the population affected by the disaster have equitable and safe access to shelter, clothing, construction materials, food production equipment and other essential supplies. Women should be consulted about a range of issues such as security and privacy, sources and means of collecting fuel for cooking and heating, and how to ensure that there is equitable access to housing and supplies. Particular attention will be needed to prevent and respond to gender-based violence and sexual exploitation. It is therefore important to encourage women's participation in the design and implementation of shelter and settlement programmes wherever possible.

Links to other chapters

Many of the standards in the other sector chapters are relevant to this chapter. Progress in achieving standards in one area often influences and sometimes even determines progress in other areas. For a response to be effective, close coordination and collaboration are required with other sectors. Coordination with local authorities and other responding agencies is also necessary to ensure that needs are met, that efforts are not duplicated, and that the quality of shelter, settlement and non-food item interventions is optimised.

For example, the complementary provision of adequate water supply and sanitation facilities in areas in which shelter assistance is being provided is necessary to ensure the health and dignity of the affected households. Similarly, the provision of adequate shelter contributes to the health and well-being of displaced households, while essential cooking and eating utensils are required to enable food assistance to be

Shelter

utilised and nutritional needs met. Reference to specific standards or guidance notes in other technical chapters is made where relevant.

Links to the standards common to all sectors

The process by which an intervention is developed and implemented is critical to its effectiveness. This chapter should be utilised in conjunction with the standards common to all sectors, which cover participation, initial assessment, response, targeting, monitoring, evaluation, aid worker competencies and responsibilities, and the supervision, management and support of personnel (see chapter 1, page 21). In particular, in any response the participation of disaster-affected people – including the vulnerable groups outlined below – should be maximised to ensure its appropriateness and quality.

Vulnerabilities and capacities of disaster-affected populations

The groups most frequently at risk in disasters are women, children, older people, disabled people and people living with HIV/AIDS (PLWH/A). In certain contexts, people may also become vulnerable by reason of ethnic origin, religious or political affiliation, or displacement. This is not an exhaustive list, but it includes those most frequently identified. Specific vulnerabilities influence people's ability to cope and survive in a disaster, and those most at risk should be identified in each context.

Throughout the handbook, the term 'vulnerable groups' refers to all these groups. When any one group is at risk, it is likely that others will also be threatened. Therefore, whenever vulnerable groups are mentioned, users are strongly urged to consider all those listed here. Special care must be taken to protect and provide for all affected groups in a non-discriminatory manner and according to their specific needs. However, it should also be remembered that disaster-affected populations possess, and acquire, skills and capacities of their own to cope, and that these should be recognised and supported.

The Minimum Standards

1 Shelter and Settlement

Shelter assistance is provided to individual households for the repair or construction of dwellings or the settlement of displaced households within existing accommodation or communities. When such dispersed settlement is not possible, shelter is provided collectively in suitable large public buildings or structures, e.g. warehouses, halls, barracks, etc. or in temporary planned or self-settled camps.

Individual household shelter solutions can be short- or long-term, subject to the level of assistance provided, land use rights or ownership, the availability of essential services and social infrastructure, and the opportunities for upgrading and expanding the dwellings.

Shelter and settlement standard 1: strategic planning

Existing shelter and settlement solutions are prioritised through the return or hosting of disaster-affected households, and the security, health, safety and well-being of the affected population are ensured.

Key indicators (to be read in conjunction with the guidance notes)

● Affected households return to the site of their original dwellings where possible (see guidance note 1).

● Affected households who cannot return to the site of their original dwellings settle independently within a host community or with host families where possible (see guidance note 2).

● Affected households who cannot return to the site of their original dwellings or who cannot settle independently within a host

Shelter

community or with host families are accommodated in mass shelters or in temporary planned or self-settled camps (see guidance note 3).

● Actual or potential threats to the security of the affected population are assessed, and the dwellings or settlements are located at a safe distance from any such external threats (see guidance note 4).

● Risks from natural hazards including earthquakes, volcanic activity, landslides, flooding or high winds are minimised, and the area is not prone to diseases or significant vector risks (see guidance notes 4-5).

● Locations are free of potentially hazardous equipment or material, and existing hazards such as dangerous structures, debris or unstable ground are identified and made safe, or access is restricted and guarded (see guidance notes 4, 6 and 7).

● Land and property ownership and/or use rights for buildings or locations are established prior to occupation and permitted use is agreed as necessary (see guidance note 8).

● Water and sanitation services, and social facilities including health care, schools and places of worship, are available or can be satisfactorily provided (see guidance note 9).

● The transportation infrastructure provides access to the settlement for personal movement and the provision of services (see guidance note 10).

● Where possible, households can access land, markets or services for the continuation or development of livelihood support activities (see guidance note 11).

Guidance notes

1. *Return:* the opportunity to return to their own land and dwellings is a major goal for most disaster-affected people. The damaged dwelling and any surrounding land are major household assets for many disaster-affected households. However, return may not always be possible, due to security concerns such as occupation of property or land, continuing violent conflict, ethnic or religious tension, fear of persecution, or landmines and

unexploded ordnance. Shelter provision through the repair of damaged dwellings supports communal coping strategies, retains established settlement patterns and enables the use of existing infrastructure.

2. ***Hosting by families and communities:*** disaster-affected people often prefer to stay in a host community, with other family members or people who share historical, religious or other ties. In cases where this preference cannot be met, hosting by other groups within the community is also possible, with due consideration being given to potential security risks or social conflict. Shelter assistance may include support to expand or upgrade an existing host family shelter and facilities to better accommodate the displaced household, or the provision of an additional separate shelter adjacent to the host family. The resulting increase in population density and demand on social facilities and infrastructure provision should be appraised and addressed. Shelter provision through the construction of additional or extended dwellings in host communities also supports communal coping strategies.

3. ***Collective settlement:*** temporary planned camps should not become a default response. Such shelter solutions may be required in areas where security threats increase the risk to isolated households, or where essential services such as water and food are limited. The provision of mass shelter in large buildings or structures can provide rapid temporary protection from the climate, and may be preferable in cold climates when there are insufficient material resources to provide the required level of thermal comfort within individual dwellings. Although school buildings are often used to accommodate affected families, alternative structures should be sought wherever possible to enable schooling to continue for children from the host and potentially also the displaced community. Care must also be taken to ensure that collective settlements do not themselves become targets for attack or pose a security risk to the surrounding population.

4. ***Risk and vulnerability assessment:*** it is critical that a comprehensive risk and vulnerability assessment is undertaken, including actual or potential security threats and the particular social or economic vulnerabilities of differing social groupings within the affected and any host community (see Initial assessment standard on page 29).

Shelter

5. ***Natural hazards:*** risks posed by the localised impact of natural hazards such as earthquakes, volcanic activity, landslides, flooding or high winds in any given location should also be assessed. Locations close to buildings or structures vulnerable to earthquake aftershocks, land formations vulnerable to landslides, low-lying sites prone to further lava flows or the build-up of exhaust gases, riverbanks and depressions at risk from further flooding and sites exposed to high winds should be avoided, until the assessed risks of returning to such locations have satisfactorily diminished.

6. ***Hazardous materials and goods:*** potentially hazardous materials and goods can be deposited or exposed following natural disasters such as earthquakes, floods and typhoons; mines and unexploded ordnance can be present due to previous or current conflicts. The presence of such items and the potential risks involved in their removal should be identified by appropriately experienced personnel. The time and expertise required for their safe removal may preclude the use of part or all of any locations affected.

7. ***Structural assessments:*** the stability of building structures in inhabited areas should be appraised by appropriately qualified personnel. Assessments should include the effects of further structural weakening from earthquake aftershocks, further flooding and high winds, etc. For mass shelters, the ability of existing building structures to accommodate any additional loading and the increased risk of the failure of building components such as floors, internal dividing walls, roofs, etc. should be assessed.

8. ***Land and building ownership and usage:*** such issues are often controversial, especially where records may not have been kept or where conflict may have affected possession. Ownership of the site or building(s) should be established and the holders of formal or customary use rights identified to the extent possible. The land or property rights of vulnerable groups should be identified and supported. This includes formal or understood rights of inheritance, particularly following a disaster in which the holder of the rights or title may have died or been displaced.

9. ***Availability of services and facilities:*** existing or repaired services or facilities should be identified and used, where there is sufficient capacity, before the construction of new facilities is considered (see Water Supply, Sanitation and Hygiene Promotion chapter on page 51).

10. ***Access to settlement locations:*** access to the settlement, the condition of local road infrastructure and proximity to airstrips, railheads or ports for the supply of relief assistance should be assessed, taking into account seasonal constraints, hazards and security risks. For mass shelters and temporary planned or self-settled camps, the site itself and any primary storage and food distribution points should be accessible by heavy trucks from an all-weather road. Other facilities should be accessible by light vehicles.

11. ***Livelihood support:*** an understanding of the pre-disaster economic activities of the affected population, and the opportunities within the post-disaster context, should guide the settling of affected populations. This should include land availability and access for cultivation and grazing; the location of and access to market areas; and the availability of and access to local services that may be essential to particular economic activities. The differing social and economic needs and constraints of particular vulnerable groups within the displaced or any host communities should also be assessed and accommodated accordingly (see Food security standards on page 119).

Shelter and settlement standard 2: physical planning

Local physical planning practices are used where possible, enabling safe and secure access to and use of shelters and essential services and facilities, as well as ensuring appropriate privacy and separation between individual household shelters.

Key indicators (to be read in conjunction with the guidance notes)

● Area or cluster planning by family, neighbourhood or village groups as appropriate supports existing social networks, contributes to security and enables self-management by the affected population (see guidance note 1).

● All members of the affected population have safe access to water, sanitary facilities, health care, solid waste disposal, graveyards and social facilities, including schools, places of worship, meeting points and recreational areas (see guidance notes 2-4).

● Temporary planned or self-settled camps are based on a minimum surface area of 45m^2 for each person (see guidance note 5).

● The surface topography is used or augmented to facilitate water drainage, and the ground conditions are suitable for excavating toilet pits where this is the primary sanitation system (see guidance note 6).

● There are roads and pathways to provide safe, secure and all-weather access to the individual dwellings and facilities (see guidance note 7).

● Mass shelters have openings to enable required access and emergency evacuation, and these openings are positioned so that access is well supervised and does not pose a security threat to occupants (see guidance note 8).

● Vector risks are minimised (see guidance note 9).

Guidance notes

1. **Cluster planning:** for collective settlements, the allocation of space within mass shelters and plots within temporary planned camps should be guided by existing social practices and the provision and maintenance of shared resources, including water and sanitation facilities, cooking, food distribution, etc. The plot layout in temporary planned camps should maintain the privacy and dignity of separate households by offsetting door openings and ensuring that each household shelter opens onto common space. Safe, integrated living areas should also be provided for vulnerable groups and displaced communities that comprise a significant number of single adults or unaccompanied children. For dispersed settlements, the principles of cluster planning also apply e.g. groups of households return to a defined geographical area or identify host families in close proximity to one another.

2. **Access to services and facilities:** access to essential services, including water supply, toilets, and health and social facilities, should be planned to

maximise the use of existing or repaired facilities whilst minimising the adverse effect on any neighbouring or host communities. Additional facilities or access points should be provided as required to meet the needs of accommodating the target population, and planned to ensure safe access by all inhabitants. The social structure and gender roles of the affected population and the requirements of vulnerable groups should be reflected in the planning and provision of services. Safe play areas should be made available for children, and access to schools and other educational facilities provided where possible (see Water Supply, Sanitation and Hygiene Promotion chapter on page 51 and Health systems and infrastructure standard 5, guidance note 1 on page 267).

3. *Handling the remains of the dead:* social customs for dealing with the remains of the dead should be respected. Where customs vary, separate areas should be available for each social group to exercise their own traditions with dignity. Where existing facilities such as graveyards or crematoria are inadequate, alternative locations or facilities should be provided. Graveyards should be at least 30 metres from groundwater sources used for drinking water, with the bottom of any grave at least 1.5m above the groundwater table. Surface water from graveyards must not enter inhabited areas. The affected community should also have access to materials to meet the needs for culturally acceptable funeral pyres and other funeral rites (see also Health systems and infrastructure standard 5, guidance note 8 on page 269).

4. *Administrative facilities and quarantine areas:* as required, provision should be made for administrative offices, warehousing and staff accommodation to support disaster response activities, and for quarantine areas (see Control of communicable diseases standard 4 on page 279).

5. *Surface area:* the planning guideline of 45m^2 per person includes household plots and the area necessary for roads, footpaths, educational facilities, sanitation, firebreaks, administration, water storage, distribution areas, markets and storage, plus limited kitchen gardens for individual households. Area planning should also consider evolution and growth of the population. If the minimum surface area cannot be provided, consideration should be given to mitigating the consequences of higher-density occupation e.g. separation and privacy between individual households, space for the required facilities, etc.

Shelter

6. **Topography and ground conditions:** for temporary planned camps the site gradient should not exceed 6%, unless extensive drainage and erosion control measures are taken, or be less than 1% to provide for adequate drainage. Drainage channels may still be required to minimise flooding or ponding. The lowest point of the site should be not less than 3 metres above the estimated level of the water table in the rainy season. Ground conditions should also inform the locations of toilets and other facilities and hence the planning of settlements e.g. fissured rock may disperse toilet waste widely; fine clays provide poor percolation and the early failure of toilet pits; volcanic rock makes the excavation of toilet pits difficult (see Excreta disposal standard 2 on page 73 and Drainage standard 1 on page 86).

7. **Access to shelter locations:** existing or new access routes should avoid proximity to any hazards. Where possible, such routes should also avoid creating isolated or screened areas that could pose a threat to the personal safety of users. Erosion as a result of the regular use of access routes should be minimised where possible through considered planning.

8. **Access and emergency escape:** mass shelters should ensure the free access of the occupants whilst enabling adequate supervision by the occupants themselves to minimise any potential security threat. Steps or changes of level close to exits to collective shelters should be avoided, and all stairways and ramps should be provided with handrails. Where possible, occupants with walking difficulties or those unable to walk without assistance should be allocated space on the ground floor, adjacent to exits or along access routes free from changes of level. All occupants of the building should be within an agreed reasonable distance of a minimum of two exits, providing a choice in the direction of escape in case of fire, and these exits should be clearly visible.

9. **Vector risks:** low-lying areas, pits, vacant buildings and excavations (such as those resulting from adobe construction) can provide breeding grounds for pests which could pose a health risk to adjacent households (see Vector control standard 2 on page 79).

Shelter and settlement standard 3: covered living space

People have sufficient covered space to provide dignified accommodation. Essential household activities can be satisfactorily undertaken, and livelihood support activities can be pursued as required.

Key indicators (to be read in conjunction with the guidance notes)

● The initial covered floor area per person is at least 3.5m^2 (see guidance notes 1-3).

● The covered area enables safe separation and privacy between the sexes, between different age groups and between separate families within a given household as required (see guidance notes 4-5).

● Essential household activities can be carried out within the shelter (see guidance notes 6 and 8).

● Key livelihood support activities are accommodated where possible (see guidance notes 7-8).

Guidance notes

1. ***Climate and context:*** in cold climates, household activities typically take place within the covered area and disaster-affected people may spend substantial time inside to ensure adequate thermal comfort. In urban settings, household activities typically occur within the covered area as there is usually less adjacent external space that can be used. In hot and humid climates, space to allow for additional air circulation is required to maintain a healthy environment. A covered floor area in excess of 3.5m^2 per person will often be required to meet these considerations. The floor to ceiling height is also a key factor, with greater height being preferable in hot and humid climates to aid air circulation, while a lower height is preferable in cold climates to minimise the internal volume that requires heating. In warmer climates, shaded external space adjacent to the shelter can be established for food preparation, cooking and sleeping.

Shelter

2. **Duration:** in the immediate aftermath of a disaster, particularly in extreme climatic conditions where shelter materials are not readily available, a covered area of less than $3.5m^2$ per person may be appropriate to save life and to provide adequate short-term shelter to the greatest number of people in need. In such instances, the shelter response should be designed to reach $3.5m^2$ per person as soon as possible, as longer durations may begin to affect the health and well-being of the people accommodated. If $3.5m^2$ per person cannot be achieved, or is in excess of the typical space used by the affected or neighbouring population, consideration should be given to the impact on dignity, health and privacy of a reduced covered area. A decision to provide less than $3.5m^2$ per person should be highlighted, along with measures to mitigate against any adverse affects on the affected population.

3. **Roof coverings:** where materials for a complete shelter cannot be provided, the provision of roofing materials and the required structural support to provide the minimum covered area should be prioritised. The resulting enclosure, however, may not provide the necessary protection from the climate, or security, privacy and dignity, and steps should be taken to meet these needs as soon as possible.

4. **Cultural practices:** existing local practices in the use of covered living space, for example sleeping arrangements and the accommodation of extended family members, should inform the covered area required. Consultation should include members of vulnerable groups, as well as those caring for mobility-impaired individuals.

5. **Safety and privacy:** women, girls and boys are vulnerable to attack and care should be given to ensuring adequate separation from potential threats to their personal safety. Within individual household shelters, opportunities for internal subdivision should be provided for. In mass shelters, the grouping of related families, well-planned access routes through the building or structure, and materials to screen personal and household space can aid the provision of adequate personal privacy and safety.

6. **Household activities:** space should be provided for sleeping, washing and dressing; care of infants, children and the ill or infirm; the storage of food, water, household possessions and other key assets; cooking and eating indoors when required; and the common gathering of the household.

7. *Design and space provision:* the flexible use of the covered space provided could potentially accommodate different activities at different times during the day or night. The design of the structure, the location of openings and the opportunities for alternative internal subdivisions should enable the internal and immediately adjacent external space to accommodate livelihood support activities where required.

8. *Other functions of shelter:* it should be acknowledged that shelter, in addition to providing protection from the climate, security and privacy for individual households, etc., also serves other purposes. These include the establishing of territorial claims or rights, serving as a location at which to receive relief assistance, and the provision of post-disaster psychosocial support through the reconstruction process. It can also represent a major household financial asset.

Shelter and settlement standard 4: design

The design of the shelter is acceptable to the affected population and provides sufficient thermal comfort, fresh air and protection from the climate to ensure their dignity, health, safety and well-being.

Key indicators (to be read in conjunction with the guidance notes)

- The design of the shelter and the materials used are familiar where possible and culturally and socially acceptable (see guidance note 1).

- The repair of existing damaged shelters or the upgrading of initial shelter solutions constructed by the disaster-affected population is prioritised (see guidance note 2).

- Alternative materials required to provide temporary shelter are durable, practical and acceptable to the affected population (see guidance note 3).

- The type of construction, materials used and the sizing and positioning of openings provides optimal thermal comfort and ventilation (see guidance notes 4-7).

Shelter

- Access to water supply sources and sanitation facilities, and the appropriate provision of rainwater harvesting, water storage, drainage and solid waste management, complement the construction of shelters (see guidance note 8).

- Vector control measures are incorporated into the design and materials are selected to minimise health hazards (see guidance note 9).

Guidance notes

1. ***Participatory design:*** each affected household should be involved to the maximum extent possible in determining the final form and materials used. Priority should be given to the opinions of those groups or individuals who typically have to spend more time within the shelters. The orientation of the individual shelter or covered area, the sizing and layout of the space provided, the positioning of door and window openings for adequate access, lighting and ventilation, and any internal subdivisions should reflect local practices where these are known to be safe. This should be informed by assessments of existing typical housing forms accommodating the respective needs (see Participation standard on page 28).

2. ***Local shelter initiatives and the repair of damaged buildings:*** disaster-affected populations often improvise shelter solutions using material salvaged from their damaged homes or otherwise locally sourced, using traditional or improvised building techniques. Material support and technical assistance to make one or more rooms habitable within a damaged house or to upgrade improvised shelters may be preferred to unfamiliar or collective shelter solutions. Risks from further natural disasters such as earthquake aftershocks and landslides, potential security threats and issues of reconciliation for households returning to areas affected by conflict, and the health and safety risks posed by damaged infrastructure or buildings, should be addressed.

3. ***Materials and construction:*** where local or familiar materials are not readily available or advisable, designs and materials that are culturally acceptable should be identified through participatory consultation with the affected community. Reinforced plastic sheeting is typically supplied to households in the initial stage of a disaster response, occasionally with rope and support materials such as locally procured timber, plastic tubing or

galvanised steel sections. Such sheeting should meet specifications accepted by the international humanitarian community.

4. *In warm, humid climates:* shelters must be oriented and designed to maximise ventilation and minimise entry of direct sunlight. Obstruction to openings, for example by neighbouring shelters, should be avoided to maximise air flow. The roof should have a reasonable slope for rainwater drainage and have large overhangs. The construction of the shelter should be lightweight, as low thermal capacity is required. Seasonal rains should be taken into account and consideration should be given to adequate surface water drainage around the shelter and to raised floors to minimise water ingress. Existing vegetation can increase water absorption into the soil.

5. *In hot, dry climates:* construction should be heavy to ensure high thermal capacity, allowing changes in night and day temperatures to alternately cool and heat the interior, or lightweight with adequate insulation. Adequate care should be taken in the structural design of heavy construction in areas with seismic risks. If only plastic sheeting or tents are available, a double-skinned roof with ventilation between the layers to reduce radiant heat gain should be provided. Door and window openings positioned away from the direction of the prevailing wind will help to minimise heating by hot winds and radiation from the surrounding ground. Shade and protection from hot winds can also be gained from adjacent shelters and surrounding natural land forms or trees. Flooring contiguous with the external walling should be provided to minimise sand penetration.

6. *In cold climates:* heavy construction with high thermal capacity is required for shelters that are occupied throughout the day. Lightweight construction with low thermal capacity and high insulation is more appropriate for shelters that are occupied only at night. Air flow through the shelter should be kept to the minimum necessary to ensure personal comfort whilst also providing adequate ventilation for space heaters or cooking stoves. Door and window openings should be designed to minimise draughts. Stoves or other forms of space heaters are essential and must be appropriate to the shelter. The loss of body heat through the floor should be minimised by ensuring that the floor is insulated and through the use of insulated sleeping mats, mattresses or raised beds (see Non-food items standard 1 on page 230 and standard 4 on page 234).

Shelter

7. **Ventilation:** adequate ventilation should be provided within the shelter design to maintain a healthy internal environment and to limit the risk of transmission of diseases such as TB spread by droplet infection.

8. **Local water acquisition, sanitation and waste management practices:** pre-disaster practices in sourcing safe water and methods of defecation and waste management should be ascertained and the opportunities and constraints of such practices in the post-disaster situation identified. The location of toilets and solid waste management facilities must not compromise the cultural, environmental, security or social aspects of the design or layout of individual shelters or of the settlement (see Water Supply, Sanitation and Hygiene Promotion chapter on page 51).

9. **Vector risk identification:** an understanding of local building practices, the patterns of shelter use by displaced people and material selection should inform the shelter design and subsequent vector control measures. Typical risks are posed by mosquitoes, rats and flies and pests such as snakes, scorpions and termites (see Vector control standards 1-3 on pages 76-82).

Shelter and settlement standard 5: construction

The construction approach is in accordance with safe local building practices and maximises local livelihood opportunities.

Key indicators (to be read in conjunction with the guidance notes)

● Locally sourced materials and labour are used without adversely affecting the local economy or environment (see guidance notes 1-2).

● Locally derived standards of workmanship and materials are achieved (see guidance note 3).

● Construction and material specifications mitigate against future natural disasters (see guidance note 4).

● The type of construction and materials used enable the maintenance and upgrading of individual household shelters using locally available tools and resources (see guidance note 5).

● The procurement of materials and labour and the supervision of the construction process are transparent, accountable and in accordance with internationally accepted bidding, purchasing and construction administration practices (see guidance note 6).

Guidance notes

1. ***Sourcing of shelter materials and labour:*** livelihood support should be promoted through the local procurement of building materials, specialist building skills and manual labour. Multiple sources, alternative materials and production processes, or the provision of regionally or internationally sourced materials or proprietary shelter systems are required if the local harvesting and supply of materials is likely to have a significant adverse impact on the local economy or the environment. The re-use of materials salvaged from damaged buildings should be promoted where feasible, either as primary construction materials (bricks or stone masonry, roof timber, roof tiles, etc.) or as secondary material (rubble for foundations or levelling roads, etc.). Ownership of or the rights to such material should be identified and agreed (see Shelter and settlement standard 6, guidance note 3 on page 228).

2. ***Participation of affected households:*** skills training programmes and apprenticeship schemes can maximise opportunities for participation during construction, particularly for individuals lacking the required building skills or experience. Complementary contributions from those less able to undertake physically or technically demanding tasks can include site monitoring and inventory control, the provision of child care or temporary accommodation and catering for those engaged in construction works, and administrative support. Consideration should be given to the other demands on the time and labour resources of the affected population. The inclusion of food-for-work initiatives can provide the necessary food security to enable affected households to actively participate. Single women, female-headed households and women with disabilities are particularly at risk from sexual exploitation in seeking assistance for the construction of their shelter. The provision of assistance from volunteer community labour teams or contracted labour could complement any beneficiary contributions (see Participation standard on page 28).

Shelter

3. **Construction standards:** standards of good practice should be agreed with the relevant authorities to ensure that key safety and performance requirements are met. In locations where applicable local or national building codes have not been customarily adhered to or enforced, incremental compliance should be agreed.

4. **Disaster prevention and mitigation:** the design should be consistent with known climatic conditions, be capable of withstanding appropriate wind-loading, and accommodate snow-loading in cold climates. Earthquake resistance and ground bearing conditions should be assessed. Recommended or actual changes to building standards or common building practices as a result of the disaster should be applied in consultation with local authorities and the disaster-affected population.

5. **Upgrading and maintenance:** as emergency shelter responses typically provide only a minimum level of enclosed space and material assistance, affected families will need to seek alternative means of increasing the extent or quality of the enclosed space provided. The form of construction and the materials used should enable individual households to incrementally adapt or upgrade the shelter or aspects of the design to meet their longer-term needs and to undertake repairs using locally available tools and materials.

6. **Procurement and construction management:** a responsive, efficient and accountable supply chain and construction management system for materials, labour and site supervision should be established that includes sourcing, procurement, transportation, handling and administration, from point of origin to the respective site as required.

Shelter and settlement standard 6: environmental impact

The adverse impact on the environment is minimised by the settling of the disaster-affected households, the material sourcing and construction techniques used.

Key indicators (to be read in conjunction with the guidance notes)

● The temporary or permanent settling of the affected population considers the extent of the natural resources available (see guidance notes 1-2).

● Natural resources are managed to meet the ongoing needs of the displaced and host populations (see guidance notes 1-2).

● The production and supply of construction material and the building process minimises the long-term depletion of natural resources (see guidance notes 2-3).

● Trees and other vegetation are retained where possible to increase water retention, minimise soil erosion and to provide shade (see guidance note 4).

● The locations of mass shelters or temporary planned camps are returned to their original condition, unless agreed otherwise, once they are no longer needed for emergency shelter use (see guidance note 5).

Guidance notes

1. *Sustainability and the management of environmental resources:* in environments where the natural resources to sustain a substantial increase in human habitation are limited, efforts should be made to contain non-sustainable demand on the environment. Sustainable external supplies of fuel and managed options for livestock grazing, agricultural production and natural resource-dependent livelihood support activities should be provided. In environments with extensive natural resources that could sustain a substantial increase in human habitation, the affected population

Shelter

should be dispersed, if necessary, into a number of small settlements, since these are less likely to cause environmental damage than large settlements. Access rights to existing natural resources, such as fuel, water, timber for construction, stone and sand, etc., and the typical use and maintenance of existing land and wooded areas should be identified.

2. *Mitigating long-term environmental impact:* where the need to provide shelter for affected populations has a significant adverse impact on the environment, e.g. through the depletion of local natural resources, efforts should be made to minimise the long-term effects through complementary environmental management and rehabilitation activities.

3. *Sourcing of construction materials:* the environmental impact of pre-disaster sourcing practices and large-scale post-disaster demands on natural resources, such as water, construction timber, sand, soil and grasses, as well as fuel for the firing of bricks and roof tiles, should be assessed. Customary users, extraction and regeneration rates and the ownership or control of these resources should be identified. Alternative or complementary sources of supply may support the local economy and reduce any long-term adverse impact on the local environment. Multiple sources and the re-use of salvaged materials, alternative materials and production processes (such as the use of stabilised earth blocks) should be specified, together with the adoption of sustainable practices such as complementary replanting or regeneration programmes.

4. *Erosion:* an assessment of typical land usage, the distribution of existing vegetation and surface water drainage patterns should be undertaken to assess the impact of any ground clearance that may be required. The use of agricultural or grazing land should be planned to minimise any adverse impact on the local natural habitat. Shelter solutions should be planned to retain existing trees and other vegetation to maintain the soil stabilisation such growth provides and to maximise the opportunities for shade and protection from the climate. Roads, pathways and drainage networks should be planned to make use of natural contours in order to minimise erosion and flooding. Where this cannot be achieved, satisfactory measures to contain any likely erosion should be provided, such as the provision of excavated drainage culverts, piped drainage runs under roadways, or planted earth banks to minimise water run-off (see Drainage standard 1 on page 86).

5. *Handover:* the natural regeneration of the environment in and around mass shelters and temporary planned or self-settled camps should be enhanced through appropriate environmental rehabilitation measures during the life of the temporary settlement. The eventual discontinuation of any such temporary settlements should be managed to ensure the satisfactory removal of all material or waste that cannot be re-used or that could have an adverse effect on the environment.

2 Non-Food Items: Clothing, Bedding and Household Items

Clothing, blankets and bedding materials meet the most personal human needs for shelter from the climate and the maintenance of health, privacy and dignity. Basic goods and supplies are required to enable families to meet personal hygiene needs, prepare and eat food, provide thermal comfort and build, maintain or repair shelters.

Non-food items standard 1: clothing and bedding

The people affected by the disaster have sufficient clothing, blankets and bedding to ensure their dignity, safety and well-being.

Key indicators (to be read in conjunction with the guidance notes)

- Women, girls, men and boys have at least one full set of clothing in the correct size, appropriate to the culture, season and climate. Infants and children up to two years old also have a blanket of a minimum 100cmx70cm (see guidance notes 1-4).

- People have access to a combination of blankets, bedding or sleeping mats to provide thermal comfort and to enable separate sleeping arrangements as required (see guidance notes 2-4).

- Those individuals most at risk have additional clothing and bedding to meet their needs (see guidance note 5).

- Culturally appropriate burial cloth is available when needed.

Guidance notes

1. ***Changes of clothing:*** individuals should have access to sufficient changes of clothing to ensure their thermal comfort, dignity and safety. This could entail the provision of more than one set of essential items, particularly underclothes, to enable laundering.

2. ***Appropriateness:*** clothing should be appropriate to climatic conditions and cultural practices, separately suitable for men, women, girls and boys, and sized according to age. Bedding materials where possible should reflect cultural practices and be sufficient in quantity to enable separate sleeping arrangements as required amongst the members of individual households.

3. ***Thermal performance:*** consideration should be given to the insulating properties of clothing and bedding and the effect of wet or damp climatic conditions on their thermal performance. An appropriate combination of clothing and bedding items should be provided to ensure a satisfactory level of thermal comfort is attained. Provision of insulated sleeping mats to combat heat loss through the ground may be more effective than providing additional blankets.

4. ***Durability:*** clothing and bedding provided should be sufficiently durable to accommodate typical wear and likely prolonged usage due to the lack of alternative items.

5. ***Special needs:*** additional changes of clothing should be provided where possible to people with incontinence problems, people with HIV/AIDS and associated diarrhoea, pregnant and lactating women, older people, disabled people and others with impaired mobility. Infants and children are more prone to heat loss than adults due to their ratio of body surface area to mass, and may require additional blankets, etc. to maintain appropriate levels of thermal comfort. Given their lack of mobility, older people and the ill or infirm, including individuals with HIV/AIDS, may also require particular attention, such as the provision of mattresses or raised beds.

Shelter

Non-food items standard 2: personal hygiene

Each disaster-affected household has access to sufficient soap and other items to ensure personal hygiene, health, dignity and well-being.

Key indicators (to be read in conjunction with the guidance notes)

● Each person has access to 250g of bathing soap per month (see guidance notes 1-3).

● Each person has access to 200g of laundry soap per month (see guidance note 1-3).

● Women and girls have sanitary materials for menstruation (see guidance note 4).

● Infants and children up to two years old have 12 washable nappies or diapers where these are typically used.

● Additional items essential for ensuring personal hygiene, dignity and well-being can be accessed (see guidance note 5).

Guidance notes

1. ***Appropriateness:*** existing cultural practices and familiar products should be assessed in specifying the items supplied. Care should be taken to avoid specifying products that would not be used due to lack of familiarity or that could be misused (e.g. being mistaken for foodstuffs). Where culturally appropriate or preferred, washing powder can be specified instead of laundry soap or the use of suitable alternatives such as ash or clean sand promoted.

2. ***Replacement:*** consideration should be given for consumables to be replaced when necessary.

3. ***Special needs:*** additional quantities of bathing and laundry soap should be provided where possible to people with incontinence problems, people with HIV/AIDS and associated diarrhoea, and older people, disabled people or others with impaired mobility.

4. *Sanitary protection:* women and girls should receive appropriate material for menstruation. It is important that these materials are appropriate and discreet and that women are involved in making decisions about what is provided.

5. *Additional items:* existing social and cultural practices may require that additional personal hygiene items can be accessed. Subject to availability, these items per person per month could include 75ml/100g of toothpaste; one toothbrush; 250ml of shampoo; 250ml of lotion for infants and children up to two years old; one disposable razor. Per household they could also include one hairbrush and/or comb, and nail clippers.

Non-food items standard 3: cooking and eating utensils

Each disaster-affected household has access to cooking and eating utensils.

Key indicators (to be read in conjunction with the guidance notes)

● Each household has access to a large-sized cooking pot with handle and a pan to act as a lid; a medium-sized cooking pot with handle and lid; a basin for food preparation or serving; a kitchen knife; and two wooden serving spoons (see guidance note 1).

● Each household has access to two 10- to 20-litre water collection vessels with a lid or cap (20-litre jerry can with a screw cap or 10-litre bucket with lid), plus additional water or food storage vessels (see guidance notes 1-2).

● Each person has access to a dished plate, a metal spoon and a mug or drinking vessel (see guidance notes 1-4).

Shelter

Guidance notes

1. **Appropriateness:** items provided should be culturally appropriate and enable safe practices to be followed. Women or those typically overseeing the preparation of food and the collection of water should be consulted when specifying items. Cooking and eating utensils and water collection vessels should be sized to suit older people, people with disabilities and children as required.

2. **Plastic goods:** all plastic goods (buckets, bowls, jerry cans, water storage vessels, etc.) should be of food-grade plastic (see also Water supply standard 3, guidance note 1 on page 70).

3. **Metallic goods:** all cutlery, bowls, plates and mugs should be of stainless steel or other non-ferrous metal.

4. **Infant feeding:** infant feeding bottles should not be provided, unless exceptional circumstances require the provision of breast milk substitutes (see General nutrition support standard 2, guidance note 1 on page 141).

Non-food items standard 4: stoves, fuel and lighting

Each disaster-affected household has access to communal cooking facilities or a stove and an accessible supply of fuel for cooking needs and to provide thermal comfort. Each household also has access to appropriate means of providing sustainable artificial lighting to ensure personal security.

Key indicators (to be read in conjunction with the guidance notes)

● Where food is cooked on an individual household basis, each household has a stove and fuel to meet essential cooking and heating needs (see guidance notes 1-2).

● Environmentally and economically sustainable sources of fuel are identified and prioritised over fuel provided from external sources (see guidance note 3).

● Fuel is obtained in a safe and secure manner, and there are no reports of incidents of harm to people in the routine collection of fuel (see guidance note 4).

● Safe fuel storage space is available.

● Each household has access to sustainable means of providing artificial lighting, e.g. lanterns or candles.

● Each household has access to matches or a suitable alternative means of igniting fuel or candles, etc.

Guidance notes

1. *Stoves:* existing local practices should be taken into account in the specification of stove and fuel solutions. Energy-efficient cooking practices should be promoted, including firewood preparation, fire management, food preparation, shared cooking, etc. This could include possible changes to the type of food to be prepared, such as any rations provided by food assistance programmes e.g. pulses require considerable cooking and hence fuel. Where displaced populations are accommodated in mass shelters, communal or centralised cooking and heating facilities are preferable to the provision of individual household stoves, to minimise fire risks and indoor smoke pollution.

2. *Ventilation:* if used inside an enclosed area, stoves should be fitted with flues to vent exhaust gases or smoke to the exterior in a safe manner. Alternatively, the positioning of the stoves and weather-protected openings within the shelter enclosure should be utilised to ensure adequate ventilation and to minimise the risk of indoor pollution and respiratory problems. Stoves should be designed to minimise the risk of fire and of indoor and outdoor pollution.

3. *Sustainable sources of fuel:* sources of fuel should be managed, and measures taken to replenish and regenerate resources to ensure sustainability of supply.

4. *Collecting fuel:* women should be consulted about the location and means of collecting fuel for cooking and heating to address issues of personal safety. The demands of collecting fuel on particularly vulnerable

Shelter

groups, such as female-headed households and households caring for PLWH/A, should be addressed. Special provisions should be made where possible e.g. the choice of less labour-intensive fuels, the use of fuel-efficient stoves and accessible fuel sources.

Non-food items standard 5: tools and equipment

Each disaster-affected household responsible for the construction or maintenance and safe use of their shelter has access to the necessary tools and equipment.

Key indicators (to be read in conjunction with the guidance notes)

● Where responsible for constructing part or all of their shelters or for carrying out essential maintenance, each household has access to tools and equipment to safely undertake each task (see guidance notes 1-2).

● Training or guidance in the use of the tools and in the shelter construction or maintenance tasks required is provided where necessary (see guidance note 3).

● Materials to reduce the spread of vector-borne disease, such as impregnated mosquito nets, are provided to protect each member of the household (see Vector control standards 1-3 on pages 76-82).

Guidance notes

1. *Typical tool sets:* subject to local practices, typical tool sets could include a hammer or mallet, an axe or machete, and a spade or shovel. The specification should be such that the tools can be easily repaired locally with available technologies. Displaced communities should also have access to sufficient tools to excavate surface water drainage channels and to handle the remains of the deceased as appropriate, through the construction of coffins, the excavation of graves and burial pits or the preparation of funeral pyres.

2. *Livelihood activities:* where possible, the tools provided should also be appropriate for livelihood support activities.

3. *Technical assistance:* female-headed households and other identified vulnerable groups may require assistance from extended family members, neighbours or contracted labour to undertake the designated construction or maintenance tasks.

Appendix 1

Shelter, Settlement and Non-Food Items Initial Needs Assessment Checklist

This list of questions serves as a guide and checklist to ensure that appropriate information is obtained that should influence post-disaster shelter response. The list of questions is not mandatory, and should be used and adapted as appropriate. It is assumed that information on the underlying causes of the disaster, the security situation, the basic demographics of the displaced and any host population and the key people to consult and contact, is separately obtained (see Initial assessment standard on page 29).

1 Shelter and Settlement

Demographics

- How many people comprise a typical household?

- Does the affected community comprise groups of individuals who do not form typical households, such as unaccompanied children, or particular minority groups with household sizes that are not typical?

- How many households are without any or with inadequate shelter and where are they?

- How many people who are not members of individual households are without any or with inadequate shelter and where are they?

Risks

- What is the immediate risk to life of the lack of shelter and inadequate shelter, and how many people are at risk?

- What are the potential risks to the lives, health and security of the affected population through the need for shelter?

● What are the potential risks to and impact on any host populations due to the presence of displaced households?

● What are the potential further risks to lives, health and security of the affected population as a result of the ongoing effects of the disaster on the provision of shelter?

● Who are the vulnerable people in the population, also considering those affected by HIV/AIDS?

● What are the particular risks for the vulnerable people and why?

Household activities

● What household and livelihood support activities typically take place in the shelters of the affected population, and how does the resulting space provision and design reflect these activities?

● What household and livelihood support activities typically take place in the external areas around the shelters of the affected population, and how does the resulting space provision and design reflect these activities?

Materials and design

● What initial shelter solutions or materials have been provided to date by the affected households or other actors?

● What existing materials can be salvaged from the damaged site (if applicable) for use in the reconstruction of shelters?

● What are the typical building practices of the displaced and host populations, and what are the different materials that are used to provide the structural frame and roof and external wall enclosures?

● What alternative design or materials solutions are potentially available and familiar or acceptable to the affected population?

● How can the potential shelter solutions identified accommodate appropriate single and multiple disaster prevention and mitigation concerns?

● How are shelters typically built and by whom?

Shelter

- How are construction materials typically obtained and by whom?

- How can women, youths and older people be trained or assisted to participate in the building of their own shelters, and what are the constraints?

Local resources and constraints

- What are the current material, financial and human resources of the affected households and the community, and the constraints to meeting some or all of their urgent shelter needs?

- What are the opportunities and constraints of current patterns of land ownership, land usage and the availability of vacant land, in helping to meet urgent shelter needs?

- What are the opportunities and constraints of the host population in accommodating displaced households within their own dwellings or on adjacent land?

- What are the opportunities and constraints of utilising existing, available and unaffected buildings or structures to temporarily accommodate displaced households?

- What is the topographical and environmental suitability of using accessible vacant land to accommodate temporary settlements?

- What are the requirements and constraints of local authority regulations in developing shelter solutions?

Essential services and facilities

- What is the current availability of water for drinking and personal hygiene, and what are the possibilities and constraints in meeting the anticipated sanitation needs?

- What is the current provision of social facilities (health clinics, schools, places of worship, etc.) and what are the constraints and opportunities of accessing these facilities?

Host community and environmental impact

- What are the issues of concern for the host community?

- What are the organisational and planning issues of accommodating the displaced households within the host community or within temporary settlements?

- What are the environmental concerns in providing the necessary shelter assistance (construction materials and access) and in supporting the displaced households (fuel, sanitation, waste disposal, grazing for animals if appropriate)?

- What opportunities are present for building local shelter and settlement provision and management capacities?

- What livelihood support opportunities can be provided through the sourcing of materials and the construction of shelter and settlement solutions?

2 Non-Food Items: Clothing, Bedding and Household Items

Clothing and bedding

- What is the customary provision of clothing, blankets and bedding for women, men, children and infants, pregnant and lactating women and older people, and what are the particular social and cultural considerations?

- How many women and men of all ages, children and infants have inadequate or insufficient clothing, blankets or bedding to provide protection from the adverse effects of the climate and to maintain their health, dignity and well-being, and why?

- What is the immediate risk to life of the lack of adequate clothing, blankets or bedding, and how many people are at risk?

- What are the potential risks to the lives, health and personal safety of the affected population through the need for adequate clothing, blankets or bedding?

Shelter

● Which social groups are most at risk, and why? How can these groups be best supported to empower themselves?

Personal hygiene

● What essential items to address personal hygiene issues did a typical household have access to before the disaster?

● What essential items do affected households no longer have access to?

● What are the particular needs of women, girls, children and infants?

● What additional items are considered socially or culturally important to maintain the health and dignity of the affected people?

Cooking and eating, stoves and fuel

● What cooking and eating utensils did a typical household have access to before the disaster?

● How many households do not have access to sufficient cooking and eating utensils, and why?

● What form of stove for cooking and heating did a typical household have access to, where did the cooking take place in relation to the existing shelter and the surrounding area, and what fuel was typically used?

● How many households do not have access to a stove for cooking and heating, and why?

● How many households do not have access to adequate supplies of fuel for cooking and heating, and why?

● What are the opportunities and constraints, in particular the environmental concerns, of sourcing adequate supplies of fuel for the displaced households and the host community as appropriate?

● What is the impact on the women in the displaced community of sourcing adequate supplies of fuel?

● What cultural and customary use and safe practice considerations should be taken into account?

Tools and equipment

● What basic tools to construct, maintain or repair a shelter do the households have access to?

● What livelihood support activities can also utilise the basic tools for shelter construction, maintenance and repair?

● Does the climate or natural environment require a ground covering to maintain appropriate standards of health and dignity, and what appropriate material solutions can be provided?

● What vector control measures, particularly the provision of mosquito nets, are required to ensure the health and well-being of households?

Shelter

Appendix 2

References

Thanks to the Forced Migration Online programme of the Refugee Studies Centre at the University of Oxford, many of these documents have received copyright permission and are posted on a special Sphere link at: http://www.forcedmigration.org

International legal instruments

The Right to Adequate Housing (Article 11 (1) of the International Covenant on Economic, Social and Cultural Rights), CECSR General Comment 4, 12 December 1991. Committee on Economic, Social and Cultural Rights.

Convention on the Elimination of All Forms of Discrimination Against Women (1981); Article 14(2)(h).

Convention on the Rights of the Child (1990); Article 27(3).

International Convention on the Elimination of All Forms of Racial Discrimination (1969), Article 5(e)(iii).

International Convention Relating to the Status of Refugees (1951), Article 21.

Universal Declaration of Human Rights (1948), Article 25.

General

Chalinder, A (1998), *Good Practice Review 6: Temporary Human Settlement Planning for Displaced Populations in Emergencies.* Overseas Development Institute/Relief and Rehabilitation Network. London.

Davis, I (1978), *Shelter After Disaster.* Oxford Polytechnic Press.

Davis, J and Lambert, R (1995), *Engineering in Emergencies: A Practical Guide for Relief Workers.* RedR/IT Publications. London.

Hamdi, N (1995), *Housing Without Houses: Participation, Flexibility, Enablement*. IT Publications, London.

ICRC (2002), *Emergency Items Catalogue*. ICRC. Geneva.

Kelly, C (2002), *Guidelines in Rapid Environmental Impact Assessment in Disasters*. Benfield Hazard Research Centre, University College London.

MSF (1997), *Guide of Kits and Emergency Items. Decision-Maker Guide. Fourth English Edition*. Médecins Sans Frontières. Belgium.

Shelterproject.org (2004), *Guidelines for the Transitional Settlement of Displaced Populations*. Cambridge.

UNDP (1995), *Emergency Relief Items, Compendium of Generic Specifications. Vol 1: Telecommunications, Shelter and Housing, Water Supply, Food, Sanitation and Hygiene, Materials Handling, Power Supply*. Inter-Agency Procurement Services Office, UNDP. Copenhagen.

UNDRO (1982), *Shelter After Disaster: Guidelines for Assistance*. UNDRO. Geneva.

UNHCR (1996), *Environmental Guidelines*. UNHCR. Geneva.

UNHCR (2002), *Environmental Considerations in the Life Cycle of Refugee Camps*. UNHCR. Geneva.

UNHCR (1993), *First International Workshop on Improved Shelter Response and Environment for Refugees*. UNHCR. Geneva.

UNHCR (1991), *Guidelines on the Protection of Refugee Women*. UNHCR. Geneva.

UNHCR (1999), *Handbook for Emergencies*. UNHCR. Geneva.

UNHCR (2001), *Policy for Older Refugees: A Resource for the Refugee Community*. UNHCR. Geneva.

UNHCR (1998), *Refugee Operations and Environmental Management: Key Principles of Decision-Making*. UNHCR. Geneva.

UNHCR (1995), *Sexual Violence Against Refugees*. UNHCR. Geneva.

USAID (1994), *Field Operations Guide for Disaster Assessment and Response*. Office of Foreign Disaster Assistance, USAID.

Shelter

Zetter, R (1995), *Shelter Provision and Settlement Policies for Refugees: A State of the Art Review.* Studies on Emergency and Disaster Relief No. 2. Noriska Afrikainstituet. Sweden.

Zetter, R, Hamdi, N and Ferretti, S (2003), *From Roofs to Reintegration.* Swiss Agency for Development and Cooperation (SDC). Geneva.

Notes

Notes

Chapter 5:
Minimum
Standards
in
Health
Services

How to use this chapter

This chapter is divided into three main sections: Health Systems and Infrastructure; Control of Communicable Diseases; and Control of Non-Communicable Diseases. The organisation of the chapter promotes a systems approach to the design, implementation, monitoring and evaluation of health services during a disaster. This is the most reliable means of ensuring that priority health needs are identified and met in an efficient and effective manner. Principles such as supporting national and local health systems, coordination and standardisation are stressed throughout.

Each of the sections contains the following:

● *the minimum standards:* these are qualitative in nature and specify the minimum levels to be attained in the provision of health services;

● *key indicators:* these are 'signals' that show whether the standard has been attained. They provide a way of measuring and communicating the impact, or result, of programmes as well as the process, or methods, used. The indicators may be qualitative or quantitative;

● *guidance notes:* these include specific points to consider when applying the standard and indicators in different situations, guidance on tackling practical difficulties, and advice on priority issues. They may also include critical issues relating to the standard or indicators, and describe dilemmas, controversies or gaps in current knowledge.

Appendices at the end of the chapter include a checklist for assessments, sample data collection forms, formulas for calculating rates of mortality and morbidity, and a select list of references, which point to sources of information on both general issues and specific technical issues relating to this chapter.

Contents

Health

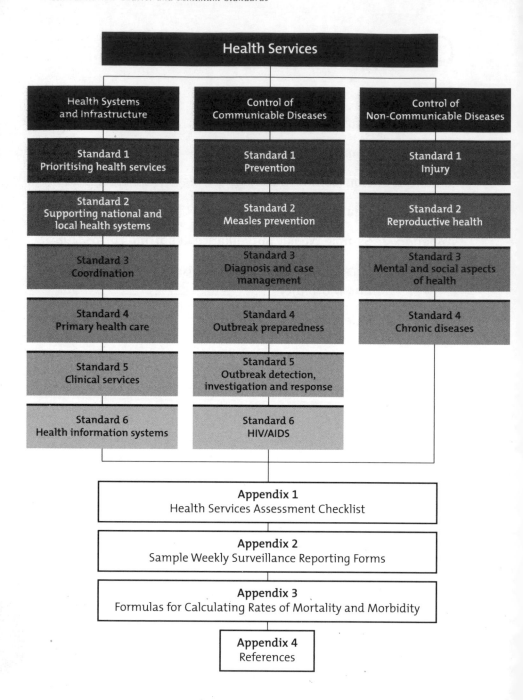

Introduction

Links to international legal instruments

The Minimum Standards in Health Services are a practical expression of the principles and rights embodied in the Humanitarian Charter. The Humanitarian Charter is concerned with the most basic requirements for sustaining the lives and dignity of those affected by calamity or conflict, as reflected in the body of international human rights, humanitarian and refugee law.

Everyone has the right to health, as recognised in a number of international legal instruments. This embraces not only the right to equal access to health care but also to the underlying determinants of health, all of which involve the fulfilment of other human rights, such as access to safe water and adequate sanitation; an adequate supply of safe food, nutrition and housing; healthy environmental conditions; access to health-related education and information; non-discrimination; and human dignity and the affirmation of individual self-worth.

The right to health can be assured only if the population is protected, if the professionals responsible for the health care system are well trained and committed to universal ethical principles and professional standards, if the system in which they work is designed to meet minimum standards of need, and if the state is disposed to establish and secure these conditions of safety and stability. Essential to this human rights perspective are the issues of dignity and equity, and the obligations of states and non-state actors in fulfilling the individual's right to health. In times of armed conflict, civilian hospitals and medical facilities may in no circumstances be the object of attack, and health and medical staff have the right to be respected and protected.

The Minimum Standards in this chapter are not a full expression of the Right to Health. However, the Sphere standards reflect the core content of the Right to Health and contribute to the progressive realisation of this right globally.

Health

The importance of health services in disasters

Health care is a critical determinant for survival in the initial stages of a disaster. Disasters almost always have significant impacts on the public health and well-being of affected populations. The public health impacts may be described as direct (e.g. injury, psychological trauma) or indirect (e.g. increased rates of infectious diseases, malnutrition, complications of chronic diseases). These indirect health impacts are usually related to factors such as inadequate quantities and quality of water, breakdowns in sanitation, interruption in food supplies, disruption of health services, overcrowding and population displacements.

The primary goals of humanitarian response to disasters are to: 1) prevent and reduce excess mortality and morbidity, and 2) promote a return to normalcy. Different types of disaster are associated with differing scales and patterns of mortality and morbidity (see table on page 257), and the public health and medical needs of an affected community will therefore vary according to the type and extent of disaster.

Prioritisation of health services requires a clear understanding of the affected community's prior health status, needs, health risks, resources and capacities. In the early stages of a disaster, information may be incomplete and important public health decisions may have to be made without all of the relevant data being available and/or analysed. A multi-sectoral assessment that includes community representatives should therefore be conducted as soon as possible to determine the public health impact of the disaster, the priority public health needs, the availability of local resources and the requirements for external assistance (see Initial assessment standard on page 29 and Appendix 1).

In general, priority public health interventions are designed to ensure that the greatest health benefit is provided to the greatest number of people. As far as possible, interventions should be based on the principle of evidence-based practice: those with a demonstrated public health benefit are preferred. Such interventions will usually include adequate quantities of safe water, sanitation, nutritional services, food aid/food security, shelter and basic clinical care. Preventive and clinical services should aim primarily to control diseases of epidemic potential.

A mass measles vaccination campaign will be a major priority for populations at risk of a measles outbreak, especially refugees and those affected by complex emergencies. In most disaster settings, referral services and hospital-based care, while important, have a smaller public health impact than primary health care interventions.

Participation of disaster-affected communities in the design, implementation, monitoring and evaluation of health services is essential. During this process there should be efforts to identify and build on existing capacities within the health sector. Building local capacity together with affected populations is probably the most effective means of helping communities to recover from disasters and to prepare them for future disasters. Refugees and internally displaced persons (IDPs) are likely to place additional strains on the health services of host populations. Humanitarian efforts should therefore aim to integrate with and support the health services of host populations as much as possible.

In most disaster situations, women and children are the main users of health care services, and it is important to seek women's views as a means of ensuring that services are equitable, appropriate and accessible for the affected population as a whole. Women can contribute to an understanding of cultural factors and customs that affect health, as well as the specific needs of vulnerable people within the affected population. They should therefore actively participate in the planning and implementation of health care services from the outset.

Links to other chapters

Many of the standards in the other sector chapters are relevant to this chapter. Progress in achieving standards in one area often influences and even determines progress in other areas. For a response to be effective, close coordination and collaboration are required with other sectors. Coordination with local authorities and other responding agencies is also necessary to ensure that needs are met, that efforts are not duplicated, and that the quality of health services is optimised. Reference to specific standards or guidance notes in other technical chapters is made where relevant.

Health

Links to the standards common to all sectors

The process by which a response is developed and implemented is critical to its effectiveness. This chapter should be utilised in conjunction with the standards common to all sectors, which cover participation, initial assessment, response, targeting, monitoring, evaluation, aid worker competencies and responsibilities, and the supervision, management and support of personnel (see chapter 1, page 21). In particular, in any response the participation of disaster-affected people – including the vulnerable groups outlined below – should be maximised to ensure its appropriateness and quality.

Vulnerabilities and capacities of disaster-affected populations

The groups most frequently at risk in emergencies are women, children, older people, disabled people and people living with HIV/AIDS (PLWH/A). In certain contexts, people may also become vulnerable by reason of ethnic origin, religious or political affiliation, or displacement. This is not an exhaustive list, but it includes those most frequently identified. Specific vulnerabilities influence people's ability to cope and survive in a disaster, and those most at risk should be identified in each context.

Throughout the handbook, the term 'vulnerable groups' refers to all these groups. When any one group is at risk, it is likely that others will also be threatened. Therefore, whenever vulnerable groups are mentioned, users are strongly urged to consider all those listed here. Special care must be taken to protect and provide for all affected groups in a non-discriminatory manner and according to their specific needs. However, it should also be remembered that disaster-affected populations possess, and acquire, skills and capacities of their own to cope, and that these should be recognised and supported.

Public Health Impact of Selected Disasters

Effect	Complex emergencies	Earthquakes	High winds (without flooding)	Floods	Flash floods/ tsunamis
Deaths	Many	Many	Few	Few	Many
Severe injuries	Varies	Many	Moderate	Few	Few
Increased risk of communicable diseases	High	Small	Small	Varies	Small
Food scarcity	Common	Rare	Rare	Varies	Common
Major population displacements	Common (may occur in heavily damaged urban areas)	Rare	Rare	Common	Varies

Source: adapted from Pan American Health Organization, *Emergency Health Management After Natural Disaster.* Office of Emergency Preparedness and Disaster Relief Coordination: Scientific Publication No. 47. Washington, DC. Pan American Health Organization, 1981.

NB: Even for specific types of disaster, the patterns of morbidity and mortality vary significantly from context to context. For example, the enforcement of building codes can dramatically reduce the number of deaths and serious injuries associated with earthquakes. In some complex emergencies communicable diseases and malnutrition are the major causes of morbidity and mortality, while in others violent trauma is the major cause of mortality and complications of chronic disease a major cause of excess morbidity.

Health

The Minimum Standards

1 Health Systems and Infrastructure

During an emergency response, when mortality rates are frequently elevated or could soon become so, priority humanitarian interventions must focus on urgent survival needs, including basic medical care. Once survival needs have been met, and mortality rates have declined to near-baseline levels, a more comprehensive range of health services should be developed. Throughout all phases of the response, a health systems approach to the design, implementation, monitoring and evaluation of services will contribute to ensuring that the most important needs are met, that coverage is appropriate, that access is optimised, and that quality is promoted.

The standards that follow apply to all disaster settings, but are particularly relevant to resource-poor settings. They are designed primarily to ensure that disaster-affected communities have access to good-quality health services during the disaster response. Promoting the sustainability of health services following disasters is especially important when there has been major disruption of health infrastructure and services. However, ensuring sustainability requires consideration of many different factors, including political, managerial, institutional, financial and technical, and is therefore beyond the scope of this document. Health agencies and staff must bear in mind that frequently decisions made during a disaster response can either help to promote or undermine the longer-term sustainability of services.

Health systems and infrastructure standard 1: prioritising health services

All people have access to health services that are prioritised to address the main causes of excess mortality and morbidity.

Key indicators (to be read in conjunction with the guidance notes)

● The major causes of mortality and morbidity are identified, documented and monitored.

● Priority health services include the most appropriate and effective interventions to reduce excess morbidity and mortality (see guidance note 1).

● All members of the community, including vulnerable groups, have access to priority health interventions (see guidance note 2).

● Local health authorities and community members participate in the design and implementation of priority health interventions.

● There is active collaboration with other sectors in the design and implementation of priority health interventions, including water and sanitation, food security, nutrition, shelter and protection.

● The crude mortality rate (CMR) is maintained at, or reduced to, less than twice the baseline rate documented for the population prior to the disaster (see guidance note 3).

● The under-5 mortality rate (U5MR) is maintained at, or reduced to, less than twice the baseline rate documented for the population prior to the disaster (see guidance note 3).

Guidance notes

1. ***Priority health interventions*** vary according to the context, including the type of disaster and its impact. Basing the design of these interventions on public health principles will ensure that the greatest health benefit is provided to the greatest number of people. Priority public health interventions include adequate supplies of safe water, sanitation,

Health

food and shelter, infectious disease control (e.g. measles vaccination), basic clinical care and disease surveillance. Expanded clinical services, including trauma care, are given higher priority following disasters that are associated with large numbers of injuries, e.g. earthquakes.

2. ***Access to health services:*** access should be based on the principle of equity, ensuring equal access according to need, without any discrimination that could lead to the exclusion of specific groups. In practice, the location and staffing of health services should be organised to ensure optimal access and coverage. The particular needs of vulnerable groups who may not have ready access should be addressed when designing health services. Where user fees are charged, arrangements should be made to ensure that those unable to afford the fees still have access, e.g. fee waivers, vouchers, etc.

3. ***Crude Mortality Rate and Under-5 Mortality Rate:*** the daily crude mortality rate (CMR) is the most specific and useful health indicator to monitor in a disaster situation. A doubling of the baseline CMR indicates a significant public health emergency, requiring immediate response. The average baseline CMR for the least developed countries is approximately 0.38 deaths/10,000 persons/day, with sub-Saharan Africa at 0.44; for industrialised countries the average CMR is approximately 0.25/10,000/day. When the baseline rate is unknown, health agencies should aim to maintain the CMR at below 1.0/10,000/day. The baseline under-5 mortality rate (U5MR) for the least developed countries is approximately 1.03 deaths/10,000 U5s/day, with sub-Saharan Africa at 1.14; for industrialised countries the rate is approximately 0.04/10,000 U5s/day. When the baseline U5MR is unknown, agencies should aim to maintain the rate at below 2.0/10,000 U5s/day (see Appendices 2-3 and the table opposite).

Baseline Reference Mortality Data by Region				
Region	CMR (deaths/ 10,000/day)	CMR emergency threshold	U5MR (deaths/ 10,000 U5s/day)	U5MR emergency threshold
Sub-Saharan Africa	0.44	0.9	1.14	2.3
Middle East and North Africa	0.16	0.3	0.36	0.7
South Asia	0.25	0.5	0.59	1.2
East Asia and Pacific	0.19	0.4	0.24	0.5
Latin America and Caribbean	0.16	0.3	0.19	0.4
Central and Eastern European Region/CIS and Baltic States	0.30	0.6	0.20	0.4
Industrialised countries	0.25	0.5	0.04	0.1
Developing countries	0.25	0.5	0.53	1.1
Least developed countries	0.38	0.8	1.03	2.1
World	0.25	0.5	0.48	1.0

Source: UNICEF's *State of the World's Children 2003* (data from 2001).

Health systems and infrastructure standard 2: supporting national and local health systems

Health services are designed to support existing health systems, structures and providers.

Key indicators (to be read in conjunction with the guidance notes)

● Representatives of the Ministry of Health lead the health sector response, whenever possible.

● When the Ministry of Health lacks the necessary capacity, an alternate agency with the requisite capacity is identified to take the lead in the health sector (see guidance notes 1-2).

Health

- Local health facilities are supported and strengthened by responding agencies (see guidance notes 1-2).

- Local health workers are supported and integrated into health services, taking account of gender and ethnic balance (see guidance note 3).

- Health services incorporate or adapt the existing national standards and guidelines of the disaster-affected or host country (see guidance note 4).

- No alternate or parallel health facilities and services are established, including foreign field hospitals, unless local capacities are exceeded or the population does not have ready access to existing services. The lead health authority is consulted on this issue (see guidance note 5).

Guidance notes

1. ***Lead health authority:*** when the Ministry of Health (MOH) lacks capacity to assume the role of lead health authority, a United Nations agency will generally take this responsibility, e.g. WHO, UNHCR, UNICEF. On occasion, when both the MOH and UN agencies lack capacity at regional, district or local level, another participating agency may be required to coordinate activities, at least temporarily. The lead health authority should ensure that responding health agencies support and strengthen the capacities of local health systems. In addition, the lead health authority will be responsible for ensuring that the activities of health agencies are coordinated and complementary.

2. ***Health sector strategy and policy:*** an important responsibility of the lead health authority is to develop an overall strategy and policy for the emergency response within the health sector. Ideally, a policy document should be produced that specifies health sector priorities and objectives and provides a framework for achieving them. This document should be developed after consultation with relevant agencies and community representatives.

3. ***Local health workers:*** health professionals and other health workers from the disaster-affected communities, including skilled/traditional birth attendants, should be integrated into health services where appropriate.

Gender balance, while always preferred, may not be practical in communities where health care providers are predominantly of one sex.

4. **National standards and guidelines:** in general, agencies should adhere to the health standards and guidelines of the country where the disaster response is being implemented, including treatment protocols and essential drug lists (see Health systems and infrastructure standard 5). These standards and guidelines should be reviewed in consultation with the MOH or lead health authority early in the disaster response to determine their appropriateness. When they are outdated or do not reflect evidence-based practice, they should be updated.

5. **Foreign field hospitals:** occasionally, field hospitals may be the only way to provide health care when existing hospitals are not functioning properly. However, it is usually more effective to provide resources to existing hospitals so that they can start working again or cope with the extra load. It may be appropriate to deploy a field hospital for the immediate care of traumatic injuries (first 48 hours), secondary care of traumatic injuries and routine emergencies (days 3-15), or as a temporary facility to substitute for a damaged local hospital until it is reconstructed (up to several years). In determining whether a field hospital deployment is appropriate, there must be a well-defined need; the field hospital must be able to provide appropriate services; it should not be a drain on local resources; and it must be cost-effective.

Health systems and infrastructure standard 3: coordination

People have access to health services that are coordinated across agencies and sectors to achieve maximum impact.

Key indicators (to be read in conjunction with the guidance notes)

● Coordination mechanisms are established at central level (national or regional) and at field level within the health sector, and between health and other sectors.

Health

- Specific responsibilities of each health agency are clarified and documented in consultation with the lead health authority to ensure optimal coverage of the population and complementarity of services (see guidance note 1).

- Regular health sector coordination meetings are held for local and external partners at both central and field levels (see guidance note 2).

Guidance notes

1. ***Coordination among health agencies:*** regardless of whether the lead health authority is the Ministry of Health or another agency, all organisations in the health sector should coordinate with national and local health services. In refugee settings, agencies should coordinate with the health system of the host country. When several health agencies are operational in the field, coordinated allocation of responsibilities will help to ensure that health sector gaps are met and that duplications are avoided.

2. ***Coordination meetings:*** these should provide a forum in which information is shared, priorities are identified and monitored, common health strategies are developed and adapted, specific tasks are allocated, and standardised protocols and interventions are agreed upon. Meetings should initially be held at least weekly.

Health systems and infrastructure standard 4: primary health care

Health services are based on relevant primary health care principles.

Key indicators (to be read in conjunction with the guidance notes)

- All people have access to health information that allows them to protect and promote their own health and well-being (see guidance note 1).

- Health services are provided at the appropriate level of the health system: household/community, peripheral health facilities, central health facilities, referral hospital (see guidance note 2).

● A standardised referral system is established by the lead health authority and utilised by health agencies. Suitable transportation is organised for patients to reach the referral facility.

● Health services and interventions are based on scientifically sound methods and are evidence-based, whenever possible.

● Health services and interventions utilise appropriate technology, and are socially and culturally acceptable.

Guidance notes

1. *Health information and education:* an active programme of community health education and promotion should be initiated in consultation with local health authorities and community representatives. It should take into account health-seeking behaviour and health beliefs of the population. It should provide information on the major endemic health problems, major health risks, the availability and location of health services, and behaviours that protect and promote good health. Public health messages and materials should utilise appropriate language and media, and be culturally sensitive. As far as possible, the content of priority health messages should be consistent among implementing health agencies.

2. *Mobile clinics:* during some disasters, it may be necessary to operate mobile clinics in order to meet the needs of isolated or mobile communities that have limited access to care. Experience has demonstrated that when operated appropriately, such clinics can fill a vital need. When operated inappropriately, mobile clinics may be under-utilised, may displace existing health services and represent an inefficient use of limited resources. They should be introduced only following consultation with the lead health authority and with local health representatives.

Health

Health systems and infrastructure standard 5: clinical services

People have access to clinical services that are standardised and follow accepted protocols and guidelines.

Key indicators (to be read in conjunction with the guidance notes)

● The number, level and location of health facilities are appropriate to meet the needs of the population (see guidance notes 1-2).

● The number, skills and gender/ethnic balance of staff at each health facility are appropriate to meet the needs of the population (see guidance notes 1-2).

● Adequate staffing levels are achieved so that clinicians are not required to consistently consult on more than 50 patients per day. If this threshold is regularly exceeded, additional clinical staff are recruited (see Appendix 3).

● Utilisation rates at health facilities are monitored and corrective measures taken if there is over- or under-utilisation (see guidance note 3).

● Standardised case management protocols are established by the lead health authority, and adhered to by health agencies (see guidance note 4).

● A standardised essential drug list is established by the lead health authority, and adhered to by health agencies (see guidance note 4).

● Clinical staff are trained and supervised in the use of the protocols and the essential drug list (see guidance notes 5-6).

● People have access to a consistent supply of essential drugs through a standardised drug management system that follows accepted guidelines (see guidance note 7).

● Drug donations are accepted only if they follow internationally recognised guidelines. Donations that do not follow these guidelines are not used and are disposed of safely.

● Bodies of the deceased are disposed of in a manner that is dignified, culturally appropriate and is based on good public health practice (see guidance note 8).

Guidance notes

1. ***Health facilities and staffing:*** the number and location of health facilities required and the number and skills of staff at each level can vary from context to context. Ensuring the presence of even one female health worker or one representative of a minority ethnic group on a staff may significantly increase the access of women or people from minority groups to health services. The carrying out of acts or activities that jeopardise the neutrality of health facilities, such as carrying arms, is prohibited.

2. ***Staffing levels:*** the following guidelines provide a useful reference, but may need to be adapted according to the context. The term 'qualified health worker' refers to a formally trained clinical provider, such as a physician, nurse, clinical officer or medical assistant.

   a. Community level: one community health worker per 500-1,000 population; one skilled/traditional birth attendant per 2,000 population; one supervisor per 10 home visitors; one senior supervisor.

   b. Peripheral health facility (for approximately 10,000 population): total of two to five staff; minimum of one qualified health worker, based on one clinician per 50 consultations per day; non-qualified staff for administering oral rehydration therapy (ORT), dressings, etc. and for registration, administration, etc.

   c. Central health facility (for approximately 50,000 population): minimum of five qualified health workers, minimum of one doctor; one qualified health worker per 50 consultations per day (out-patient care); one qualified health worker per 20-30 beds, 24-hour services (in-patient care). One non-qualified health worker for administering ORT; one/two for pharmacy; one/two for dressings, injections, sterilisation. One lab technician. Non-qualified staff for registration, security, etc.

   d. Referral hospital: variable. At least one doctor with surgical skills; one nurse for 20-30 beds per shift.

Health

3. **Utilisation rate of health services:** attendance at health facilities will help to determine the utilisation rate. There is no definitive threshold for utilisation, as this will vary from context to context, and often from season to season. However, it usually increases significantly among disaster-affected populations. Among stable populations, utilisation rates are approximately 0.5-1.0 new consultations/person/year. Among displaced populations, an average of 4.0 new consultations/person/year may be expected. If the rate is lower than expected, it may indicate inadequate access to health facilities, e.g. due to insecurity or poor capacity of health services. If the rate is higher, it may suggest over-utilisation due to a specific public health problem (e.g. infectious disease outbreak), or under-estimation of the target population. In analysing utilisation rates, consideration should also be given to gender, age, ethnic origin and disability, to ensure that vulnerable groups are not under-represented (see Appendix 3).

4. **Standardised treatment protocols and essential drug lists:** most countries have established essential drug lists or national formularies, and many have treatment protocols for the management of common diseases and injuries. These protocols and drug lists should be reviewed in consultation with the Ministry of Health or lead health authority early in the disaster response to determine their appropriateness. Occasionally, alterations to established national protocols and drug lists may be necessary, e.g. if there is evidence of resistance to recommended antibiotics or anti-malarial agents. If protocols and/or essential drug lists do not exist, guidelines established by WHO or UNHCR should be followed, e.g. New Emergency Health Kit.

5. **Training and supervision of staff:** health workers should have the proper training and skills for their level of responsibility. Health agencies have an obligation to train staff to ensure that their knowledge is up-to-date. Training and supervision will be high priorities especially where staff have not received continuing education, or new health systems and protocols are introduced. As far as possible, training programmes should be standardised and linked to national programmes.

6. **Patients' rights:** many factors associated with disasters may make it difficult to consistently enforce a patient's rights to privacy, confidentiality and informed consent. However, as far as possible, health personnel

should attempt to safeguard and promote these rights. Health facilities and services should be designed in a manner that ensures privacy and confidentiality (see Health systems and infrastructure standard 6, guidance note 3). Informed consent should be sought from patients prior to medical or surgical procedures. Patients have a right to know what each procedure involves, as well as its expected benefits, potential risks, costs and duration.

7. **Drug management:** in addition to utilising the essential drug list, health agencies need to establish an effective system of drug management. The goal of such a system is to ensure the efficient, cost-effective and rational use of drugs. This system should be based on the four key elements of the drug management cycle: selection, procurement, distribution and use (see Management Sciences for Health (1997), *Managing Drug Supply. Second Edition)*.

8. **Handling the remains of the dead:** when disasters result in high mortality, the management of a large number of dead bodies will be required. Bodies should not be disposed of unceremoniously in mass graves, as this cannot be justified as a public health measure, violates important social norms and may waste scarce resources. The mass management of human remains is often based on the false belief that they represent an epidemic hazard if not buried or burned immediately. In fact, the health hazard presented by dead bodies is usually negligible. In only a few special cases do human remains pose health risks and require specific precautions, e.g. deaths resulting from cholera or haemorrhagic fevers. Families should have the opportunity to conduct culturally appropriate funerals and burials. When those being buried are victims of violence, forensic issues should be considered (see also Shelter and settlement standard 2, guidance note 3 on page 217).

Health

Health systems and infrastructure standard 6: health information systems

The design and development of health services are guided by the ongoing, coordinated collection, analysis and utilisation of relevant public health data.

Key indicators (to be read in conjunction with the guidance notes)

- A standardised health information system (HIS) is implemented by all health agencies to routinely collect relevant data on demographics, mortality, morbidity and health services (see guidance notes 1-2 and Appendices 2-3).

- A designated HIS coordinating agency (or agencies) is identified to organise and supervise the system.

- Health facilities and agencies submit surveillance data to the designated HIS coordinating agency on a regular basis. The frequency of these reports will vary according to the context, e.g. daily, weekly, monthly.

- A regular epidemiological report, including analysis and interpretation of the data, is produced by the HIS coordinating agency and shared with all relevant agencies, decision-makers and the community. The frequency of the report will vary according to the context, e.g. daily, weekly, monthly.

- Agencies take adequate precautions for the protection of data to guarantee the rights and safety of individuals and/or populations (see guidance note 3).

- The HIS includes an early warning component to ensure timely detection of and response to infectious disease outbreaks (see Control of communicable diseases standard 5 on page 281).

- Supplementary data from other relevant sources are consistently used to interpret surveillance data and to guide decision-making (see guidance note 4).

Guidance notes

1. *Health information system (HIS):* the HIS builds upon the pre-existing surveillance system whenever possible. In some emergencies, a new or parallel system may be required and this is determined in consultation with the lead health authority. The HIS should be designed to be flexible and should evolve over time. During the disaster response health data should include, but not be limited to, the following:

   a. crude mortality rate

   b. under-5 mortality rate

   c. proportional mortality

   d. cause-specific mortality rate

   e. incidence rates for most common diseases

   f. health facility utilisation rate

   g. number of consultations per clinician per day.

2. *Disaggregation of data:* data should be disaggregated by age and sex as far as is practical in order to guide decision-making. Detailed disaggregation may be difficult during the early stages of a disaster. However, mortality and morbidity data for children under five years old should be documented from the outset, as this group is usually at special risk. In addition, gender breakdown for mortality and morbidity is useful for detecting gender-specific differences. As time and conditions allow, more detailed disaggregation should be sought, to detect further differences according to age (e.g. 0-11 months, 1-4 years, 5-14 years, 15-49 years, 50-59 years, 60+ years) and sex.

3. *Confidentiality:* confidentiality of medical records and data should be ensured. Adequate precautions should be taken to protect the safety of the individual, as well as the data itself. Staff members should never share patient information with anyone not directly involved in the patient's care without the patient's permission. Data that relates to trauma caused by torture or other human rights violations must be treated with the utmost care. Consideration may be given to passing on this information to appropriate actors or institutions, if the individual gives their consent.

Health

4. *Sources of other data:* sources of relevant health data include laboratory reports, surveys, case reports, quality of service measurements and other programmatic sectors.

See Appendix 2 for sample weekly mortality and morbidity forms and Appendix 3 for formulas for calculating rates of mortality and morbidity.

2 Control of Communicable Diseases

Increased rates of morbidity and mortality due to communicable diseases occur more frequently in association with complex emergencies than other disasters. In many of these settings, especially those occurring in developing countries, between 60% and 90% of deaths have been attributed to one of four major infectious causes: measles, diarrhoea, acute respiratory infections and malaria. Acute malnutrition is often associated with increased case fatality rates of these diseases, especially among young children. There have also been outbreaks of other communicable diseases, such as meningococcal meningitis, yellow fever, viral hepatitis and typhoid, in certain settings.

Outbreaks of communicable diseases are far less commonly associated with acute onset natural disasters. When they do occur, they are generally associated with disruptions of sanitation and poor water quality. The potential use of biological agents as weapons by terrorists and military forces raises new concerns for disaster response agencies and those involved in humanitarian assistance. The response to incidents involving biological weapons is not specifically addressed in the following standards, although several of the standards and indicators are applicable to such incidents.

Control of communicable diseases standard 1: prevention

People have access to information and services that are designed to prevent the communicable diseases that contribute most significantly to excess morbidity and mortality.

Key indicators (to be read in conjunction with the guidance notes)

● General prevention measures are developed and implemented in coordination with other relevant sectors (see guidance note 1).

● Community health education messages provide individuals with information on how to prevent common communicable diseases and how to access relevant services (see Health systems and infrastructure standard 4 on page 264).

● Specific prevention measures, such as a mass measles vaccination campaign and Expanded Programme on Immunisation (EPI), are implemented as indicated (see guidance note 2 and Control of communicable diseases standard 2).

Guidance notes

1. *General prevention measures:* most of these interventions are developed in coordination with other sectors, including:

   – water and sanitation: sufficient water quantity and quality; sufficient sanitation; hygiene promotion; vector control, etc. (see Water, Sanitation and Hygiene Promotion, page 51).

   – food security, nutrition and food aid: access to adequate food and management of malnutrition (see Food Security, Nutrition and Food Aid, page 103).

   – shelter: sufficient and adequate shelter (see Shelter, Settlement and Non-Food Items, page 203).

2. *Prevention of measles and Expanded Programme on Immunisation (EPI):* because measles has high potential for outbreaks and mortality, mass vaccination of children against the disease is often a high priority among disaster-affected populations, especially those who are displaced and/or affected by conflict. Vaccination against other childhood diseases through EPI is generally a lesser priority, as outbreaks of these diseases are less frequent and the health risks associated with them are lower. Therefore, other EPI vaccines are generally introduced only when the immediate needs of the population have been met. The exceptions to this guideline include ongoing outbreaks of diseases such as pertussis or diphtheria, when vaccination against these diseases also becomes a priority.

Control of communicable diseases standard 2: measles prevention

All children aged 6 months to 15 years have immunity against measles.

Key indicators (to be read in conjunction with the guidance notes)

● An estimation of measles vaccination coverage of children aged 9 months to 15 years is made at the outset of the emergency response, to determine the prevalence of susceptibility to measles (see guidance note 1).

● If vaccination coverage is estimated to be less than 90%, a mass measles vaccination campaign for children aged 6 months to 15 years (including administration of vitamin A to children aged 6-59 months) is initiated. The vaccination campaign is coordinated with national and local health authorities, including the Expanded Programme on Immunisation (see guidance note 2).

● Upon completion of the campaign:
  – at least 95% of children aged 6 months to 15 years have received measles vaccination;
  – at least 95% of children aged 6-59 months have received an appropriate dose of vitamin A.

Health

● All infants vaccinated between 6-9 months of age receive another dose of measles vaccine upon reaching 9 months (see guidance note 3).

● Routine ongoing vaccination of 9-month-old children is established to ensure the maintenance of the minimum 95% coverage. This system is linked to the Expanded Programme on Immunisation.

● For mobile or displaced populations, an ongoing system is established to ensure that at least 95% of newcomers aged between 6 months and 15 years receive vaccination against measles.

Guidance notes

1. **Measles prevention:** measles is one of the most contagious viruses known and can be associated with high mortality rates. Whenever there are crowded emergency settings, large population displacements and high levels of malnutrition, there is a high risk of a measles outbreak. Mass measles vaccination campaigns should therefore be given the highest priority at the earliest possible time in these settings. The necessary personnel, vaccine, cold chain equipment and other supplies to conduct a mass campaign should be assembled as soon as possible. If the vaccination coverage for the population is unknown, the campaign should be carried out on the assumption that the coverage is inadequate.

2. **Age ranges for measles vaccination:** some older children may have escaped both previous measles vaccination campaigns and measles disease. These children remain at risk of measles and can serve as a source of infection for infants and young children who are at higher risk of dying from the disease. This is the reason for the recommendation to vaccinate up to the age of 15 years. In resource-poor settings, however, it may not be possible to vaccinate all children aged 6 months to 15 years. In these settings, priority should be given to children aged 6-59 months.

3. **Repeat measles vaccination for children aged 6-9 months:** the repeat measles vaccination should be administered as soon as the child reaches 9 months of age, except for children who received their first dose after 8 months of age. These children should receive the repeat dose after a minimum interval of 30 days.

Control of communicable diseases standard 3: diagnosis and case management

People have access to effective diagnosis and treatment for those infectious diseases that contribute most significantly to preventable excess morbidity and mortality.

Key indicators (to be read in conjunction with the guidance notes)

- Standardised case management protocols for diagnosis and treatment of the most common infectious diseases are consistently used (see guidance note 1; see also Health systems and infrastructure standard 5).

- Public health education messages encourage people to seek early care for fever, cough, diarrhoea, etc., especially children, pregnant women and older people.

- In malaria-endemic regions, a protocol is established to ensure early (<24 hours) diagnosis of fever cases and treatment with highly effective first-line drugs (see guidance note 2).

- Laboratory services are available and utilised when indicated (see guidance note 3).

- A tuberculosis control programme is introduced only after consideration of recognised criteria (see guidance note 4).

Guidance notes

1. *Integrated management of childhood illness:* where the integrated management of childhood illness (IMCI) has been developed in a country, and clinical guidelines adapted, these guidelines should preferably be incorporated into the standardised protocols. IMCI has been demonstrated to improve the quality of care provided to children under the age of five years.

2. *Malaria:* malaria incidence is likely to rise within a few days/weeks of mass population movements in endemic areas. Because of widespread and increasing resistance to chloroquine and sulphadoxine-pyrimethamine

Health

(Fansidar), more efficacious anti-malarial drugs may be required. This will be especially important for non-immune and vulnerable populations exposed to falciparum malaria. Combination therapies utilising artemisinin derivatives are preferable. Drug choice should be determined in consultation with the lead health authority, following a consideration of drug efficacy data. Standardised WHO protocols should be used to evaluate drug efficacy.

3. ***Laboratory services:*** establishing a clinical laboratory is not a priority during the initial phase of most disasters. The most common communicable diseases can usually be diagnosed clinically and treatment will generally be presumptive. Laboratory testing is most useful for confirming the diagnosis during a suspected outbreak for which mass immunisation may be indicated (e.g. meningococcal meningitis) or where culture and antibiotic sensitivity testing may influence case management decisions (e.g. dysentery). Therefore, it will be important to identify an established laboratory either nationally or in another country that can conduct the appropriate microbiological investigations. Guidelines on correct specimen collection and transportation will be required.

4. ***Tuberculosis control:*** a high prevalence of TB has frequently been documented among refugees and other war-affected populations. However, poorly implemented TB control programmes can potentially do more harm than good, by prolonging infectivity and by contributing to the spread of multi-drug-resistant bacilli. While the management of individual patients with TB may be possible during emergencies, a comprehensive programme of TB control should only be implemented following a consideration of recognised criteria (see WHO, *Tuberculosis Control in Refugee Situations: An Interagency Field Manual*). When implemented, TB control programmes in these settings should be integrated with the national/host country programme and follow the well-established DOTS strategy (Directly-Observed Therapy, Short-course).

Control of communicable diseases standard 4: outbreak preparedness

Measures are taken to prepare for and respond to outbreaks of infectious diseases.

Key indicators (to be read in conjunction with the guidance notes)

● An outbreak investigation and control plan is prepared (see guidance note 1).

● Protocols for the investigation and control of common outbreaks are available and distributed to relevant staff.

● Staff receive training in the principles of outbreak investigation and control, including relevant treatment protocols.

● Reserve stocks of essential drugs, medical supplies, vaccines and basic protection material are available and can be procured rapidly (see guidance note 2).

● Sources of vaccines for relevant outbreaks (e.g. measles, meningococcal meningitis, yellow fever) are identified for rapid procurement and use. Mechanisms for rapid procurement are established (see guidance note 2).

● Sites for the isolation and treatment of infectious patients are identified in advance, e.g. cholera treatment centres.

● A laboratory is identified, whether locally, regionally, nationally or in another country, that can provide confirmation of diagnoses (see guidance note 3).

● Sampling materials and transport media for the infectious agents most likely to cause a sudden outbreak are available on-site, to permit transfer of specimens to an appropriate laboratory. In addition, several rapid tests may be stored on-site (see guidance note 4).

Health

Guidance notes

1. **Outbreak investigation and control plan:** the following issues should be addressed in the plan:

   a. the circumstances under which an outbreak control team is to be convened;

   b. composition of the outbreak control team, including representatives from appropriate sectors, e.g. health, water and sanitation;

   c. specific roles and responsibilities of organisations and positions on the team;

   d. arrangements for consulting and informing authorities at local and national level;

   e. the resources/facilities available to investigate and respond to outbreaks.

2. **Reserve stocks:** on-site reserves should include material to use in response to likely outbreaks. Such stocks might include oral rehydration salts, intravenous fluids, antibiotics, vaccines and consumable medical supplies. Single use/auto-destruct syringes and safe needle containers should be available, to prevent the spread of viral hepatitis and HIV. A pre-packaged cholera kit may be indicated in some circumstances. It may not be practical to keep some stocks on-site, such as meningococcal vaccine. For these items, the mechanisms for rapid procurement, shipment and storage should be determined in advance so that they can be rapidly available.

3. **Reference laboratories:** a reference laboratory should also be identified either regionally or internationally that can assist with more sophisticated testing, e.g. antibiotic sensitivity for *Shigella*, serological diagnosis of viral haemorrhagic fevers.

4. **Transport media and rapid tests:** sampling materials (e.g. rectal swabs) and transport media (e.g. Cary-Blair, Amies' or Stuarts' media for cholera, *Shigella*, *E. Coli* and *Salmonella*; Translocate for meningitis) should be available on-site, or readily accessible. In addition, several new rapid tests are available that can be useful in confirming diagnoses of communicable diseases in the field, including malaria and meningitis.

Control of communicable diseases standard 5: outbreak detection, investigation and response

Outbreaks of communicable diseases are detected, investigated and controlled in a timely and effective manner.

Key indicators (to be read in conjunction with the guidance notes)

● The health information system (HIS) includes an early warning component (see guidance notes 1-2).

● Initiation of outbreak investigation occurs within 24 hours of notification.

● The outbreak is described according to time, place and person, leading to the identification of high-risk groups. Adequate precautions are taken to protect the safety of both individuals and data.

● Appropriate control measures that are specific to the disease and context are implemented as soon as possible (see guidance notes 3-4).

● Case fatality rates are maintained at acceptable levels (see guidance note 5):

  – cholera: 1% or lower

  – *Shigella* dysentery: 1% or lower

  – typhoid: 1% or lower

  – meningococcal meningitis: varies (see guidance note 6).

Guidance notes

1. ***Early warning system for infectious disease outbreaks:*** the key elements of such a system will include:

   – case definitions and thresholds defined and distributed to all reporting health facilities;

   – community health workers (CHWs) trained to detect and report potential outbreaks from within the community;

Health

- reporting of suspected outbreaks to the next appropriate level of the health system within 24 hours of detection;

- communications systems established to ensure rapid notification of relevant health authorities, e.g. radio, telephone.

2. **Confirmation of the existence of an outbreak:** it is not always straightforward to determine whether an outbreak is present and clear definitions of outbreak thresholds do not exist for all diseases.

   a. Diseases for which a single case may indicate an outbreak: cholera, measles, yellow fever, *Shigella,* viral haemorrhagic fevers.

   b. Meningococcal meningitis: for populations above 30,000, 15 cases/100,000 persons/week in one week indicates an outbreak; however, with high outbreak risk (i.e. no outbreak for 3+ years and vaccination coverage <80%), this threshold is reduced to 10 cases/100,000/week. In populations of less than 30,000, an incidence of five cases in one week or a doubling of cases over a three-week period confirms an outbreak.

   c. Malaria: less specific definitions exist. However, an increase in the number of cases above what is expected for the time of year among a defined population in a defined area may indicate an outbreak.

3. **Outbreak control:** control measures must be specifically developed to halt transmission of the agent causing the outbreak. Often, pre-existing knowledge about the agent can guide the design of appropriate control measures in specific situations. In general, response activities include:

   - controlling the source. Interventions may include improving water quality and quantity (e.g. cholera), prompt diagnosis and treatment (e.g. malaria), isolation (e.g. dysentery), controlling animal reservoirs (e.g. plague, Lassa fever).

   - protecting susceptible groups. Interventions may include immunisation (e.g. measles, meningitis, yellow fever), chemoprophylaxis (e.g. malaria prevention for pregnant women), improved nutrition (e.g. acute respiratory infections).

   - interrupting transmission. Interventions may include hygiene promotion (e.g. for all diseases spread by the faeco-oral route), vector control (e.g. malaria, dengue).

(See also chapter 2: Water, Sanitation and Hygiene Promotion on page 51).

4. **Vector control and malaria:** during a malaria outbreak, vector control measures such as indoor residual spraying and the distribution of insecticide-treated bed net (ITN) programmes should be guided by entomological assessments and expertise. These interventions require substantial logistical support and follow-up that may not be available in the initial phase of the disaster. For populations that already have a high level of ITN usage (>80%), rapid re-impregnation of nets with pyrethroids may help to stem transmission (see Vector control standards 1-2 on pages 77-81).

5. **Case fatality rates (CFRs):** if CFRs exceed these specified levels, an immediate evaluation of control measures should be undertaken, and corrective steps taken to ensure CFRs are maintained at acceptable levels.

6. **CFRs for meningococcal meningitis:** the acceptable CFR for meningococcal meningitis varies according to the general context and accessibility to health services. In general, health agencies should aim for a CFR that is as low as possible, though during outbreaks it may be as high as 20%.

Control of communicable diseases standard 6: HIV/AIDS

People have access to the minimum package of services to prevent transmission of HIV/AIDS.

Key indicators (to be read in conjunction with the guidance notes)

● People have access to the following essential package of services during the disaster phase:

– free male condoms and promotion of proper condom use;

– universal precautions to prevent iatrogenic/nosocomial transmission in emergency and health-care settings;

– safe blood supply;

Health

- relevant information and education so that individuals can take steps to protect themselves against HIV transmission;

- syndromic case management of sexually transmitted infections (STIs);

- prevention and management of the consequences of sexual violence;

- basic health care for people living with HIV/AIDS (PLWH/A).

● Plans are initiated to broaden the range of HIV control services in the post-disaster phase (see guidance note 1).

Guidance note

1. HIV control: during the post-emergency and rehabilitation phase of disasters, the expansion of HIV control activities will be based on an assessment of local needs and circumstances. Involvement of the community, especially people living with HIV/AIDS (PLWH/A) and their carers, in the design, implementation, monitoring and evaluation of the programme will be crucial to its success. In addition to services already implemented during the initial phase, more comprehensive surveillance, prevention, treatment, care and support services should be introduced. The provision of antiretroviral medications to treat PLWH/A is not currently feasible in most post-disaster humanitarian settings, although this may change in the future as financial and other barriers to their use fall. Protection and education programmes to reduce stigma and to protect people against discrimination should be implemented as soon as is feasible.

Note

Caritas Internationalis members cannot endorse standard 6 in the Control of Communicable Diseases section as it relates to the promotion of condom use, or standard 2 in the Control of Non-Communicable Diseases section concerning the Minimum Initial Service Package (MISP). By the same token, Caritas Internationalis members cannot endorse standards related to the use of condoms or the MISP which might appear in other parts of this handbook.

3 Control of Non-Communicable Diseases

Increases in morbidity and mortality due to non-communicable diseases are a common feature of many disasters. Injury is usually the major cause following acute onset natural disasters, such as earthquakes and hurricanes. Injury due to physical violence is also associated with all complex emergencies, and can be a major cause of excess mortality during such crises. The reproductive health (RH) needs of disaster-affected populations have received increased attention in recent years, especially in light of the greater awareness of problems such as HIV/AIDS, gender-based violence, emergency obstetric care needs and the poor availability of even basic RH services in many communities. The need for improved RH programmes has been especially recognised in association with complex emergencies, but it is also relevant to many other types of disaster.

Although difficult to quantify, mental health and psychosocial problems can be associated with any type of disaster and post-disaster setting. The horrors, losses, uncertainties and other stressors associated with disasters can place people at increased risk of various psychiatric, psychological and social problems. Finally, there is evidence to suggest that there is an increased incidence of acute complications from chronic diseases associated with disasters. These complications are generally due to disruptions of ongoing treatment regimens. However, a variety of other stressors may also precipitate an acute deterioration of a chronic medical condition.

Control of non-communicable diseases standard 1: injury

People have access to appropriate services for the management of injuries.

Key indicators (to be read in conjunction with the guidance notes)

● In situations with a large number of injured patients, a standardised system of triage is established to guide health care providers on assessment, prioritisation, basic resuscitation and referral (see guidance notes 1-2).

● Standardised guidelines for the provision of first aid and basic resuscitation are established (see guidance note 3).

● Standardised protocols for the referral of injured patients for advanced care, including surgery, are established. Suitable transportation is organised for patients to reach the referral facility.

● Definitive trauma and surgical services are established only by agencies with appropriate expertise and resources (see guidance note 4).

● In situations with a potentially large number of injured patients, contingency plans for the management of multiple casualties are developed for relevant health care facilities. These plans are related to district and regional plans.

Guidance notes

1. *Prioritising trauma services:* in most disasters, it is not possible to determine the number of injured persons who will require clinical care. Following acute onset disasters such as earthquakes, 85-90% of those rescued alive are generally extracted by local emergency personnel or by their neighbours and families within 72 hours. Therefore, in planning relief operations in disaster-prone regions the major emphasis should be on preparing local populations to provide the initial care. It is important to note

that priority health interventions are designed to reduce preventable excess mortality. During armed conflict, most violent trauma deaths occur in insecure regions away from health facilities and therefore cannot usually be prevented by medical care. Interventions that aim to protect the civilian population are required to prevent these deaths. Health interventions implemented during conflict should emphasise community-based public health and primary care, even in situations where there is a high incidence of violent injury.

2. **Triage:** triage is the process of categorising patients according to the severity of their injuries or illness, and prioritising treatment according to the availability of resources and the patients' chances of survival. The underlying principle of triage is allocating limited resources in a manner that provides the greatest health benefit to the greatest number. Triage does not necessarily mean that individuals with the most serious injuries receive priority. In the setting of multiple casualties with limited resources, those with severe, life-threatening injuries may, in fact, receive lower priority than those with more survivable injuries. There is no standardised system of triage, and internationally several are in use. Most systems specify between two and five categories of injury, with four being the most common.

3. **First aid and basic medical care:** definitive trauma and surgical care may not be readily available, especially in resource-poor settings. But it is important to note that first aid, basic resuscitation and non-operative procedures can be life-saving for even severe injuries. Simple procedures such as clearing the airway, controlling haemorrhage and administering intravenous fluids may help to stabilise individuals with life-threatening injuries before transfer to a referral centre. The quality of the initial medical management provided can therefore significantly affect a patient's chances of survival. Other non-operative procedures, such as cleaning and dressing wounds, and administering antibiotics and tetanus prophylaxis, are also important. Many severely injured patients can survive for days or even weeks without surgery, provided that appropriate first aid, medical and nursing care are provided.

4. **Trauma and surgical care:** all health-care providers should be able to provide first aid and basic resuscitation to injured patients. In addition, life-saving triage capacity at strategic points, with a linkage to a referral system, is important. However, definitive trauma care and war surgery are

Health

specialised fields that require specific training and resources that few agencies possess. Inappropriate or inadequate surgery may do more harm than doing nothing. Only organisations and professionals with the relevant expertise should therefore establish these sophisticated services.

Control of non-communicable diseases standard 2: reproductive health

People have access to the Minimum Initial Service Package (MISP) to respond to their reproductive health needs.

Key indicators (to be read in conjunction with the guidance notes)

● An organisation(s) and individual(s) are identified to facilitate the coordination and implementation of the MISP in consultation with the lead health authority (see guidance note 1).

● Steps are taken by health agencies to prevent and manage the consequences of gender-based violence (GBV), in coordination with other relevant sectors, especially protection and community services (see guidance note 2).

● The number of cases of sexual and other forms of GBV reported to health services, protection and security officers is monitored and reported to a designated lead GBV agency (or agencies). Rules of confidentiality are applied to data collection and review.

● The minimum package of services to prevent the transmission of HIV/AIDS is implemented (see Control of communicable diseases standard 6).

● Adequate numbers of clean delivery kits, based on the estimated number of births in a given time period, are available and distributed to visibly pregnant women and skilled/traditional birth attendants to promote clean home deliveries.

● Adequate numbers of midwife delivery kits (UNICEF or equivalent) are distributed to health facilities to ensure clean and safe deliveries.

- A standardised referral system is established and promoted within the community, incorporating midwives and skilled/traditional birth attendants, to manage obstetric emergencies. Suitable transportation is organised for patients to reach the referral facility (see guidance note 3).

- Plans are initiated to implement a comprehensive range of reproductive health services integrated into primary health care as soon as possible (see guidance note 4).

Guidance notes

1. *Minimum Initial Service Package:* the MISP is designed to respond to the reproductive health (RH) needs of the affected population in the early phase of a disaster. The MISP is not only a set of equipment and supplies, but also a series of specific health activities. Its objectives are to: identify an organisation(s) or individual(s) to facilitate its coordination and implementation; prevent and manage the consequences of gender-based violence; reduce HIV transmission; prevent excess neonatal and maternal mortality and morbidity; and plan for the provision of comprehensive RH services. The UNFPA RH Kit has been designed specifically to facilitate the implementation of the MISP. It consists of a series of 12 sub-kits that can be used at each sequential level of care: community/health post, health centre and referral centre.

2. *Gender-based violence (GBV)* is a common feature of many complex emergencies and even many natural disasters. It includes abuses such as rape, domestic violence, sexual exploitation, forced marriage, forced prostitution, trafficking and abduction. The prevention and management of GBV requires collaboration and coordination among members of the community and between agencies. Health services should include medical management for sexual assault survivors, confidential counselling and referral for other appropriate care. The layout of settlements, distribution of essential items, and access to health services and other programmes should be designed to reduce the potential for GBV. Sexual exploitation of disaster-affected populations, especially children and youth by relief agency staff, military personnel and others in positions of influence must be actively prevented and managed. Codes of conduct should be

Health

developed and disciplinary measures established for any violations (see Aid worker competencies and responsibilities standard on page 40).

3. *Emergency obstetric care:* approximately 15% of pregnant women will develop complications that require essential obstetric care and up to 5% of pregnant women will require some type of surgery, including Caesarean section. Basic essential obstetric care services should be established at the health centre level as soon as possible and should include initial assessment; assessment of foetal well-being; episiotomy; management of haemorrhage; management of infection; management of eclampsia; multiple birth; breech delivery; use of vacuum extractor; and special care for women who have undergone genital mutilation. Comprehensive essential obstetric care should be available at the referral hospital as soon as possible and should include Caesarean section; laparotomy; repair of cervical and third-degree vaginal tears; care for the complications of unsafe abortion; and safe blood transfusion.

4. *Comprehensive reproductive health services:* health agencies should plan for the subsequent integration of comprehensive RH services into primary health care. RH services should not be established as separate, vertical programmes. In addition to interventions addressed in the MISP, other important elements of comprehensive, integrated RH services include safe motherhood; family planning and counselling; comprehensive GBV services; comprehensive management of STIs and HIV/AIDS; the specific RH needs of youth; and monitoring and surveillance.

Control of non-communicable diseases standard 3: mental and social aspects of health

People have access to social and mental health services to reduce mental health morbidity, disability and social problems.

Key social intervention indicators[1] (to be read in conjunction with the guidance notes)

During the acute disaster phase, the emphasis should be on social interventions.

- People have access to an ongoing, reliable flow of credible information on the disaster and associated relief efforts (see guidance note 1).

- Normal cultural and religious events are maintained or re-established (including grieving rituals conducted by relevant spiritual and religious practitioners). People are able to conduct funeral ceremonies (see guidance note 2).

- As soon as resources permit, children and adolescents have access to formal or informal schooling and to normal recreational activities.

- Adults and adolescents are able to participate in concrete, purposeful, common interest activities, such as emergency relief activities.

- Isolated persons, such as separated or orphaned children, child combatants, widows and widowers, older people or others without their families, have access to activities that facilitate their inclusion in social networks.

---

[1] Social and psychological indicators are discussed separately. The term 'social intervention' is used for those activities that primarily aim to have social effects. The term 'psychological intervention' is used for interventions that primarily aim to have a psychological (or psychiatric) effect. It is acknowledged that social interventions have secondary psychological effects and that psychological interventions have secondary social effects, as the term 'psychosocial' suggests.

Health

- When necessary, a tracing service is established to reunite people and families.

- Where people are displaced, shelter is organised with the aim of keeping family members and communities together.

- The community is consulted regarding decisions on where to locate religious places, schools, water points and sanitation facilities. The design of settlements for displaced people includes recreational and cultural space (see Shelter and settlement standards 1-2, pages 211-218).

Key psychological and psychiatric intervention indicators
(to be read in conjunction with the guidance notes)

- Individuals experiencing acute mental distress after exposure to traumatic stressors have access to psychological first aid at health service facilities and in the community (see guidance note 3).

- Care for urgent psychiatric complaints is available through the primary health care system. Essential psychiatric medications, consistent with the essential drug list, are available at primary care facilities (see guidance note 4).

- Individuals with pre-existing psychiatric disorders continue to receive relevant treatment, and harmful, sudden discontinuation of medications is avoided. Basic needs of patients in custodial psychiatric hospitals are addressed.

- If the disaster becomes protracted, plans are initiated to provide a more comprehensive range of community-based psychological interventions for the post-disaster phase (see guidance note 5).

Guidance notes

1. *Information:* access to information is not only a human right but it also reduces unnecessary public anxiety and distress. Information should be provided on the nature and scale of the disaster and on efforts to establish physical safety for the population. Moreover, the population should be informed on the specific types of relief activities being undertaken by the government, local authorities and aid organisations, and their location.

Information should be disseminated according to principles of risk communication i.e. it should be uncomplicated (understandable to local 12-year-olds) and empathic (showing understanding of the situation of the disaster survivor).

2. **Burials:** families should have the option to see the body of a loved one to say goodbye, when culturally appropriate. Unceremonious disposal of bodies of the deceased should be avoided (see Health systems and infrastructure standard 5, guidance note 8 on page 269).

3. **Psychological first aid:** whether among the general population or among aid workers, acute distress following exposure to traumatic stressors is best managed following the principles of psychological first aid. This entails basic, non-intrusive pragmatic care with a focus on listening but not forcing talk; assessing needs and ensuring that basic needs are met; encouraging but not forcing company from significant others; and protecting from further harm. This type of first aid can be taught quickly to both volunteers and professionals. Health workers are cautioned to avoid widespread prescription of benzodiazepines because of the risk of dependence.

4. **Care for urgent psychiatric complaints:** psychiatric conditions requiring urgent care include dangerousness to self or others, psychoses, severe depression and mania.

5. **Community-based psychological interventions:** interventions should be based on an assessment of existing services and an understanding of the socio-cultural context. They should include use of functional, cultural coping mechanisms of individuals and communities to help them regain control over their circumstances. Collaboration with community leaders and indigenous healers is recommended when feasible. Community-based self-help groups should be encouraged. Community workers should be trained and supervised to assist health workers with heavy caseloads and to conduct outreach activities to facilitate care for vulnerable and minority groups.

Health

Control of non-communicable diseases standard 4: chronic diseases

For populations in which chronic diseases are responsible for a large proportion of mortality, people have access to essential therapies to prevent death.

Key indicators (to be read in conjunction with the guidance notes)

- A specific agency (or agencies) is designated to coordinate programmes for individuals with chronic diseases for which an acute cessation of therapy is likely to result in death (see guidance note 1).

- Individuals with such chronic diseases are actively identified and registered.

- Medications for the routine, ongoing management of chronic diseases are available through the primary health care system, provided that these medications are specified on the essential drug list.

Guidance note

1. *Chronic diseases:* no generally accepted guidance on the management of chronic diseases during disasters has previously been established. During recent complex emergencies in countries where patients had previously had access to ongoing treatment for chronic diseases, priority was given to those conditions for which an acute cessation of therapy was likely to result in death, including dialysis-dependent chronic renal failure, insulin-dependent diabetes and certain childhood cancers. These were not new programmes, but a continuation of ongoing life-saving therapy. In future disasters, programmes for other chronic diseases may also be relevant. It is not appropriate to introduce new therapeutic regimens or programmes for the management of chronic diseases during the relief effort if the population did not have access to these therapies prior to the disaster. The routine, ongoing management of stable chronic diseases should be available through the primary health care system, using medications from the essential drug list.

Appendix 1

Health Services Assessment Checklist

Preparation

● Obtain available information on the disaster-affected population and resources from host country and international sources.

● Obtain available maps and aerial photographs.

● Obtain demographic and health data from host country and international sources.

Security and access

● Determine the existence of ongoing natural or human-generated hazards.

● Determine the overall security situation, including the presence of armed forces or militias.

● Determine the access that humanitarian agencies have to the affected population.

Demographics and social structure

● Determine the total disaster-affected population and proportion of children under five years old.

● Determine age and sex breakdown of the population.

● Identify groups at increased risk, e.g. women, children, older people, disabled people, people living with HIV/AIDS, members of certain ethnic or social groups.

● Determine the average household size and estimates of female- and child-headed households.

● Determine the existing social structure, including positions of authority/influence and the role of women.

Background health information

● Identify pre-existing health problems and priorities in the disaster-affected area prior to the disaster. Ascertain local disease epidemiology.

● Identify pre-existing health problems and priorities in the country of origin if refugees are involved. Ascertain disease epidemiology in the country of origin.

● Identify existing risks to health, e.g. potential epidemic diseases.

● Identify previous sources of health care.

● Determine the strengths and coverage of local public health programmes in refugees' country of origin.

Mortality rates

● Calculate the crude mortality rate (CMR).

● Calculate the under-5 mortality rate (U5MR: age-specific mortality rate for children under 5 years of age).

● Calculate cause-specific mortality rates.

Morbidity rates

● Determine incidence rates of major diseases that have public health importance.

● Determine age- and sex-specific incidence rates of major diseases where possible.

Available resources

● Determine the capacity of and the response by the Ministry of Health of the country or countries affected by the disaster.

● Determine the status of national health facilities, including total number, classification and levels of care provided, physical status, functional status and access.

● Determine the numbers and skills of available health staff.

● Determine the capacity and functional status of existing public health programmes, e.g. Expanded Programme on Immunisation (EPI), maternal and child health services.

● Determine the availability of standardised protocols, essential drugs, supplies and equipment.

● Determine the status of existing referral systems.

● Determine the status of the existing health information system (HIS).

● Determine the capacity of existing logistics systems, especially as they relate to procurement, distribution and storage of essential drugs, vaccines and medical supplies.

Consider data from other relevant sectors

● Nutritional status

● Environmental conditions

● Food and food security.

Health

Appendix 2 Sample Weekly Surveillance Reporting Forms

Mortality Surveillance Form 1*

Site ....

Date from Monday ....To Sunday: ....

Total population at beginning of this week: ....

Births this week: ....Deaths this week:..................................

Arrivals this week (if applicable):................................Departures this week: ....

Total population at end of week:................................Total under 5 years population: ....

	0-4 yrs		5+ yrs		Total
	male	female	male	female	
Immediate cause					
Acute lower resp. infection					
Cholera (suspected)					
Diarrhoea – bloody					
Diarrhoea – watery					
Injury – non-accidental					
Malaria					
Maternal death – direct					
Measles					
Meningitis (suspected)					
Neonatal (0-28 days)					
Other					
Unknown					
Total by age and sex					
Underlying cause					
AIDS (suspected)					
Malnutrition					
Maternal death – indirect					
Other					
Total by age and sex					

* This form is used when there are many deaths and therefore more detailed information on individual deaths cannot be collected due to time limitations.
 – Frequency of reporting (i.e. daily or weekly) depends upon the number of deaths.
 – Other causes of mortality can be added according to the context and epidemiological pattern.
 – Ages can be further disaggregated (0-11 mths, 1-4 yrs, 5-14 yrs, 15-49 yrs, 50-59 yrs, 60+ yrs) as feasible.
 – Deaths should not be reported solely from site health facilities, but should include reports from site and religious leaders, community workers, women's groups and referral hospitals.
 – Whenever possible, case definitions should be put on back of form.

Mortality Surveillance Form 2*

Site:..

Date from Monday........................To Sunday:........................

Total population at beginning of this week:........................

Births this week: ....Deaths this week:........................

Arrivals this week (if applicable):........................Departures this week:........................

Total population at end of week:........................Total under 5 years population:........................

No	Sex (m, f)	Age (days=d mths=m yrs=y)	Acute lower resp. infection	Cholera (suspected)	Diarrhoea – bloody	Diarrhoea – watery	Injury – non-accidental	Malaria	Maternal death – direct	Measles	Meningitis (suspected)	Neonatal (0-28 days)	Other (specify)	Unknown	AIDS (suspected)	Malnutrition	Maternal death – indirect	Other (specify)	Date (dd/mm /yy)	Location in site (e.g. block no.)	Died in hospital or at home

Direct Cause of Death | *Underlying Causes*

1
2
3
4
5
6
7
8
9
10

* This form is used when there is enough time to record data on individual deaths; it allows analysis by age, outbreak investigation by location and facility utilisation rates.

– Frequency of reporting (i.e. daily or weekly) depends upon the number of deaths.

– Other causes of death can be added as fits the situation.

– Deaths should not be reported solely from site health facilities, but should include reports from site and religious leaders, community workers, women's groups and referral hospitals

– Whenever possible, case definitions should be put on back of form.

Weekly Morbidity Surveillance Reporting Form

Site ....

Date from Monday: .... To Sunday: ....

Total population at beginning of this week: ....

Births this week: .... Deaths this week: ....

Arrivals this week (if applicable): .... Departures this week: ....

Total population at end of week: .... Total under 5 years population: ....

Morbidity	Under 5 years (new cases)			5 years and over (new cases)			Total	Repeat cases
Diagnosis*	Male	Female	Total	Male	Female	Total	new cases	Total
Acute respiratory infections**								
AIDS (suspected)								
Anaemia								
Cholera (suspected)								
Diarrhoea – bloody								
Diarrhoea – watery								
Eye diseases								
Malaria								
Malnutrition								
Measles								
Meningitis (suspected)								
Injuries – accidental								
Injuries – non-accidental								
Sexually transmitted infections								
Genital ulcer disease								
Male urethral discharge								
Vaginal discharge								
Lower abdominal pain								
Scabies								
Skin diseases (excluding scabies)								
Worms								
Others								
Unknown								
Total								

* More than one diagnosis is possible; diseases can be removed or added as fits the current situation.

** Acute respiratory tract infections: in some countries, this category may be divided into upper and lower tract infections.

– Causes of morbidity can be added or subtracted according to context and epidemiological pattern.

– Ages can be further disaggregated (0-11 mths, 1-4 yrs, 5-14 yrs, 15-49 yrs, 50-59 yrs, 60+ yrs) as feasible.

Visits to	Under 5 years			5 years and over			Total	
health facility	Male	Female	Total	Male	Female	Total	Male	Female
Total visits								

Utilisation rate: Number of visits per person per year to health facility = total number of visits in 1 week / total population x 52 weeks

– Ages can be further disaggregated (0-11 mths, 1-4 yrs, 5-14 yrs, 15-49 yrs, 50-59 yrs, 60+ yrs) as feasible.

Number of consultations per clinician: Number of total visits (new and repeat) / FTE clinician in health facility/ number of days health facility functioning per week.

Appendix 3

Formulas for Calculating Rates of Mortality and Morbidity

Crude Mortality Rate (CMR)

- *Definition:* The rate of death in the entire population, including both sexes and all ages. The CMR can be expressed with different standard population denominators and for different time periods, e.g. deaths per 1,000 population per month or deaths per 1,000 population per year.

- *Formula most commonly used during disasters:*

$$\frac{\text{Total number of deaths during time period}}{\text{Total population}} \times \frac{10{,}000 \text{ persons}}{\text{No. days in time period}}$$

= deaths/10,000 persons/day

Under-5 Mortality Rate (U5MR)

- *Definition:* The rate of death among children below 5 years of age in the population.

- *Formula most commonly used during disasters* (age-specific mortality rate for children less than 5 years):

$$\frac{\text{Total number of deaths in children} <5 \text{ years during time period}}{\text{Total number of children} <5 \text{ years}} \times \frac{10{,}000 \text{ persons}}{\text{No. days in time period}}$$

= deaths/10,000 /day

Incidence Rate

● *Definition:* The number of new cases of a disease that occur during a specified period of time in a population at risk of developing the disease.

● *Formula most commonly used during disasters:*

Number of new cases due to specific   1,000 persons
disease in time period

Population at risk of developing disease   x   No. months in time period

= new cases due to specific disease/1,000/month

Case Fatality Rate (CFR)

● *Definition:* The number of people who die of a disease divided by the number of people who have the disease.

● *Formula:*

Number of people dying from disease during time period

People who have the disease during time period   x   100   = x%

Health Facility Utilisation Rate

● *Definition:* The number of out-patient visits per person per year. Whenever possible, a distinction should be drawn between new and old visits, and new visits should be used to calculate this rate. However, it is often difficult to differentiate between new and old visits, so they are frequently combined as total visits during a disaster.

● *Formula:*

Total number of visits in one week

     Total population   x   52 weeks

= visits/person/year

Number of Consultations per Clinician per Day

● *Definition:* Average number of total consultations (new and repeat cases) seen by each clinician per day.

● *Formula:*

Total number of consultations (new and repeat) ÷ Number of days health
Number FTE* clinicians in health facility   facility open per week

* FTE ('full-time equivalent') refers to the equivalent number of clinicians working in a health facility. For example, if there are six clinicians working in the out-patient department but two of them work half-time, then the number of FTE clinicians = 4 full-time staff + 2 half-time staff = 5 FTE clinicians.

Appendix 4

References

Thanks to the Forced Migration Online programme of the Refugee Studies Centre at the University of Oxford, many of these documents have received copyright permission and are posted on a special Sphere link at: http://www.forcedmigration.org

International legal instruments

The Right to the Highest Attainable Standard of Health (Article 12 of the International Covenant on Economic, Social and Cultural Rights), CESCR General comment 14, 11 August 2000, U.N. Doc. E/C.12/2000/4. Committee on Economic, Social and Cultural Rights.

Baccino-Astrada, A (1982), *Manual on the Rights and Duties of Medical Personnel in Armed Conflicts*. ICRC. Geneva.

Mann, J, Gruskin, S, Grodin, M, Annas, G (eds.) (1999), *Health and Human Rights: A Reader*. Routledge.

WHO (2002), *25 Questions and Answers on Health and Human Rights*. World Health Organisation. http://www.who.int/hhr

Health Systems and Infrastructure

Beaglehole, R, Bonita, R, Kjellstrom, T (1993), *Basic Epidemiology*. World Health Organisation. Geneva.

Management Sciences for Health (1997), *Managing Drug Supply (Second Edition)*. Kumarian Press. Bloomfield, CT.

Médecins Sans Frontières (1993), *Clinical Guidelines. Diagnostic and Treatment Manual*. Médecins Sans Frontières. Paris.

Médecins Sans Frontières (1997), *Refugee Health. An Approach to Emergency Situations*. Macmillan. London.

Noji, E (ed.) (1997), *The Public Health Consequences of Disasters*. Oxford University Press. New York.

Perrin, P (1996), *Handbook on War and Public Health*. International Committee of the Red Cross. Geneva.

UNHCR/WHO (1996), *Guidelines for Drug Donations*. World Health Organisation and United Nations High Commissioner for Refugees. Geneva.

UNHCR (2001), *Health, Food, and Nutrition Toolkit: Tools and Reference Materials to Manage and Evaluate Health, Food and Nutrition Programmes* (CD-ROM). United Nations High Commissioner for Refugees. Geneva.

WHO/PAHO (2001), *Health Library for Disasters* (CD-ROM). World Health Organisation/Pan-American Health Organization. Geneva.

WHO (1998), *The New Emergency Health Kit 1998*. World Health Organisation. Geneva.

WHO (1999), *Rapid Health Assessment Protocols for Emergencies*. World Health Organisation. Geneva.

WHO (1994), *Health Laboratory Facilities in Emergencies and Disaster Situations*. World Health Organisation. Geneva.

Control of Communicable Diseases

Chin, J (2000), *Control of Communicable Diseases Manual (17th Edition)*. American Public Health Association. Washington, DC.

Cook, GC, Zumla, AI, Weir, J (2003), *Manson's Tropical Diseases*. WB Saunders.

Inter-Agency Standing Committee Reference Group on HIV/AIDS in Emergency Settings (2003), *Guidelines for HIV Interventions in Emergency Settings*. UNAIDS. Geneva (in press). (This document will replace UNAIDS, 1998, *Guidelines for HIV Interventions In Emergency Settings*).

International Rescue Committee (2003), *Protecting the Future: HIV Prevention, Care and Support Among Displaced and War-Affected Populations*. Kumarian Press. Bloomfield, CT.

Pasteur Institute: http://www.pasteur.fr

Health

UNAIDS: http://www.unaids.org

WHO (1993), *Guidelines for Cholera Control*. World Health Organisation. Geneva.

WHO (2002), *Guidelines for the Collection of Clinical Specimens During Field Investigation of Outbreaks*. World Health Organisation. Geneva.

WHO (1997), *Immunisation in Practice. A Guide for Health Workers Who Give Vaccines*. Macmillan. London.

WHO (2003), *Malaria Control in Complex Emergencies: An Interagency Handbook*. World Health Organisation. Geneva (in press).

WHO (1993), *The Management and Prevention of Diarrhoea: Practical Guidelines*. World Health Organisation. Geneva.

Control of Non-Communicable Diseases

Injury

Hayward-Karlsson, J, Jeffrey, S, Kerr, A et al (1998), *Hospitals for War-Wounded: A Practical Guide for Setting Up and Running a Surgical Hospital in an Area of Armed Conflict*. International Committee of the Red Cross. Geneva.

Médecins Sans Frontières (1989), *Minor Surgical Procedures in Remote Areas*. Médecins Sans Frontières. Paris.

PAHO-OPS (1995), *Establishing a Mass Casualty Management System*. Pan-American Health Organization. Geneva.

WHO (1991), *Surgery at the District Hospital: Obstetrics, Gynaecology, Orthopaedics and Traumatology*. World Health Organisation. Geneva.

Reproductive health

Reproductive Health for Refugees Consortium (1997), *Refugee Reproductive Health Needs Assessment Field Tools*. RHR Consortium.

Interagency Working Group (1999), *An Inter-Agency Field Manual for Reproductive Health in Refugee Situations*. United Nations High Commissioner for Refugees. Geneva.

UNFPA: http://www.unfpa.org

UNFPA (2001), *The Reproductive Health Kit for Emergency Situations (Second Edition)*. UNFPA.

UNHCR (2003), *Sexual and Gender-Based Violence Against Refugees, Returnees and Internally Displaced Persons: Guidelines for Prevention and Response*. Draft for field-testing, 8 July 2002. (This document will replace the UNHCR 1995 *Sexual Violence Against Refugees: Guidelines on Prevention and Response*.)

WHO (2001), *Clinical Management of Survivors of Rape*. World Health Organisation. Geneva.

Mental and social aspects of health

National Institute of Mental Health (2002), *Mental Health and Mass Violence: Evidence-Based Early Psychological Interventions for Victims/Survivors of Mass Violence. A Workshop to Reach Consensus on Best Practices*. (NIH Publication No. 02-5138). US Government Printing Office. Washington, DC. http://www.nimh.nih.gov

WHO (2003), *Mental Health in Emergencies: Mental and Social Aspects of Populations Exposed to Extreme Stressors*. World Health Organisation. Geneva.

WHO/UNHCR (1996), *Mental Health of Refugees*. World Health Organisation. Geneva. http://whqlibdoc.who.int

Chronic diseases

Ahya, SN, Flood, K, Paranjothi, S et al (eds.), *The Washington Manual of Medical Therapeutics (30th Edition)*. Lippincott Williams & Wilkins Publishers.

Braunwald, E, Fauci, AS, Kasper, DL et al (eds.) (2001), *Harrison's Principles of Internal Medicine (15th Edition)*. McGraw Hill Professional. New York.

Tierny, LM, McPhee, SJ, Papadakis, MA (eds.), *Current Medical Diagnosis and Treatment 2003 (42nd Edition)*. McGraw-Hill/Appleton & Lange. New York.

Health

Websites

Centers for Disease Control and Prevention: http://www.cdc.gov

Centre for Research on the Epidemiology of Disasters: http://www.cred.be

International Committee of the Red Cross: http://www.icrc.org

International Federation of the Red Cross and Red Crescent Societies: http://www.ifrc.org

Pan-American Health Organization: http://www.paho.org

United Nations High Commissioner for Refugees: http://www.unhcr.ch

UNICEF: http://www.unicef.org

World Health Organisation: http://www.who.int

Notes

Notes

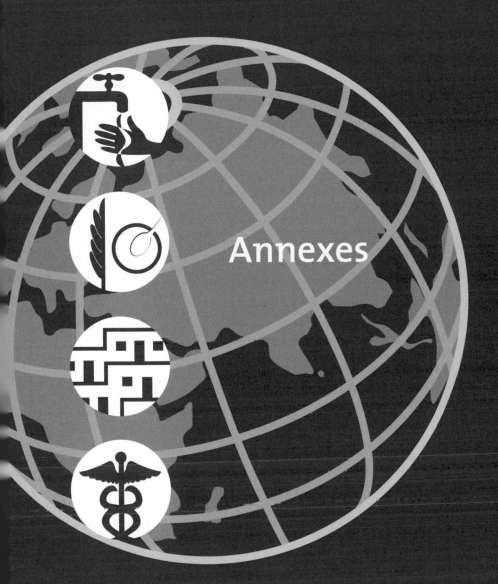

Annexes

1 Legal Instruments Underpinning the Sphere Handbook

The following instruments inform the Humanitarian Charter and the Minimum Standards in Disaster Response:

Universal Declaration of Human Rights 1948.

International Covenant on Civil and Political Rights 1966.

International Covenant on Economic, Social and Cultural Rights 1966.

International Convention on the Elimination of All Forms of Racial Discrimination 1969.

The four Geneva Conventions of 1949 and their two Additional Protocols of 1977.

Convention relating to the Status of Refugees 1951 and the Protocol relating to the Status of Refugees 1967.

Convention against Torture and Other Cruel, Inhuman or Degrading Treatment or Punishment 1984.

Convention on the Prevention and Punishment of the Crime of Genocide 1948.

Convention on the Rights of the Child 1989.

Convention on the Elimination of All Forms of Discrimination Against Women 1979.

Convention relating to the Status of Stateless Persons 1960.

Guiding Principles on Internal Displacement 1998.

2 The Code of Conduct for the International Red Cross and Red Crescent Movement and Non-Governmental Organisations (NGOs) in Disaster Relief

Prepared jointly by the International Federation of Red Cross and Red Crescent Societies and the ICRC[1]

Purpose

This Code of Conduct seeks to guard our standards of behaviour. It is not about operational details, such as how one should calculate food rations or set up a refugee camp. Rather, it seeks to maintain the high standards of independence, effectiveness and impact to which disaster response NGOs and the International Red Cross and Red Crescent Movement aspires. It is a voluntary code, enforced by the will of the organisation accepting it to maintain the standards laid down in the Code.

In the event of armed conflict, the present Code of Conduct will be interpreted and applied in conformity with international humanitarian law.

Note

1. Sponsored by: Caritas Internationalis*, Catholic Relief Services*, The International Federation of Red Cross and Red Crescent Societies*, International Save the Children Alliance*, Lutheran World Federation*, Oxfam*, The World Council of Churches*, The International Committee of the Red Cross (* members of the Steering Committee for Humanitarian Response).

The Code of Conduct is presented first. Attached to it are three annexes, describing the working environment that we would like to see created by Host Governments, Donor Governments and Inter-Governmental Organisations in order to facilitate the effective delivery of humanitarian assistance.

Definitions

NGOs: NGOs (Non-Governmental Organisations) refers here to organisations, both national and international, which are constituted separately from the government of the country in which they are founded.

NGHAs: For the purposes of this text, the term Non-Governmental Humanitarian Agencies (NGHAs) has been coined to encompass the components of the International Red Cross and Red Crescent Movement – The International Committee of the Red Cross, The International Federation of Red Cross and Red Crescent Societies and its member National Societies – and the NGOs as defined above. This code refers specifically to those NGHAs who are involved in disaster response.

IGOs: IGOs (Inter-Governmental Organisations) refers to organisations constituted by two or more governments. It thus includes all United Nations Agencies and regional organisations.

Disasters: A disaster is a calamitous event resulting in loss of life, great human suffering and distress, and large-scale material damage.

The Code of Conduct

Principles of Conduct for The International Red Cross and Red Crescent Movement and NGOs in Disaster Response Programmes

1 The humanitarian imperative comes first

The right to receive humanitarian assistance, and to offer it, is a fundamental humanitarian principle which should be enjoyed by all citizens of all countries. As members of the international community, we recognise our obligation to provide humanitarian assistance wherever it is needed. Hence the need for unimpeded access to affected populations is of fundamental importance in exercising that responsibility. The prime motivation of our response to disaster is to alleviate human suffering amongst those least able to withstand the stress caused by disaster. When we give humanitarian aid it is not a partisan or political act and should not be viewed as such.

2 Aid is given regardless of the race, creed or nationality of the recipients and without adverse distinction of any kind. Aid priorities are calculated on the basis of need alone

Wherever possible, we will base the provision of relief aid upon a thorough assessment of the needs of the disaster victims and the local capacities already in place to meet those needs. Within the entirety of our programmes, we will reflect considerations of proportionality. Human suffering must be alleviated whenever it is found; life is as precious in one part of a country as another. Thus, our provision of aid will reflect the degree of suffering it seeks to alleviate. In implementing this approach, we recognise the crucial role played by women in disaster-prone communities and will ensure that this role is supported, not diminished, by our aid programmes. The implementation of such a universal, impartial and independent policy, can only be effective if we and our partners have access to the necessary resources to provide for such equitable relief, and have equal access to all disaster victims.

3 Aid will not be used to further a particular political or religious standpoint

Humanitarian aid will be given according to the need of individuals, families and communities. Notwithstanding the right of NGHAs to espouse particular political or religious opinions, we affirm that assistance will not be dependent on the adherence of the recipients to those opinions. We will not tie the promise, delivery or distribution of assistance to the embracing or acceptance of a particular political or religious creed.

4 We shall endeavour not to act as instruments of government foreign policy

NGHAs are agencies which act independently from governments. We therefore formulate our own policies and implementation strategies and do not seek to implement the policy of any government, except in so far as it coincides with our own independent policy. We will never knowingly – or through negligence – allow ourselves, or our employees, to be used to gather information of a political, military or economically sensitive nature for governments or other bodies that may serve purposes other than those which are strictly humanitarian, nor will we act as instruments of foreign policy of donor governments. We will use the assistance we receive to respond to needs and this assistance should not be driven by the need to dispose of donor commodity surpluses, nor by the political interest of any particular donor. We value and promote the voluntary giving of labour and finances by concerned individuals to support our work and recognise the independence of action promoted by such voluntary motivation. In order to protect our independence we will seek to avoid dependence upon a single funding source.

5 We shall respect culture and custom

We will endeavour to respect the culture, structures and customs of the communities and countries we are working in.

6 We shall attempt to build disaster response on local capacities

All people and communities – even in disaster – possess capacities as well as vulnerabilities. Where possible, we will strengthen these capacities by employing local staff, purchasing local materials and trading with local companies. Where possible, we will work through local NGHAs as partners in planning and implementation, and co-operate with local government structures where appropriate. We will place a high priority on the proper co-ordination of our emergency responses. This is best done within the countries concerned by those most directly involved in the relief operations, and should include representatives of the relevant UN bodies.

7 Ways shall be found to involve programme beneficiaries in the management of relief aid

Disaster response assistance should never be imposed upon the beneficiaries. Effective relief and lasting rehabilitation can best be achieved where the intended beneficiaries are involved in the design, management and implementation of the assistance programme. We will strive to achieve full community participation in our relief and rehabilitation programmes.

8 Relief aid must strive to reduce future vulnerabilities to disaster as well as meeting basic needs

All relief actions affect the prospects for long-term development, either in a positive or a negative fashion. Recognising this, we will strive to implement relief programmes which actively reduce the beneficiaries' vulnerability to future disasters and help create sustainable lifestyles. We will pay particular attention to environmental concerns in the design and management of relief programmes. We will also endeavour to minimise the negative impact of humanitarian assistance, seeking to avoid long-term beneficiary dependence upon external aid.

9 We hold ourselves accountable to both those we seek to assist and those from whom we accept resources

We often act as an institutional link in the partnership between those who wish to assist and those who need assistance during disasters. We therefore hold ourselves accountable to both constituencies. All our dealings with donors and beneficiaries shall reflect an attitude of openness and transparency. We recognise the need to report on our activities, both from a financial perspective and the perspective of effectiveness. We recognise the obligation to ensure appropriate monitoring of aid distributions and to carry out regular assessments of the impact of disaster assistance. We will also seek to report, in an open fashion, upon the impact of our work, and the factors limiting or enhancing that impact. Our programmes will be based upon high standards of professionalism and expertise in order to minimise the wasting of valuable resources.

10 In our information, publicity and advertising activities, we shall recognise disaster victims as dignified humans, not hopeless objects

Respect for the disaster victim as an equal partner in action should never be lost. In our public information we shall portray an objective image of the disaster situation where the capacities and aspirations of disaster victims are highlighted, and not just their vulnerabilities and fears. While we will cooperate with the media in order to enhance public response, we will not allow external or internal demands for publicity to take precedence over the principle of maximising overall relief assistance. We will avoid competing with other disaster response agencies for media coverage in situations where such coverage may be to the detriment of the service provided to the beneficiaries or to the security of our staff or the beneficiaries.

The Working Environment

Having agreed unilaterally to strive to abide by the Code laid out above, we present below some indicative guidelines which describe the working environment we would like to see created by donor governments, host governments and the inter-governmental organisations – principally the agencies of the United Nations – in order to facilitate the effective participation of NGHAs in disaster response.

These guidelines are presented for guidance. They are not legally binding, nor do we expect governments and IGOs to indicate their acceptance of the guidelines through the signature of any document, although this may be a goal to work to in the future. They are presented in a spirit of openness and cooperation so that our partners will become aware of the ideal relationship we would seek with them.

Annex I : Recommendations to the governments of disaster-affected countries

1 Governments should recognise and respect the independent, humanitarian and impartial actions of NGHAs

NGHAs are independent bodies. This independence and impartiality should be respected by host governments.

2 Host governments should facilitate rapid access to disaster victims for NGHAs

If NGHAs are to act in full compliance with their humanitarian principles, they should be granted rapid and impartial access to disaster victims, for the purpose of delivering humanitarian assistance. It is the duty of the host government, as part of the exercising of sovereign responsibility, not to block such assistance, and to accept the impartial and apolitical action of NGHAs. Host governments should facilitate the rapid entry of relief staff, particularly by waiving requirements for transit, entry and exit visas, or arranging that these are rapidly granted. Governments should grant over-flight permission and landing rights for aircraft transporting international relief supplies and personnel, for the duration of the emergency relief phase.

3 Governments should facilitate the timely flow of relief goods and information during disasters

Relief supplies and equipment are brought into a country solely for the purpose of alleviating human suffering, not for commercial benefit or gain. Such supplies should normally be allowed free and unrestricted passage and should not be subject to requirements for consular certificates of origin or invoices, import and/or export licences or other restrictions, or to importation taxation, landing fees or port charges.

The temporary importation of necessary relief equipment, including vehicles, light aircraft and telecommunications equipment, should be facilitated by the receiving host government through the temporary waiving of licence or registration restrictions. Equally, governments should not restrict the re-exportation of relief equipment at the end of a relief operation.

To facilitate disaster communications, host governments are encouraged to designate certain radio frequencies, which relief organisations may use in-country and for international communications for the purpose of disaster communications, and to make such frequencies known to the disaster response community prior to the disaster. They should authorise relief personnel to utilise all means of communication required for their relief operations.

4 Governments should seek to provide a coordinated disaster information and planning service

The overall planning and coordination of relief efforts is ultimately the responsibility of the host government. Planning and coordination can be greatly enhanced if NGHAs are provided with information on relief needs and government systems for planning and implementing relief efforts as well as information on potential security risks they may encounter. Governments are urged to provide such information to NGHAs.

To facilitate effective coordination and the efficient utilisation of relief efforts, host governments are urged to designate, prior to disaster, a single point-of-contact for incoming NGHAs to liaise with the national authorities.

5 Disaster relief in the event of armed conflict

In the event of armed conflict, relief actions are governed by the relevant provisions of international humanitarian law.

Annex II : Recommendations to donor governments

1 Donor governments should recognise and respect the independent, humanitarian and impartial actions of NGHAs

NGHAs are independent bodies whose independence and impartiality should be respected by donor governments. Donor governments should not use NGHAs to further any political or ideological aim.

2 Donor governments should provide funding with a guarantee of operational independence

NGHAs accept funding and material assistance from donor governments in the same spirit as they render it to disaster victims; one of humanity and independence of action. The implementation of relief actions is ultimately the responsibility of the NGHA and will be carried out according to the policies of that NGHA.

3 Donor governments should use their good offices to assist NGHAs in obtaining access to disaster victims

Donor governments should recognise the importance of accepting a level of responsibility for the security and freedom of access of NGHA staff to disaster sites. They should be prepared to exercise diplomacy with host governments on such issues if necessary.

Annex III : Recommendations to inter-governmental organisations

1 IGOs should recognise NGHAs, local and foreign, as valuable partners

NGHAs are willing to work with UN and other inter-governmental agencies to effect better disaster response. They do so in a spirit of partnership which respects the integrity and independence of all partners. Inter-governmental agencies must respect the independence and impartiality of the NGHAs. NGHAs should be consulted by UN agencies in the preparation of relief plans.

2 IGOs should assist host governments in providing an overall coordinating framework for international and local disaster relief

NGHAs do not usually have the mandate to provide the overall coordinating framework for disasters which require an international response. This responsibility falls to the host government and the relevant United Nations authorities. They are urged to provide this service in a timely and effective manner to serve the affected state and the national and international disaster response community. In any case, NGHAs should make all efforts to ensure the effective co-ordination of their own services.

In the event of armed conflict, relief actions are governed by the relevant provisions of international humanitarian law.

3 IGOs should extend security protection provided for UN organisations to NGHAs

Where security services are provided for inter-governmental organisations, this service should be extended to their operational NGHA partners where it is so requested.

4 IGOs should provide NGHAs with the same access to relevant information as is granted to UN organisations

IGOs are urged to share all information, pertinent to the implementation of effective disaster response, with their operational NGHA partners.

3 Acknowledgements

Sphere Project Staff Team

Project Manager: Nan Buzard

Training Manager: Sean Lowrie

Project Officer: Veronica Foubert

Project Senior Assistant: Elly Proudlock

Sphere Project Management Committee

InterAction ◊ Save the Children Alliance ◊ CARE International ◊ The Lutheran World Federation (LWF/ACT) ◊ Voluntary Organisations in Cooperation in Emergencies (VOICE) ◊ Mercy Corps ◊ Action by Churches Together (ACT) ◊ Oxfam GB ◊ Steering Committee for Humanitarian Response ◊ International Committee of the Red Cross ◊ International Federation of the Red Cross and Red Crescent Societies ◊ International Council of Voluntary Agencies (ICVA) ◊ Caritas Internationalis

Donors

In addition to contributions by the member organisations listed above, funding for the Sphere Project was provided by:

The Australian Agency for International Development (AusAID) ◊ The Belgian Ministry of Development ◊ The Canadian International Development Agency (CIDA) ◊ Caritas Spain ◊ Danish International Development Assistance (DANIDA) ◊ The Disaster Emergency Committee (DEC) ◊ The Finnish Government Development Agency (FINIDA) ◊ The European Community Humanitarian Office (ECHO) ◊ The Ford Foundation ◊ Development Cooperation Ireland (DCI) ◊ The Netherlands Ministry of Foreign Affairs Humanitarian Aid Division ◊ The New Zealand Ministry of Foreign Affairs and Trade ◊ The Foreign Ministry of Norway ◊ The Swedish International Development Cooperation Agency (Sida) ◊ The Swiss Agency for Development and Cooperation (SDC) ◊ The United Nations Children's Fund (UNICEF) ◊ The United Kingdom Department for International Development (DFID)

◊ The United States Department of State Bureau of Refugees and Migration (US-PRM) ◊ The United States Agency for International Development Office of Foreign Disaster Assistance (US-OFDA)

Technical Chapter Focal Points

Water, Sanitation and Hygiene Promotion: Andy Bastable, Oxfam GB

Food Security: Helen Young, Tufts University

Nutrition: Anna Taylor, Save the Children UK

Food Aid: John Solomon, CARE USA and NM Prusty, CARE India

Shelter, Settlement and Non-Food Items: Graham Saunders, Catholic Relief Services

Health Services: Richard J Brennan, International Rescue Committee

Common Standards: in addition to the focal points and cross-cutters, the following contributed to this chapter: Jock Baker, Nan Buzard, Jim Good, Maurice Henderson, Susanne Jaspars, Charles Kelly, Ron Ockwell, Sylvie Robert

Cross-Cutting Issue Coordinators

Children: Jane Gibreel, Save the Children UK

Older People: Nadia Saim, HelpAge International

Disabled People: Beverly Ashton, Action on Disability and Development

Gender: Rosemarie McNairn, Oxfam GB

Protection: Ed Schenkenberg, ICVA

HIV/AIDS: Paul Spiegel, UNHCR/CDC

Environment: Mario Pareja, CARE/UNHCR

Handbook Revision Meetings Facilitator: Isobel McConnan

Editor: David Wilson

Many thanks

The Sphere standards and indicators are built on the collective experience and good practice of individuals and agencies active in many different areas of humanitarian work. As with the first edition of the handbook, this revision would have been impossible to undertake without the collaboration of many people around the world. In all, thousands of individuals in 80 countries, representing more than 400 agencies, participated in the process, volunteering significant time and expertise.

The emphasis throughout the development of the handbook was on consultation, with networks of peer review groups involved at all stages of the process. In particular, aid workers based in countries where disasters are a regular occurrence, and who are using the handbook in the field, provided detailed feedback. The result does not represent the view of any one agency. Rather, it represents the active and deliberate will of the humanitarian community to join together to share an extensive body of experience and learning, in an effort to improve the quality and accountability of humanitarian action. Thanks to all who helped to make this a reality.

While Sphere gratefully acknowledges the contribution of everyone who has participated, both in the original handbook and in this revision, it would take more than 40 pages to list individual names and space does not allow this. However, a full listing of all agencies and individuals who have contributed can be found on the Sphere website at: http://www.sphereproject.org

4 Acronyms

ACC/SCN:
> United Nations Administrative Committee on Coordination/Subcommittee on Nutrition

ACT:
> Action by Churches Together

ALNAP:
> Active Learning Network for Accountability in Practice

CDC:
> Centers for Disease Control and Prevention

DAC:
> Development Assistance Committee (OECD)

FAO:
> Food and Agriculture Organisation

IAPSO:
> Inter-Agency Procurement Services Office (UNDP)

ICRC:
> International Committee of the Red Cross

INFCD:
> International Nutrition Foundation for Developing Countries

LWF:
> The Lutheran World Federation

MISP:
> Minimum Initial Service Package

MSF:
> Médecins Sans Frontières

NCHS:
> National Centre for Health Statistics

NGO:
> Non-governmental organisation

OCHA:
   UN Office for the Coordination of Humanitarian Affairs

OECD:
   Organisation for Economic Cooperation and Development

OFDA:
   Office of Foreign Disaster Assistance (USAID)

PTSS:
   Programme and Technical Support Section (UNHCR)

SCHR:
   Steering Committee for Humanitarian Response

UNDP:
   United Nations Development Programme

UNDRO:
   United Nations Disaster Relief Organisation

UNEP:
   United Nations Environment Programme

UNHCR:
   United Nations High Commissioner for Refugees

UNICEF:
   United Nations Children's Fund

USAID:
   United States Agency for International Development

WCRWC:
   Women's Commission for Refugee Women and Children

WFP:
   World Food Programme

WHO:
   World Health Organisation

WMO:
   World Meteorological Organisation

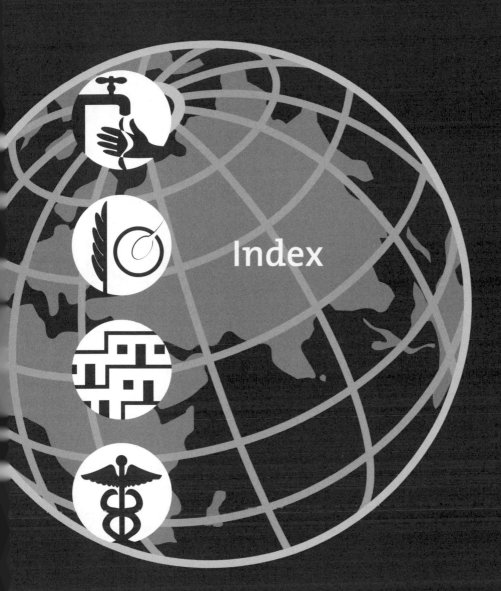

Index

Index

The Sphere Project Training

This new pack features excellent training materials, developed and field-tested by Sphere Trainers. The pack contains:

1 TRAINING MATERIALS

400pp, A4, 8¼ x 11½, Canadian wire-bound

Four training modules covering:

- Introduction to Sphere
- The Humanitarian Charter
- The Project Cycle
- Sphere in Disaster Preparedness

Modules feature:

- training sessions
- background notes
- exercise ideas
- visual aids

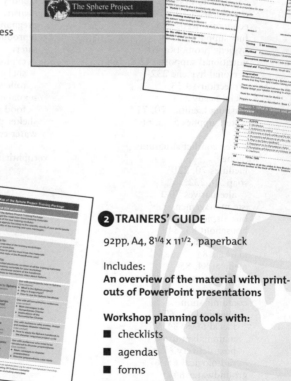

2 TRAINERS' GUIDE

92pp, A4, 8¼ x 11½, paperback

Includes:
An overview of the material with print-outs of PowerPoint presentations

Workshop planning tools with:

- checklists
- agendas
- forms
- templates

Information on:

- training methodologies
- participant selection
- training tips
- maximising learning

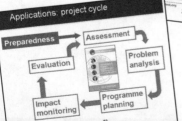

ackage

❸ CD-ROM

Features:

- Trainers' Guide and Training Materials:
  i)   as an RTF file - to be customised to suit individual needs
  ii) in PDF - easily downloaded for clear printing
  iii) in HTML - for easy navigation and search of content by topic (eg project cycle, advocacy, etc).

- 9-minute Sphere video (1999)

- full text of *The Sphere Handbook* 2004 edition

The fully photocopiable training materials include references to both 2000 and 2004 editions of the Handbook throughout, so that they can be used with either version.

THE SPHERE PROJECT TRAINING PACKAGE
A4, 8¹/₄ x 11¹/², 400pp, Canadian wiro-bound;
A4, 8¹/₄ x 11¹/², 92pp, paperback;
CD-ROM
0 85598 509 7 • November 2003 • £30.00 / US$48.00
Sold as a set. Items are not available separately.

The Sphere Project Film:
An Introduction to Humanitarian Challenges

This specially filmed full-colour footage from Sierra Leone and other locations introduces the Sphere principles and practices in a real field situation. It forms an ideal orientation package for humanitarian and development aid workers.

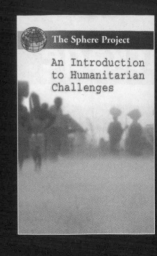

Through testimonies from experienced practitioners and real-life examples of the use of the Sphere Handbook, the film explores broader themes such as:

■ What is the history of humanitarian action?
■ What is the humanitarian identity?
■ What role do legal instruments play in disaster response?
■ How does one move from principles to action?
■ What does participation really mean in a disaster response?
■ Where is humanitarianism going?

Published by The Sphere Project

0 85598 506 2 • November 2003
English NTSC video version of 45 min film
£9.95 + VAT (£11.70) / US$16.50

0 85598 518 6 • November 2003 • French
0 85598 520 8 • November 2003 • Spanis

0 85598 507 0 • November 2003
English PAL video version of 45 min film
£9.95 + VAT (£11.70) / US$16.50

0 85598 517 8 • November 2003 • French
0 85598 519 4 • November 2003 • Spanis

0 85598 508 9 • November 2003
NTSC DVD version of 45 min film in
English, French and Spanish
£9.95 + VAT (£11.70) / US$16.50

0 85598 516 x • November 2003
PAL DVD version of 45 min film in Englis
French and Spanish
£9.95 + VAT (£11.70) / US$16.50

NB Charges for video/DVD cover the cost o
duplication and packaging. All DVDs are
multi-zone.